Praise for *The Art of ClearCase® Deployment*

"An essential read for any organization using change management. Whether you are new to ClearCase or an experienced user, this book addresses key points that will drive you to a successful ClearCase deployment and usage model."

—*Adam Levensohn*
Manager, ClearCase Technical Support, IBM Rational Software

"Buckley and Pulsipher offer the voice of hard-won experience leavened with significant amounts of humor, which is not exactly what one expects from a book about configuration management (or any computer science book, for that matter). The way I see it, a book that offers advice about 'how to reduce build cycle times for large, multi-site products' in terms of 'eating an elephant, one bite at a time' is definitely worth reading. Thanks to these guys, I'm the proud owner of a brand-new VOB, and after I read the detailed advice herein about how to configure it, it works like a charm!"

—*Kendall Scott*
Author, UML Explained

The Art of ClearCase® Deployment

The Addison-Wesley Object Technology Series

Grady Booch, Ivar Jacobson, and James Rumbaugh, Series Editors

For more information, check out the series web site at www.awprofessional.com/otseries.

Ahmed/Umrysh, *Developing Enterprise Java Applications with J2EE™ and UML*

Arlow/Neustadt, *Enterprise Patterns and MDA: Building Better Software with Archetype Patterns and UML*

Arlow/Neustadt, *UML and the Unified Process: Practical Object-Oriented Analysis and Design*

Armour/Miller, *Advanced Use Case Modeling: Software Systems*

Bellin/Simone, *The CRC Card Book*

Bergström/Råberg, *Adopting the Rational Unified Process: Success with the RUP*

Binder, *Testing Object-Oriented Systems: Models, Patterns, and Tools*

Bittner/Spence, *Use Case Modeling*

Booch, *Object Solutions: Managing the Object-Oriented Project*

Booch, *Object-Oriented Analysis and Design with Applications, 2E*

Booch/Bryan, *Software Engineering with ADA, 3E*

Booch/Rumbaugh/Jacobson, *The Unified Modeling Language User Guide*

Box/Brown/Ewald/Sells, *Effective COM: 50 Ways to Improve Your COM and MTS-based Applications*

Carlson, *Modeling XML Applications with UML: Practical e-Business Applications*

Collins, *Designing Object-Oriented User Interfaces*

Conallen, *Building Web Applications with UML, 2E*

D'Souza/Wills, *Objects, Components, and Frameworks with UML: The Catalysis(SM) Approach*

Douglass, *Doing Hard Time: Developing Real-Time Systems with UML, Objects, Frameworks, and Patterns*

Douglass, *Real-Time Design Patterns: Robust Scalable Architecture for Real-Time Systems*

Douglass, *Real Time UML, 3E: Advances in The UML for Real-Time Systems*

Eeles et al., *Building J2EE™ Applications with the Rational Unified Process*

Fontoura/Pree/Rumpe, *The UML Profile for Framework Architectures*

Fowler, *Analysis Patterns: Reusable Object Models*

Fowler et al., *Refactoring: Improving the Design of Existing Code*

Fowler, *UML Distilled, 3E: A Brief Guide to the Standard Object Modeling Language*

Gomaa, *Designing Concurrent, Distributed, and Real-Time Applications with UML*

Gomaa, *Designing Software Product Lines with UML*

Graham, *Object-Oriented Methods, 3E: Principles and Practice*

Heinckiens, *Building Scalable Database Applications: Object-Oriented Design, Architectures, and Implementations*

Hofmeister/Nord/Dilip, *Applied Software Architecture*

Jacobson/Booch/Rumbaugh, *The Unified Software Development Process*

Jordan, *C++ Object Databases: Programming with the ODMG Standard*

Kleppe/Warmer/Bast, *MDA Explained: The Model Driven Architecture™: Practice and Promise*

Kroll/Kruchten, *The Rational Unified Process Made Easy: A Practitioner's Guide to the RUP*

Kruchten, *The Rational Unified Process, 3E: An Introduction*

Lau, *The Art of Objects: Object-Oriented Design and Architecture*

Leffingwell/Widrig, *Managing Software Requirements, 2E: A Use Case Approach*

Manassis, *Practical Software Engineering: Analysis and Design for the .NET Platform*

Marshall, *Enterprise Modeling with UML: Designing Successful Software through Business Analysis*

McGregor/Sykes, *A Practical Guide to Testing Object-Oriented Software*

Mellor/Balcer, *Executable UML: A Foundation for Model-Driven Architecture*

Mellor et al., *MDA Distilled: Principles of Model-Driven Architecture*

Naiburg/Maksimchuk, *UML for Database Design*

Oestereich, *Developing Software with UML, 2E: Object-Oriented Analysis and Design in Practice*

Page-Jones, *Fundamentals of Object-Oriented Design in UML*

Pohl, *Object-Oriented Programming Using C++, 2E*

Pollice et al. *Software Development for Small Teams: A RUP-Centric Approach*

Quatrani, *Visual Modeling with Rational Rose 2002 and UML*

Rector/Sells, *ATL Internals*

Reed, *Developing Applications with Visual Basic and UML*

Rosenberg/Scott, *Applying Use Case Driven Object Modeling with UML: An Annotated e-Commerce Example*

Rosenberg/Scott, *Use Case Driven Object Modeling with UML: A Practical Approach*

Royce, *Software Project Management: A Unified Framework*

Rumbaugh/Jacobson/Booch, *The Unified Modeling Language Reference Manual*

Schneider/Winters, *Applying Use Cases, 2E: A Practical Guide*

Smith/Williams, *Performance Solutions: A Practical Guide to Creating Responsive, Scalable Software*

Stevens/Pooley, *Using UML, Updated Edition: Software Engineering with Objects and Components*

Unhelkar, *Process Quality Assurance for UML-Based Projects*

van Harmelen, *Object Modeling and User Interface Design: Designing Interactive Systems*

Wake, *Refactoring Workbook*

Warmer/Kleppe, *The Object Constraint Language, 2E: Getting Your Models Ready for MDA*

White, *Software Configuration Management Strategies and Rational ClearCase®: A Practical Introduction*

The Component Software Series

Clemens Szyperski, Series Editor

For more information, check out the series web site at www.awprofessional.com/csseries.

Allen, *Realizing eBusiness with Components*

Apperly et al., *Service- and Component-based Development: Using the Select Perspective™ and UML*

Atkinson et al., *Component-Based Product Line Engineering with UML*

Cheesman/Daniels, *UML Components: A Simple Process for Specifying Component-Based Software*

Szyperski, *Component Software, 2E: Beyond Object-Oriented Programming*

Whitehead, *Component-Based Development: Principles and Planning for Business Systems*

The Art of ClearCase® Deployment

The Secrets to Successful Implementation

Christian D. Buckley

Darren W. Pulsipher

✦ Addison-Wesley

Boston • San Francisco • New York • Toronto • Montreal
London • Munich • Paris • Madrid
Capetown • Sydney • Tokyo • Singapore • Mexico City

Many of the designations used by manufacturers and sellers to distinguish their products are claimed as trademarks. Where those designations appear in this book, and Addison-Wesley was aware of a trademark claim, the designations have been printed with initial capital letters or in all capitals.

The authors and publisher have taken care in the preparation of this book, but make no expressed or implied warranty of any kind and assume no responsibility for errors or omissions. No liability is assumed for incidental or consequential damages in connection with or arising out of the use of the information or programs contained herein.

IBM, Rational and ClearCase are registered trademarks of International Business Machines Corporation in the United States, other countries, or both.

The publisher offers discounts on this book when ordered in quantity for bulk purchases and special sales. For more information, please contact:

U.S. Corporate and Government Sales
(800) 382-3419
corpsales@pearsontechgroup.com

For sales outside of the U.S., please contact:

International Sales
(317) 581-3793
international@pearsontechgroup.com

Visit Addison-Wesley on the Web: www.awprofessional.com

Library of Congress Cataloging-in-Publication Data
Buckley, Christian D.
     The art of ClearCase deployment : the secrets to successful implementation / Christian D. Buckley, Darren W. Pulsipher.
          p.   cm.
     Includes index.
     ISBN 0-321-26220-4 (pbk. : alk. paper)
     1. Software configuration management. 2. Rational Clearcase. I. Pulsipher, Darren W. II. Title.
QA76.76.C69B82 2004
005.1—dc22   2004010532

ISBN: 0-321-26220-4
Text printed on recycled paper
1 2 3 4 5 6 7 8 9 10—ML—0807060504
First printing, July 2004

To my wife, Kendal
—*CDB*

To my wife, Stacy
—*DWP*

Contents

Foreword

My first exposure to the term *configuration management*—well, the first exposure I was required to notice—was early in my career when I was managing software tools, porting, and acquisitions for several divisions of a major test instrumentation company. In this case, a group of software development managers came to me and said, "We must do configuration management. Find us a configuration management tool." I thought for a moment and replied with the first question that came to mind. In retrospect, this question has turned out to be one of the most profound of my career: "What is configuration management?" Their reply was equally profound: "Er ... uh ... we don't know, but we think it has something to do with RCS."

In the years since that seminal exchange, I have observed that when people say they "want to do configuration management" or even say "we are doing configuration management," they often have no idea what configuration management is, or what gain they should be deriving from its use. Why, then, would they want to do configuration management if they don't know what it is or why they should use it? The answer lies, I believe, in human nature. When walking in uncharted territory over complex terrain, our survival tends to depend on our actions being under control. In that respect, the desire to do configuration management can almost be categorized as instinctual. This notion conforms to my experience and tends to explain the behavior of those original managers. They knew they were dealing with new product development that included the often-overwhelming complexity of software development projects. They instinctually felt that they needed to control what was going on, even if they couldn't articulate that need.

What follows, then, is the definition of software configuration management (SCM) that I like the most: "Software configuration management is what you do to control the evolution of software projects." It is a simple definition, and others are certainly more detailed, but the one I like is accurate, easy to remember, and easy to articulate.

Some years later, I found myself in a job with Atria Software that allowed me to deploy the ClearCase product in many different organizations. Each organization I visited suffered to some degree with the problem illustrated by that question-and-answer exchange I first experienced those many years earlier: "What is configuration management? We don't know, but we think we need to do it." In every case, these organizations were already doing some form of software configuration management, usually using a simple version control tool such as RCS or CVS, but they really couldn't say why they were doing it or what benefit they were getting from their practice. In every case, though, they had identified that their current way of doing software configuration management was not providing the level of control required to deal with the complexity of the development they were doing. They knew instinctually that they needed more control but were largely unable to articulate exactly what kind of control or exactly what they expected to gain from that control.

I found that part and parcel of each implementation was a need to describe the kinds of things that a good software configuration management scheme would allow you to do. I found it also useful to note that just because you can do something doesn't mean you have to. A good SCM system should allow you to tailor your control rather than dictate it to you. This ability to tailor your SCM to suit your organization, however, brings with it the need to know not only how the SCM system works, but also what suits your organization. The second part of that equation, defining how your organization wants to work, is actually the harder part.

In working through these deployments, I found that the following principles were reliable guidelines:

- **If you can't articulate your vision, no one will want to follow you.** This is important if you want to gain advocates for the changes you desire in your organization. These advocates can then win others over, saving you much time, effort, and frustration. It all starts with your knowing what you want to do and being able to explain it clearly (assuming that what you want to do is a good idea in the first place!).

- **There's no substitute for knowing what you're talking about.** This means not only knowing what tools you want to use and the technical details of how they work, but also the more difficult task of understanding how your organization currently works: what works well, what is broken, and how your plan offers a net gain for the organization.

The other thing I learned in these deployments was that beyond the haze surrounding the somewhat theoretical discussion of what SCM is and what you should get from it is the part where you have to make it work. So, to the two preceding principles, I add this one:

- **At the end of the day, your solution must work.** Your solution must function technically, but it also must be useable. I've seen many organizations spend tens or hundreds of thousands of dollars implementing an SCM system only to discover, after it is rolled out and developers start using it, that it just doesn't work. Either the system itself doesn't work because of technical flaws, or it is so cumbersome and painful to use that developers rebel and won't use it—or worse, sabotage its use.
  The deadly temptation that leads to this disaster is usually trying to do too much. Remember, just because you can do

something doesn't mean you have to. I've found it best to keep SCM simple at first and then iterate into complexity rather than trying to engineer a complex and arcane SCM scheme before anyone gets to try it.

This book is grounded in these fundamental principles. First, the authors are explicit about what software configuration management is and what you should get from it. Second, they are clear about the need to articulate that vision, the techniques you'll need to use, and to whom you should be prepared to articulate your vision. Finally, this book isn't just a theoretical treatise on software configuration management principles; it also has the "make it work" piece. *The Art of ClearCase® Deployment* is appropriate for the individual or the organization new to deploying ClearCase, as well as for those who have done it many times before. The extensive hands-on, how-to information on managing a ClearCase deployment project is material I wish I had when I first started deploying ClearCase, and I still find it valuable today.

Tom Milligan
IBM Rational Software

Preface

How This Book Came About

When we began writing for Rational Software back in 1998 for the now-defunct *Rose Architect* magazine, our intent was to provide project managers, product managers, and various other nonengineers with a grounding in some fairly technical material, allowing them to stand shoulder to shoulder with their technical team and not feel clueless. Initially, our article topics varied widely depending on our own interests and current projects. But as time went on, we slowly began to articulate some broader themes, and we developed an outline of topics that began to explore the critical topics in configuration management, and in ClearCase specifically. As *Rose Architect* magazine was retired, the articles we wrote shifted from best practices in generic software development to all of the steps involved in developing an integrated, enterprise-wide change management solution.

For those of you who are not familiar with the history of Rational Software and its various content efforts, a brief recap: As Rational's flagship visual modeling magazine, *Rose Architect,* was discontinued, we redirected our efforts toward the Catapulse portal, a Rational spin-off company that was eventually spun back into Rational—and then became the foundation for the Rational Developers Network (RDN). Then came Big Blue. RDN is now part of IBM's developer-Works family of content. Throughout all of these changes, we continued to develop content around ClearCase and Unified Change Management (UCM), attempting to help people understand the pitfalls and complexities of building and maintaining a multi-site change management solution.

Back in early 2003, Addison-Wesley approached us about writing a book. At the time, we were both fully engaged in our current projects—Christian was developing a Web-based team collaboration tool, and Darren was inventing a grid-based workflow application—and we just could not make the time to add a book to our list of tasks. But the seed was planted, and we occasionally talked about it. We slowly began to investigate current authors and titles, and ultimately we outlined a book concept that we thought the market needed. Based on our individual experiences and our shared understanding of both ClearCase and UCM, we decided that the book would provide an introduction to these topics for beginners and seasoned users alike.

The Goal of This Book

Spend any time in a bookstore or online and you'll see that the market is flush with titles on software configuration management (SCM or CM), software development, and various object-oriented development themes. For us, the problem with most such books is not so much the content but the writing style. For the "nontechnical" reader, most of these books are just too, well, technical. The majority of books on the market are written like textbooks. The first one or two chapters are generally very basic, but the subsequent chapters immediately jump off the deep end, drowning the reader in technical jargon and architectural diagrams. Almost every single one of these books assumes the reader already has some kind of background in software engineering. And frankly, most of them are dry and boring.

We believe there are a number of problems with the approach taken by these books:

- They emphasize installation and configuration, not the underlying reasons for deploying a comprehensive change management solution—much less the decisions project managers must make before the software is even installed.

- They jump very quickly from an overview to the main content; they tend to require previous experience in a specific technology or methodology.

- Many of the diagrams and case studies in these books are simply too complicated for the nontechnical reader.

- None of these titles was written with the project manager, analyst, or nonengineer in mind.

- For the most part, humor is absent from all of these titles.

The Art of ClearCase® Deployment follows some of the same technical footsteps as these other books, but we present the material in a way that a broader group of project personnel can use. When people ask us, "Why this book?" our answer is that we hope to provide members of the extended project team and burgeoning CM managers with a better understanding of how an end-to-end change management solution, in general, can enhance an organization's ability to deliver better products—and deliver them faster. But we also hope to show how ClearCase, specifically, best meets those needs.

You may ask: What problems will this book solve? What questions will it answer? This book will help you to understand the fundamentals of software configuration management and ClearCase. It will demystify many aspects of the technology and help you understand the business value of an integrated change management solution. And most important, it will help you to make better decisions about the planning and management of your software development efforts.

We chose the title *The Art of ClearCase® Deployment* because deploying and maintaining ClearCase really is an art. Sure, there are some basic configurations that are mandatory for any ClearCase install, but overall the tool is powerful and flexible, allowing the CM manager and ClearCase users to retain a large amount of control over the solution they develop. Building and maintaining a ClearCase deployment is an iterative process. You'll make mistakes, and you'll constantly find areas for improvement—but over time, you'll also learn to further integrate ClearCase into your company's business processes. In fact, a finely tuned change management solution will become a major factor in your company's ability to stay competitive.

Our Writing Style

We've received a lot of feedback about our writing style. Admittedly, our language use and tone can be colloquial at times, but we prefer to write in the voice with which we are most comfortable. Both of us present and teach on a regular basis, and we like to have fun with what we do. We want to ease the reader into the subject matter, by using humor and by sharing specific examples of our own project experiences. And so the book follows a natural progression, moving from broad concepts of project and change management to the more technical aspects of a ClearCase deployment. Unlike other books, we gradually introduce the reader to important concepts, explaining at each step how the various acronyms and activities fit into the bigger picture. We walk through the nuances of working within a modeling paradigm, and we help the reader understand the actors, the use cases, and the complete problem domain before embarking on a change management implementation of any size. Whether or not you will be the primary user of your new CM system, this book will help you understand how the system works, and where you fit into the overall process.

Learning is a circular process. Most people cannot read a textbook from cover to cover and retain all of that information. Readers need some repetition of material throughout a book, to help reinforce key concepts, but they also need an organized presentation of the subject matter, so they can readily explore each topic and find the information they seek. Our writing follows a specific pattern. Many chapters review basic concepts covered in previous sections, because we feel that certain ideas need to be highlighted. As you advance through the book, it is important to keep noticing these underlying themes to help drive them home.

Unlike other books in the broader category of software-development best practices, this book provides insight into the management, communication, and implementation issues surrounding the components of a change management solution. It also covers issues and tactical responses to implementing both small, team-based ClearCase installations, as well as large, multi-site deployments found in many of today's global enterprises. The book also shows how ClearCase can best serve these organizations.

Most chapters contain actionable steps that a project manager can follow, along with relevant examples—with a story or theme to keep things interesting. The unifying factor in this book is the use of real-world examples, with practical guidelines for designing and deploying an end-to-end solution, all taken from our own experiences in building these kinds of solutions. We use a healthy dose of humor—in the form of stories, quotes, and anecdotes—to help make our points and keep the reader engaged. And whenever a picture can help to make a point or to illustrate a concept, we include diagrams and visual examples to demonstrate new concepts and ideas.

To be honest, there are numerous books on the market that support the many different faces of change management—from configuration management tools to detailed methodologies, most with case studies on huge implementations. Some of these books we even recommend (after you read this one, of course; see the bibliography). However, most of these books fail to mention all of the different tools in the change management continuum and how they work together with ClearCase—and even fewer attempt to explain the process and techniques with the nonengineer in mind. What is missing from the libraries of most project and CM managers is a book that clearly articulates the strategies and practical guidelines for scoping and deploying ClearCase, from the initial modeling activities through the handoff to the training and support teams.

Who Should Read This Book

The Art of ClearCase® Deployment is targeted toward those readers who want to learn about the end-to-end change management product family with ClearCase at the core, and how each component fits into the larger product development organization—mostly from the standpoint of the project manager (and the nondeveloper). Although some of the material in this book is very technical, we assume the majority of readers have minimal knowledge of change management tools, object-oriented analysis and design, programming, or any modeling methodologies. This book should serve as a guide for ClearCase novices and as a desktop reference for more experienced CM managers.

We view our book as a "bridge" to many of the more technical books already on the market—books that are more focused on the implementation of specific tools within the change management continuum, such as Brian White's *Software Configuration Management Strategies and Rational ClearCase* (Addison-Wesley, 2000).

Our intended readers belong to an extended development organization: project managers and nonengineers intimidated by the complexity and technical background needed to understand the official ClearCase documentation; technical writers and analysts who will participate in the rollout of a ClearCase solution and want to better understand the requirements of deployment within a corporation; product managers and marketing personnel who have a vested interest in the quick and efficient creation of products; and of course, current users of ClearCase who want to strengthen their understanding of the fundamentals.

The Structure of This Book

Chapter 1—The Role of the Change Agent
Preparing to deploy any large software solution takes planning and coordination with many groups within your company, and you need

to be ready for the challenge. This chapter sets the tone for the book, with some recommendations on how to prepare yourself for this challenge.

Chapter 2—The Current Software Dilemma
Why do so many software projects fail? This chapter outlines the problems and shows how ClearCase can help overcome the fundamental challenges in software development.

Chapter 3—Standards Enforcement Using Configuration Management Tools
This chapter is a brief history of standards in software development, and it offers a lesson on how CM tools can help manage or reinforce your own standards.

Chapter 4—Selling ClearCase into the Rest of Your Organization
There are many paths that might lead you toward ClearCase, but are you prepared to answer some of the basic questions for deploying a company-wide change management solution? This chapter will help prepare you for the reasoning and politics behind a ClearCase deployment.

Chapter 5—Mapping the Manufacturing Process
There is more to creating a viable product than just writing and building software. Creating software products involves many of the same processes found in the manufacturing process. It is important to understand these similarities, recognize all of the phases of development, and plan accordingly for a successful product launch.

Chapter 6—Ground-Level View of a Product Release
Understanding the product launch is another concept largely lost on the average software development organization. The handoff between engineering and the business office is critical. But with proper planning, you'll better understand the timing and interactions between engineering and marketing, and how to plan accordingly.

Chapter 7—Planning Your ClearCase Deployment
ClearCase is not something you can just install and start using out of the box. Because it affects numerous people and processes, planning

out your ClearCase deployment from the perspectives of both technology and resources can make your deployments less painful. This chapter covers the fundamental questions you must ask yourself before setting up your ClearCase system.

Chapter 8—Modeling Your Configuration Management System
With most deployments, there is a driving factor for getting the system up and running quickly (usually a large number of projects with deadlines), but in this rush to go live, many mistakes can be made in your install. By taking the time to properly plan your system and understand the gaps within your processes, you'll build a better solution—and avoid a lot of potholes down the road.

Chapter 9—Using Configuration Management to Control Process
CM tools can help you to automate your systems and processes, and they can play an important role in preparing for internal or external audits. This chapter outlines the basic process controls available through ClearCase.

Chapter 10—Planning for the Rational Unified Process
This chapter gives an overview of the role of the Rational Unified Process (RUP) as it relates to ClearCase, including all of the major actors and their tasks, and how they fit into your ClearCase planning activities.

Chapter 11—Build-and-Release Basics
Once you have your system up and running, this chapter will provide you with a solid foundation in the day-to-day build-and-release basics, including frequency, automation, communication with your team and management, and where to start looking at optimization.

Chapter 12—Understanding Branching and Labeling
This is a brief overview of branching and labeling strategies, naming conventions, versioning, configuration specs, and other key terms.

Chapter 13—Deploying ClearCase
Building on the previous chapters, you are now ready to start moving on to your new system. This chapter provides a checklist of activities

and prescribes specific tasks for moving from other well-known source-code management systems.

Chapter 14—ClearCase Integration Analysis
Integration with other tools and systems is a key to making your ClearCase deployment successful—ClearCase must work fluidly with your other tools. This chapter outlines the primary actors, primary tools, and systems you'll want to consider, and it discusses the specific benefits and limitations of your integrations.

Chapter 15—ClearCase UCM Integration
For those unfamiliar with Unified Change Management, this chapter presents an outline of the basic objects, workflow, development activities, and policy management in UCM.

Chapter 16—Lone Eagle Management
Many teams have individuals who work remotely. This chapter helps you understand how these individuals fit into your ClearCase deployment, and how to better manage them.

Chapter 17—Integrating Multi-Site Teams in Your Spare Time
This chapter focuses on the primary actors, tools, and phases that you need to understand for multi-site development, with some important recommendations on how to be more successful.

Chapter 18—Hot Rods and Hardware
This chapter outlines the hardware considerations for a ClearCase deployment.

Chapter 19—The Magical World of VOB Sizing
Here you'll find everything you need to know about the best way to design your versioned object base (VOB) configuration, and how to deploy an efficient ClearCase system.

Chapter 20—Constructing Your CM System
With your system up and running, it's now time to start refining your system and processes, using ClearCase as your development tools repository.

Chapter 21—Training and Scripting to Control Process
This chapter offers a brief lesson on the best practices around
scripts, and how best to utilize training with your team.

Chapter 22—Trigger-Happy
This is a fairly comprehensive outline of the many types of triggers
and how to manage them. The chapter defines the major trigger
types, offers suggestions for installation and control, and provides
insight into both the benefits and the pitfalls.

Chapter 23—Efficiencies in Your CM System
Here we present a history of collaboration technologies and show
where ClearCase fits into all of them. Understanding this history will
help you to plan your ClearCase strategies and find additional opportunities for collaboration.

Chapter 24—Reducing Build Cycle Times
This chapter goes through several solutions for build-cycle reduction, from make system reconstruction to hardware options.

Chapter 25—The Drag Coefficient of Test-Cycle Reduction
This chapter outlines the different levels of testing and discusses
several strategies for improving testing efficiencies.

*Chapter 26—What to Do When Things Go Wrong: Solving Problems
with ClearCase*
We offer some recommendations for minimizing problems with
ClearCase, including how to protect your VOBs, how to access your
logs, how to identify issues with your multi-site deployment, and
where to go to find the experts.

Chapter 27—Bringing It All Together
Finally, the book concludes with a brief wrap-up and reaffirmation of
the role of the change agent.

About the Authors

Christian Buckley describes himself as the "king of side projects." In addition to his writing projects for IBM Rational, he maintains several weblogs, including www.PLMblog.com, his ongoing analysis of collaboration technology. A partner with Red Hill Partners (www.redhill-partners.com) in San Ramon, California, Christian is an entrepreneur coach and consultant with a passion for technology—especially collaboration and product lifecycle management technologies—and enjoys advising and consulting startups. He has provided services to companies across North America, Asia-Pacific, and Europe, including such technology stalwarts as Hewlett-Packard, IBM, Hitachi, Visa International, SBC, Nortel, Matsushita, and Seagate Technology. He also co-founded the East Bay I.T. Group (www.ebig.org), a nonprofit technology forum serving more than 4000 members in the Bay Area. Christian has a B.A. in Marketing and an M.B.A. in Technology Management, with plans to pursue a Ph.D. in Social Informatics of Collaboration Technology. He lives in the San Francisco East Bay with his wife and four children. He can be reached at buckley@redhillpartners.com

Darren Pulsipher started his career as a software developer and system administrator working for both large and small companies. He quickly became disenchanted with the lack of quality in most software products and decided to go back to school and augment his B.S. in Computer Science from Brigham Young University. He focused his studies on software development processes and management and earned his M.B.A. in Technology Management. He has been using and promoting Rational tools and methodology for more than ten years through conferences and articles. His most recent focus has been on grid technology, and he serves as chairman of several working groups in the Global Grid Forum standards body. Darren recently moved his lovely wife and four kids from the rat race of the Silicon Valley out to Utah, where he finds life moves at a much more reasonable pace. He can be reached at darren@pulsipher.org

Acknowledgments

The idea for compiling this book arose a couple years back at the urging of our editors at Rational Software, pre-IBM. If not for the support of people such as Lisa Dornell, Gary Clarke, Rebecca Bence, and Richard Alden, this project would never have come together. We'd also like to recognize Joe Taylor—as the third member of the original trio when all of these writings began—for helping us on our path. We miss the spirited conversations over late-night burgers.

We'd also like to thank Kendall Scott for his input over the years, and for being brave enough to move out of civilization and into the back-woods of Tennessee, where we're convinced he walks around shirt-less and barefoot in overalls, shooting at squirrels from his back porch and yelling at imaginary houseguests—all while working on his latest book. (He denies all of this, but we know it to be true.)

Christian would like to thank his wife, Kendal, for all of her love and support during the three start-ups, years of long commutes down to the peninsula, and various nonprofit activities; and his children, Audrey, Preston, Nicholas, and Joshua, for making life more enjoyable. Christian would also like to thank Floyd Andrus for his example and encouragement during his formative years, and his seventh-grade wood-shop teacher, Mr. Forrest, for making a deep impression regarding the importance of perseverance.

Darren would like to thank the love of his life—his wife, Stacy. Her patience with him during the last 14 years has helped him get through it all: years of schooling, hours of commuting, late nights at home yelling at his computer, and weeks of being gone, conference-hopping. Additionally, Darren would like to thank his kids, Matthew, Dallin, Jacob, and Julianne, for making life enjoyable and very interesting and for giving him lots of good writing material.

1

The Role of the Change Agent

Hermes, Morpheus, Shiva, Olin, and Veltha. What in the world do you have in common with these ancient gods and goddesses? Examine the following list:

- Hermes—Greek god of change

- Morpheus—Greek god of dreams and change

- Shiva—Hindu god of change, transformation, and destruction

- Olin—Aztec god of change

- Veltha—Etruscan god of change and seasons

In his article "Honoring the Forces of Transformation," author John Snyder describes the traits of Hermes and Apollo, and how together those characteristics can effect great change.[1] Hermes is not only the messenger of the gods, he is also the "god of change, transformation, movement, lightness of touch, and everything powered by those energies. What happens when Hermes enters the room? You can't predict, but it's bound to be interesting. Whomever Hermes touches rediscovers a youthful perspective and a refreshing playfulness."

Are you like Hermes, or are you more like Shiva, the Hindu god of change and destruction? One of Hermes' qualities is his ability to make people *want* to change. Therein lies the lesson: you cannot force change onto people. They will not only resist the change, but they will actually work against it, sometimes doing anything to stop it outright—even changes that might, ultimately, benefit them.

So maybe we all want to be more like Hermes, "supple, pragmatic, and refreshing," as Snyder calls him. Some people seem to have an uncanny ability to persuade others into doing things they wouldn't normally do, or to convince previously sedentary folks to take action. But most of us need to work at persuading others to move in a desired direction. Having original ideas and helping people to think outside of the box are two parts of the skill necessary to persuade, but we also need to be just a little like Apollo. He represents "measure, order, and balance in thinking," according to Snyder. If we can combine the characteristics of these two gods and use them, then we have found a vehicle for real change. Snyder says it best: "Apollo erects great monuments to the disciplined intellect; Hermes, in his role as Divine Graffiti Artist, leaves his irreverent, spray-painted question mark and is gone long before the Mind Police arrive."

Are You a Change Agent?

Okay, there are probably a few of you out there who believe your company should already start erecting statues and temples praising your great accomplishments as a god of change. Maybe you'll settle for the title *change agent*. Not as grandiose, but sometimes you need

1. The article is available online at
   http://www.thinksmart.com/2/articles/MP_2-2-4.html

to take what you can get. But for those who consider themselves movers and shakers within their companies, what makes you think you have what it takes to be a change agent? Here's what we believe qualifies someone for this title:

- **Commitment.** You must be committed to change, and passionate about the changes you are trying to make. Just as animals can sense fear, people can sense apathy toward an idea and toward change. You must believe in what you are doing—or don't do it. Or at least don't try to convince others to do it.

- **Communication.** You must have strong communication skills, including writing and public speaking. You will need to take your passion and convey it to the masses—or at least to the people you want to change. But you should realize that not all people are at the same level. You will need to be able to communicate with executives, managers, and workers about your ideas, and successfully demonstrate both an understanding of the complexities of the undertaking and your willingness to see the project through to the end.

- **Intuition.** You must have a good ability to sense and manage concerns and controversy. When people have concerns, these concerns need to be addressed quickly. A small question at the back of the room left unanswered can grow and swell, diverting the momentum of an entire group that is in the process of making a change.

- **Stamina.** You must understand, and be able to defend, the change. There is nothing more defective than some middle manager or self-proclaimed change agent attempting to push a change through an organization just because he or she was told to. The manager may be passionate about it but may not know a thing about the technology—or the effects of the change. You must become knowledgeable about the technology behind the change, and the effects it may have on everyone making the change. Most people can see right through a "phony" change agent.

Secrets of the Trade

If you possess these traits, then you are ready to wear the banner of change agent. However, don't let it go to your head—this is just the beginning of the process. Here are some secrets that can help you become even more effective in your role.

Be Genuine

Be real. People can see right through insincerity. If you are not truly committed to yourself and the changes you propose, people will not want to make the change themselves.

Have Thick Skin

People hate change. It makes them uncomfortable. How many times have you heard someone say, "We have always done it that way, and it seems to work fine. Why change it?" Be prepared to be verbally and emotionally (but hopefully not physically) abused by people resisting the change. You may feel isolated from others until they come on board, so be ready.

Be Motivated from Within

This advice goes hand in hand with "have thick skin," but there is more to it than that. Change agents do not seek approval to determine their success. They make change happen; they don't wait for change to happen. What motivates them is something inside them, and they do not rely on approval from others. Okay, it is nice to get approval every once in a while (especially when you cannot authorize purchases over $100)—but don't make it the core of your decision-making process.

Don't Be Afraid to Fail

This may be one of the main reasons people don't like change: they are flat-out afraid of failing. What is interesting is that we have all learned to accept change in our own lives. Learning to walk when we were very young, for example, was a huge change in our lives. But we learned, and now we can walk.

If we are afraid to take chances and fail, we will never learn. The key is to learn from our mistakes. Some say the definition of *insanity* is making the same mistakes over and over again but each time expecting a different result. We must learn from our failures. Can you imagine everyone crawling into your office because they were afraid to learn to walk? Of course not. But how often do we see teams and companies crawling along with old technology, outdated methodologies, and ancient business practices?

Enable Others

Effective change comes from getting others involved. Rarely does a change really take hold with just one person pushing it forward. If your goal is to produce a lasting cultural change, you need to enlist other people. Remember, they need to be fully converted to the change to become change agents as well.

One technique found in the advertising world is to simply tell someone that everyone else is buying the product. While it sounds stupid and manipulative (people can't be that gullible, can they?), the influence of peers can steer decision making. Because other people use a product or accept a change, people will more readily accept a change. In fact, the more endorsements and colleagues you have backing you, the more people will accept change—time and time again.

Commit to Priorities

Work on the things that are most important first. You can quickly get bogged down in the trivial and lose the vision and passion of the change. Keep the end goal in mind, and make sure that you constantly work toward that end.

Remember to Have Fun

If you are not having fun, you will quickly burn out. Furthermore, people around you will start noticing that you are no longer having fun, and they will equate that to a lack of passion. Without passion, they will see this as a sign that you are not committed to the changes you are admonishing others to make. You need to keep your chin up and press forward.

Get Away from It All

Honestly, being a change agent can take a lot of energy. Every so often, take some downtime from the constant pressures. Take a real vacation—not one with the cell phone attached to your ear on the beach. On a regular basis, everyone needs to get away from everything. Don't worry about the work you've left behind. Look at it this way: because most people resist change, chances are that absolutely nothing will change while you are gone.

Conclusion

As you set out to undertake any large project, make sure you have the support and direction to accomplish your task. Are you willing to stand up and count yourself as an agent of change? It is not an easy job, but it can be very rewarding—especially if people accept and embrace the change. You never know—you may just get one of those statues or temples after all. Just don't charge the raw marble to your corporate card.

2

The Current Software Dilemma

Death, taxes, and change are the only constants in life. But while most people have learned to deal with death and taxes, the fear of change endures as one of the greatest maladies of modern society. So why haven't we mastered our fear of change? Well, for one thing, it can be downright scary. In the business world, change is commonly associated with negative results, such as department reorganizations, politically motivated technology decisions, and the dreaded D-word: *downsizing*. Life has taught us that, in general, people have a difficult time making adjustments to their individual comfort levels. Compound their anxiety by throwing the word *change* into the mix, with all of its negative connotations, and suddenly asking your team to "expand their area of expertise" becomes as simple as home dentistry.

But you are an "evangelist of change." Your role is to bring your organization up to speed with the latest technology, to ensure your developers and systems are used efficiently and effectively.

Effective Change Through Communication

So how does a manager effectively "persuade" his team into moving from a shareware and largely home-brewed configuration management solution to ClearCase? Let's set the record straight: this is no small task. But every project has a beginning. The first step is to build a relationship of trust with your team. It takes preparation and a lot of listening, but once established, this relationship will allow you to help others recognize the benefits of implementing object-oriented methodologies *by removing the fear*. People fear what they do not understand. The next step is to help them recognize the benefits (and the risks) of the change by providing detailed answers to their questions. People are driven by what they feel. Present a clear and concise message by offering a well-organized tactical and strategic plan for each level of the organization, thoroughly outlining the roles and responsibilities of each team member. If people understand the proposed change, they are less likely to fear it.

The three greatest barriers to change are communication, communication, and communication. If you cannot effectively communicate your ideas for change, you will not succeed. As the "evangelist of change," you must uncover the concerns of the project team and be prepared to provide solutions. This is especially difficult in such a large undertaking as adding or changing a source-code management tool such as ClearCase. Even an experienced team with years of working together will have issues, so be prepared—and keep the dialog flowing between all team members. That's the key.

Communication is a two-way street. You must listen to your team's questions without bias until you fully understand their concerns and are able to respond with the appropriate solutions. As stated by Stephen R. Covey, "Seek first to understand, then to be understood."[1] Remember that the move to object-oriented systems is a fundamental change in the way your engineers have been trained—a change in the way they think. Don't mandate change; instead, *invite* your team to make this shift in paradigms. For change to be successful, people must willingly follow.

---

1. *The Seven Habits of Highly Effective People* (Simon and Schuster, 1990)

But don't think you have to go through all of this alone. During pre-liminary steps of the process, you will begin to identify those in your company who embrace your ideas, and who will act as change agents within each level of the organization. If you set an example by keeping on top of your team's questions, resolving the concerns that will undoubtedly pop up at every phase of the project, potential change agents will feel empowered to come forward and offer their support. Ultimately, without their help you will be unable to wage your multilevel attack. Understand the magnitude of this change—and realize that you cannot do it alone. Every organization within the company and all departments involved in the project need to buy into the idea of change. Inevitably, each business area will have different concerns about the project and the move to an object-oriented methodology.

Managing Management

OK. You now have a plan, your team is behind you, and you have change agents strategically entrenched throughout your organization, all of them ready to make the move to ClearCase. There's just one small group of individuals standing between you and the successful implementation of your strategic goals: management. When the opportunity to make your proposal arrives, you will most likely feel like you are walking into a lion's den. Undoubtedly, they will counter your proposals with a barrage of calculated questions designed to pick apart even the most water-tight project plans: How much will it cost? How long will it take? What will make this project a success? Is this just another fad in software development? What will the company have to learn? Will we be inadequate with this new technology? Have our competitors also made this change? What will this do to our bottom line?

Before you have a chance to catch your breath, middle managers may sense any doubts you exhibit and decide to pounce. They want to know: How am I going to get this product out on time? How do I keep my engineers happy and productive? Is this just another fad in software development? What will I have to learn? Will I be inadequate in this new technology?

Your breathing is slow and deliberate as you pull yourself from the floor—your body bruised and beaten. As the lions surround you, waiting for you to run or assume some kind of defensive position, you reach desperately for your briefcase, searching for something to stay these beasts . . . and you find it. Your detailed project plan with time and cost estimates. Your work breakdown structure. Your systems architecture design and specification documents. Your business and process flows. Your descriptions of employee roles and responsibilities.

The lions back down for a moment, but they have seen these tactics before and start to move in for the final attack. But what they do not realize is that the key to your entire proposal goes beyond this documentation. You understand the need to clearly demonstrate the advanced utility and scalability of the powerful new channel of communication you are propounding. High-level presentations and cleverly written proposals are insufficient for communication of today's complex systems.

Communication Is the Solution

To help close the deal and sell your entire organization on the move to ClearCase, you will need to convince both the business team and the technical team of its benefits.

Following a Unified Modeling Language (UML)-compatible methodology, you explain to your technical team that marketing, working together with business analysts and technical writers, builds its requirements based on use cases and use case diagrams. Using these fundamental building blocks, they are able to piece together the specific functionality and tangible results of the project. Once the basic system components have been established, scenarios and sequence diagrams are used to define processes, relationships, and communications between components.

From there, engineering uses marketing's activity diagrams to expand the project, tying objects together using collaboration diagrams. As the project becomes more complex, groups of objects become classes, and the engineers create class diagrams and state diagrams that describe the behavior and identify attributes of the key classes of the system. Following this flow, classes are allocated to language-specific components for creation and implementation of code.

QA and manufacturing also use the sequence diagrams created by marketing and engineering to further the project. While QA may improve or introduce new product scenarios, manufacturing utilizes deployment diagrams to construct the system or product.

The key to this process, you explain, is that every part of the company is working from the same set of models. If one group makes changes, everyone will see the changes and instantly understand the connections to and effects on their teams and processes. This instant communication and visibility into the linkages between projects is the greatest selling point of ClearCase.

While a common change management solution is essential to the fast-paced development of products in today's competitive marketplace—one that can be utilized, ideally, by all departments and levels of the company, from engineers to marketing management, business analysts to the VP of Sales—the crux of your business proposal cannot be presented with a simple UML diagram.

To convince your management team and move your project forward, you must be able to explain the basic business value of a corporate-wide configuration management solution, and the resource efficiencies and cost reductions that will come as a result. Sometimes easier said than done, but key to getting management commitment. The process is very similar to the steps you followed with your technical team: begin with the requirements for the system, outline the use cases for the system, and work your way toward an explanation of how each of these use cases solves specific business concerns.

A Common Solution

Communication channels must be kept open for any project to be successful. Whether your focus is manufacturing, software engineering, information systems, or telecommunications, a common change management solution is the key to your project mastery. All departments and all levels of your company must buy into the idea that it is critical to align your development efforts under a single communication methodology. Driving your organization toward a ClearCase reality may seem as difficult as making the Earth move. In fact, convincing your team to adopt this new paradigm may be one of the biggest challenges of your career—but it isn't impossible.

Start with your team relationships. It is critical to build relationships of trust, recognizing and quickly removing the fear factor through clear communication of the benefits of ClearCase, and by providing solutions. Present a clear and concise message by offering a well-organized tactical and strategic plan for each level of the organization, thoroughly outlining the roles and responsibilities of each team member, and most important, establishing ClearCase as the de facto communication vehicle.

If people understand change, they are less likely to fear it. And if you remove the fear, you can accomplish anything.

Understanding the Scope

Once you have a clear communication channel with your team, you can then begin to collect the data and requirements necessary for scoping your solution. Without it, management of daily interactions with a demanding set of customers, internal or external, can be a time-consuming and sometimes frustrating endeavor. Something as complex as the deployment of a software configuration management system can get even more complex when rolled out across several different teams, and several different office locations.

Control of an expanding project definition is a battle hard fought. The users want more gadgets, faster processing time, less back-end management. And then some managers seem to invite every other software vendor to give a presentation on the latest products—after which you are buried under a barrage of phone calls and e-mails asking, "Can our software do this too?" or "What would it take to add in this functionality?" or even "I've changed my mind about that capability—I'm really more interested in taking the software in this direction."

Come to think of it, talking to internal customers sometimes resembles conversations with teenagers. What a fickle lot. How do you talk to a teenager, anyway? That's one of the questions passed down from generation to generation—and one that may never be completely answered. It seems that each and every day is full of new problems, new adventures, and growing pains. The same is true with most users, and we'd like to illustrate these similarities by analyzing four of the most prevalent issues affecting most projects (in no particular order): unrealistic timelines, scope creep, funding issues, and changes in technology decisions.

Unrealistic Timelines

Users have been known to make requests with unrealistic timelines. While their intentions may be good, they are often unfamiliar with the process and tools necessary to complete the task, or they may not comprehend the impacts on your scarce team resources. Teenagers, on the other hand, are known to make unrealistic time estimates—whether it affects your time or their time—when dealing with such topics as cleaning their room, mowing the lawn, or taking the family car out to "get some gas." In these situations, they clearly do not comprehend (if you're an optimist) or are ignoring (for those of us who are pessimists) the family ground rules.

Scope Creep

Scope creep is the dreaded expansion of a product or project in which the goals have not been clearly defined and, more than likely, documentation is not being tracked. What usually happens is an agreement is reached on some limited functionality, but as soon as the project is underway, the scope falls under attack. Compare this to teenagers. No matter how clear you are on "house rules" or "family guidelines," teenagers will push definitions of the finer points of your instructions to the legal limit. Don't fall into the all-too-familiar trap of "You said to be home by 10, but you didn't specifically say 10 p.m.!" Most teenagers find safety in the "gray area" of even the most explicit statements, always expanding the scope of your original intentions.

Funding Issues

Users want a Mercedes, but they only want to pay for a Yugo. Who doesn't want the best possible product for the least possible cash outlay? This problem is usually the result of the aforementioned project scope creep. While the project definition gets tweaked, adjusted, expanded, altered, refitted—whatever you want to call it—rarely (if ever) is the financial support appropriately expanded. Do we need to even interpret the parallels to teenagers on this point? Let us put it this way: How many times have we given our teenagers money for work and chores they should be doing anyway? (cleaning their rooms, doing the dishes, and so on)

Changes in Technology

One major fear is the perceived technological jump amidst a major development effort. Not that most of us fear change in general, or the wealth of technological leaps and jumps being made in many industries, but users are often drawn like mosquitoes to a lightbulb when a vendor plays the technology card. Even more applicable than the insect analogy is that of teenagers and any consumer product. They endlessly pursue the latest/greatest toy, gadget, or trinket. Hey, who are we fooling? This is one problem that extends to all of us. We want the newest car, the latest fashions, and the fastest computer. Why would it be any different with our users?

Project Risk

A major driver for all projects is planning for and minimizing risk. Proper planning, clarification of scope, detailed understanding of financial issues, and mastery of the technology all help manage risk. Taking time in your planning to specifically identify the risks around not only the project mechanics, but also the softer issues—such as user adoption, management support, and business process change—will go a long way in securing the success of your project.

Seek First to Understand . . .

So what does all of this mean? What we're trying to illustrate is that both customers and teenagers can be demanding, temperamental, and even illogical. Most of us can relate to some of these examples, having lived through them on a number of projects. Now that we've identified some of the major problems, let's discuss the process for obtaining solutions.

You're about to undertake a major effort by implementing ClearCase. How do you get past these barriers in communication, allowing you to fully realize your customers' needs and to build a system that meets their software development requirements? Here's the secret: you need to understand your users.

We know what you're thinking: this is an oversimplified answer to a very complex issue. How does one "understand" a given project? The answer can be gained through business modeling. The purpose of business modeling is to determine who and what the customer is—but not necessarily the requirements of the project. The point is to seek to understand the client's perspective (which, in this case, is your software development organization) and not make any judgments about possible solutions or what the customer thinks he or she needs. We are not trying to identify the requirements at this stage—the business model is the *problem domain*, while the requirements are the *solution domain*, which comes later in the development process. Instead, it is critical to know what you are building and why. And yet this step is often downplayed. In fact, we would venture that business modeling is the most undervalued part of the software development process.

Let us put it to you this way. A sick man enters a doctor's office with severe pain in his chest and abdomen. The doctor doesn't simply prescribe medicine based on the external symptoms the man is exhibiting. The doctor examines the patient, takes x-rays, and performs blood tests. Only when he truly understands the cause of the symptoms does the doctor assign a prescription. And yet many developers dive right into solving their customer's problems without truly understanding the root cause. Business modeling begins much like normal system modeling, but we need to remember that the focus is on the current state of the business—that is, on the problem domain, and not the solution domain.

To further illustrate our point, let's take a look at how most development efforts begin. How often do we start the development of a system with the use case analysis? Although this is an integral part of the model, we really are putting the cart before the horse. Instead of thoroughly defining and understanding the customers and their mode of operation, we often create several use cases for what we perceive to be the customers' needs, only to have the customer come back and make changes later in the development cycle. This process of building blindly continues throughout the development of the system unless recognized and corrected up front. The result? Unrealistic timelines. Scope creep. Funding issues. Poor technology decisions. Ultimately, without understanding the business needs behind the system, your company will end up building the wrong product.

Stephen Covey hit the right note when he suggested the secret to communication is "Seek first to understand, and then to be understood." To fall back on our original analogy, the process of understanding your teenagers (and your customers) begins with listening. And we mean really listening—not just to the words that come out of their mouths, but also to the meaning behind the words. How often do we lecture our teenagers without actually listening to them first? Think about how easy it is to jump to the wrong conclusions when all of the pertinent data are not before us. As consultants, software developers, and managers, it is our role to anticipate the needs of our customers (as with our teenagers) by looking beyond the words and, like the doctor, revealing the illness behind the symptoms.

Business modeling is a mechanism that guides you through the listening phase of your project, helping you to understand every part of the system being designed and to properly integrate all of the functions. The modeling process helps to organize the information gathered from the customer and the users of the system. The Rational Unified Process (RUP) includes many steps and deliverables that, if met, will start you out in the right direction.

The RUP helps define the roles that each member of your team plays by defining the activities in which they will participate and the artifacts they will produce or help produce. This book covers many aspects of the RUP, but specifically it focuses on the Configuration Management role, as described in the RUP. Chapter 9 has more information about RUP and how configuration management ties into the process.

The System Glossary

This living document establishes a common vocabulary for your project and, if properly maintained, will prove invaluable to the success of your project. The glossary is developed from common words and phrases used throughout the business, and it is regularly updated and revised by modifying use case names to fit those in the glossary, and vice versa. Sometimes a word can be used to mean several different things; this should be noted and tracked. Having a common vocabulary will strengthen communication. It is important that new terms are documented and presented to the customer as soon as possible.

The Use Case Model

This thoroughly describes the functional roles and processes of the current business. Just as in the normal system analysis, the use case model defines the boundaries of the problem by identifying the actors of the problem domain. An actor can be a computer, a human being, or even a Web service that provides a specific function. Although it seems to be fairly simple, this step can take a considerable amount of customer interaction and communication. Don't get into the trap of making the boundary of your system too broad or too narrow. After the actors have been found, begin identifying the use cases that they employ in the current system, and the interactions between them. Once use cases have been identified, scenarios need to be developed. Start with the most common scenario for the use case. Each use case should, at the very least, have its most common scenario developed. It is also important to describe the scenarios that you and your customer consider the highest risk. Don't forget to consult and modify the system glossary for consistency. For those of you who are relatively new to the world of actors and use cases, we recommend you take a look at *UML Explained,* by Kendall Scott (Addison-Wesley).

You may, at this point, find it difficult to keep from jumping into the solution phase. Remember to model the current system, not the future system.

The Class Model

In the previous step of the process, we defined the use cases and scenarios of the business and the problem domain. Each scenario has objects and messages between those objects. The next step is to segregate those objects into classes. Many times these objects will be deliverables, documents, or physical things that are currently used by the business and its processes. It may be beneficial to stereotype these classes according to delivcrable type. Sometimes, depending on the customer, it may be beneficial to design an icon for the stereotype to aid in communication. Once again, this should capture what is happening now, not what will happen later.

The Business Specification

Many times customers require documentation for the newly developed model. The business specification is the culmination of all of your efforts to understand: the system glossary, the use case model, and the class models are the deliverables that define your understanding of the customer and his or her problems. The result of these steps should be a detailed description of what your project or process looks like today. These pieces are combined into one document and used to convey your understanding to the customer, and once ratified by the customer, this document becomes the foundation of the solution phase of the development effort.

...And Then to Be Understood

When focusing on business modeling, the key is to remember that you are not trying to solve the problem outright. Instead, your purpose is to meticulously capture and document the state of the business, therefore revealing a clear picture of the problem your software must help solve. Now that you understand the customer and the customer agrees with your assessment of the current state of the system, it is time to work on the second half of Covey's equation: how to be understood. Basically, you go about this with the same level of detail applied to your efforts to understand the system. We highly recommend finding and following a well-crafted methodology and sound software development practices—a topic for later chapters. See Chapter 5, "Mapping the Manufacturing Process," in particular.

More gadgets, faster processing time, less back-end management. Each and every workday can be full of new problems, new adventures, and maybe even one or two adjustments to the technological direction of your company. The purpose of our user/teenager analogy was to present the concept of understanding your users and customers—and to illustrate that it all begins with listening. Hopefully we have accomplished this. Listening is not a problem if you understand the underlying motivations behind your user requests. If you can identify the current system first, your development efforts will more aptly deal with the unrealistic timelines, scope creep, funding issues, and changes in technology decisions that will inevitably crop up during the project. We would be naive to think that this method is a catchall for every possible system issue. But you will find that by taking the time to document the current system up front, many potential problems will be diverted, and your chances for success will increase exponentially.

And then it will be time for management approval.

The Principles of Change Management

There's never enough time to do it right,
but there's always enough time to do it over.
—*Jack Bergman*

There are typically three project management variables that can be
used in software or system development efforts to regulate project
fluctuations: time, resources, and money. With most projects, however, time is not a variable to be considered. Last time we checked
with Father Time (a.k.a. the demanding customer), he would not let
things slip—no matter how hard we pushed. As for resources and
money, they've always been scarce.

So . . . when you are faced with a development schedule that seems
impossible, what do you do? As projects progress, it is inevitable that
time schedules become increasingly tight. The proverbial "window of
opportunity" has become smaller and smaller as time-to-market
demands have grown. Competition has increased and qualified engineers have become more difficult to secure.

So what can you do? Hire more people to come up with a solution?
Have your existing team work longer hours? Bring in an outside consulting team to "fix" your systems? Scrap your entire system and start
over again? None of these are reasonable solutions. You need to solve
your problems in a timely manner with your current resources and
within your budget parameters. In a nutshell, you need to find ways
to enable your engineering team to work in parallel.

Defining the Layers of the System

You have clear communication with your team, the scope has been
clearly defined and shared throughout the company, and it is now
time to move your project forward. Take a look at the way many
companies—and your own company in particular—approach problems. Do different divisions or business units define a problem from

their individual perspectives, without taking into account the "big picture"? Some companies have recognized this approach to problem solving as a weakness, and they have taken steps to reverse segmented business practices. Many fall far short of what is truly needed, unleashing instead a series of well-intended policies, requirements meetings, and joint application design sessions that do not solve the problems. "Concurrent engineering" is about as overused a phrase and draws as much excitement from development teams as "cross-functional," "paradigm shifts," and "total quality management." Somewhere behind the well-intended jargon hides the formula these organizations need to move forward, but they just can't break the cycle.

As a result, time is lost. Time you can't afford to lose. What most organizations lack is a process for communication and an understanding of how to develop software and systems in parallel. You cannot afford to hire more people, even if you could find them. A consulting group is probably not going to do much better, what with ramp-up time and a tight budget. And scrapping the system is not a viable solution. You need to work smarter.

There are several approaches to parallel development. One approach is to work on several releases at the same time. ClearCase can aid your software team in setting up parallel branches of development. Some of our customers have tried and failed to develop multiple releases of a product at the same time. The largest problem with this simplistic approach is determining (1) where defects or enhancements are implemented and (2) when to propagate the changes to the other releases being developed concurrently. Many companies have already learned that they cannot sustain the level of overhead required to merge code to and from their releases.

Another approach to parallel development is to define specific layers of the system. Breaking the system into multiple components—to be built individually—can increase parallel development dramatically, but it too must be carefully planned and monitored.

Component(ize) the Architecture— Component(ize) Engineering

The key to parallel development is the identification of logical divisions in the software or system, dividing them into separate components that can be developed autonomously. As shown in Figure 2.1, think of each component as a system unto itself, and follow the same development techniques you would use on the complete system. Begin by defining the component responsibilities and interfaces. Devise use cases and scenarios—derived from the complete system use cases and scenarios—to define the responsibilities and interface of the system.

Keep in mind that the complete system use case analysis must be completed first. The second step is to have the system architect define the component boundaries and the interfaces between components. Once the component boundaries and interfaces have been defined, the torch can be passed to others. Small teams of engineers can then take each component to work on as their "system." The interfaces should be the first to be implemented. The Interface Definition Language (IDL) is a great language for this step. (For information on the IDL, see the CORBA IDL specification at

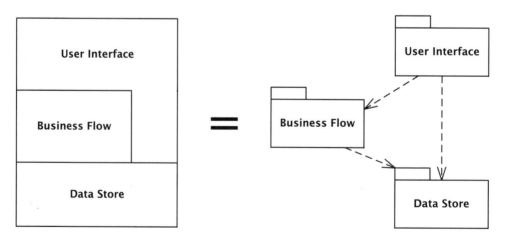

Figure 2.1 *Divide Your System into Components*

http://www.omg.org.) Remember that any change to the interface will mean coordination between your group and other groups, and it will require coordination through the system architecture group. (After all, they need something to do.)

Each team of engineers should develop its component as if it were a standalone product—one that will ultimately be delivered to a customer. Okay, the customer just happens to be the group in the "cube farm" next door, but they should be treated as a customer all the same.

Because each component will go through several releases, coordination is critical. The first release of your component will be the interface. This will allow other components to communicate with your component right away. Subsequent releases, however, should be based on a system plan covering the complete system. It is a very logical process. Features required by the complete system should be supported by the separate components of the system. Think about it: it does not do any good to develop code that implements a feature that will not be needed until the next major release of the complete system. Your time is critical. If you focus on such low-priority features, you will be guilty of ignoring the features that need to be finished for this release. Communication is always important—at all levels of the organization—but in this case, a good defect/enhancement-tracking and work task-tracking program will come in very handy.

Your initial focus should be on components with the most dependencies and the highest risk. If a component has several high-level dependencies, it is typically your highest-risk component and should be worked on first. However, this is not always the case. A component without the obvious high-level dependencies may use a new technology or language. Therefore, this component may be your highest risk. Although such special cases should be considered, the rule of thumb is to start with the component with the highest dependencies.

Coordinating Component Releases

At the center of any parallel development effort is the coordination of component releases and the dependencies between the components.

A strong project management team is essential to your success. Any number of issues or undefined tasks can add dimensions of complexity. If one component schedule slips, what will be the impact on other schedules? How can you minimize risk, avoiding failure of the entire project? The answer is an iterative development approach. As shown in Figure 2.2, if each component has a release cycle that is very short—let's say every two to six weeks—problems will pop up quickly. These problems can be addressed immediately, with resources shifted as needed. A short cycle leads to a tighter focus, improving the process of identifying problems and finding solutions.

Another benefit of several short iterations is the adaptability to change. By building change into the process, your team becomes more adept at identifying problems and making adjustments. There is nothing worse than trying to pound a square peg into a round hole because that is what your fuzzy requirements call for. With short cycles, changes can occur quickly—in one iteration.

Points to Consider

Circular Dependencies
Nothing kills productivity and increases complexity more than having two components dependent on each other. One of the biggest

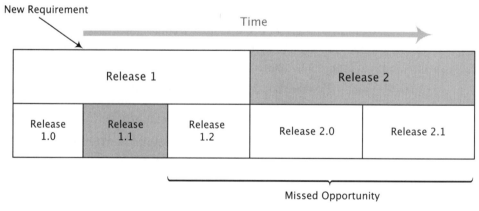

Figure 2.2 *Iterative Development*

problems is determining what component to build first. We have had customers build the same code twice to make sure that the circular dependency was handled properly, or so they thought. They seemed to have a problem rebuilding a particular release of their product. As illustrated in Figure 2.3, it is the same problem that biologists have been trying to solve for thousands of years: Which came first—the chicken or the egg?

Overhead

If engineers and managers are spending all of their time filling out paperwork and status reports, productivity will decrease, and frustration will increase. Use a good defect/enhancement-tracking tool that is accessible by those who need information about the components and the system as a whole. When people are able to look into the system for what they need, they do not have to interrupt someone else to ask.

Too Many Pieces

Be careful not to divide your system into too many components. The overhead of coordination of component development cycles can be costly in time and resources.

Finger Pointing

Watch out. One of the difficulties that typically arise is the "It's not my code causing the problem" syndrome. Finger pointing can

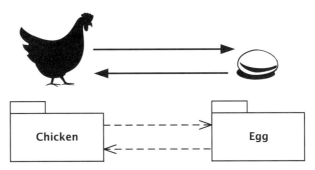

Figure 2.3 *Which Came First?*

become corrosive to the organization as a whole. Avoid setting up groups to compete against each other for reward, resources, or recognition.

Look at the Big Picture

There is an old Indian story, often told by environmental educators, entitled "The Blind Men and the Elephant." In the story, six blind men encircle an elephant trying to outdo one another in explaining what the elephant is. One of the men feels the side of the animal and declares, "Elephants are like walls." Another man grabs hold of a tusk and says, "Elephants are sharp and dangerous." Yet another takes hold of an ear and claims, "They are like fans." "They are like soft fire hoses," says another as he handles the trunk. "No, they are like tree trunks," protests another as he holds onto a leg. "They are like whips," exclaims yet another with the tail in hand.

This story is told to illustrate the complexity of the elephant, and to suggest that to properly comprehend a subject we must back off a bit and at least see it from several sides. Each of the blind men walked away with a different understanding of the elephant. While each of their descriptions contained what they believed to be the truth—and from each perspective, it was the truth—none of them had a full understanding of the situation.

Do not fall into this trap. Remember that each component plays a role in the development of a larger system. Know how each piece fits into the puzzle and, above all, communicate, communicate, communicate.

Getting Started

You now have a better idea of how to approach parallel development. It's all about working smarter, not harder. But this process calls for change—in the way your team operates, and in the way problems are analyzed. By building change into the process, however, your team will become more adept at identifying problems and making adjustments. Just remember these six steps:

1. Identify logical divisions in your software or system.

2. Divide your system into separate components that can be developed autonomously and assigned to small development teams.

3. Define the component boundaries and interfaces.

4. Coordinate between components.

5. Reduce risk by focusing on components with the most dependencies.

6. And always look at the big picture.

3

Standards Enforcement Using Configuration Management Tools

Configuration Management Is Man's Best Friend

STANDARD, CRITERION, GAUGE, YARDSTICK, TOUCHSTONE mean a means of determining what a thing should be. STANDARD applies to any definite rule, principle, or measure established by authority . . . . CRITERION may apply to anything used as a test of quality whether formulated as a rule or principle or not . . . . GAUGE applies to a means of testing a particular dimension . . . or figuratively a particular quality or aspect . . . . YARDSTICK is an informal substitute for CRITERION that suggests quantity more often than quality . . . . TOUCHSTONE suggests a simple test of the authenticity or value of something intangible . . . .

—*From* Merriam-Webster's Collegiate Dictionary, 11th Edition.
© *2003 by Merriam-Webster, Incorporated. Used with permission.*

A Continuing Story about Life Without Standards...

Changing jobs is always an interesting proposition. Because people get so accustomed to the environments in which they work, change can be difficult. Now try moving from an established, process-driven environment to a start-up. Instead of detailed processes, you're more likely to find "shoot-from-the-hip" management styles and a "get the product out at any cost" mentality. And in that rush of building the latest, greatest technology that everyone wants and everyone needs and everyone else is trying to build "so we better get ours out there first"—we sometimes push standards to the bottom of the priority list. In the long run, the product, and the company, will most likely suffer.

So what's the big deal about working without standards? We're not talking about anything that can seriously impede our development progress, like ethics (or personal hygiene). A lone engineer can create a product without having to follow some complicated methodology as defined by an organization with a funny name, right? A team of engineers can also probably survive. It's been done before; it can be done again. Granted, it may take longer than projects following a defined process. And there's not much chance of reusing the process or components if there is no clear documentation. But hey—you got the product out the door, right?

From a technical standpoint, how much do any of us think about standards when we work? The fact is, we apply standards to our everyday lives that we may not even consider standards. For example, you could not read this chapter if we didn't have a standard written language. Before you jump to the conclusion that this is a silly comparison, think about how written language came about. People spoke the language before they learned to write it. Can you get along in life without reading? Sure. But how far can you really get in life? Our ancestors were relatively smart people. But once they could write, efficiencies soared. Creativity grew by leaps and bounds. There was that slightly odd period called the Dark Ages, but otherwise things have progressed quite nicely.

Another fine example of standardization is the automobile industry. Can you imagine what would have happened to user acceptance if each and every auto manufacturer had decided to support its own type of liquid fuel? There would need to be different fuel stations for each brand of car on the road. Maybe you'd see some consolidation as a few major manufacturers worked together, but it still would be a mess out on the road. There would have been fewer choices for consumers, as smaller manufacturers fought to gain market share. Rural customers would have even more limited choices—or no choice at all if the only regional manufacturer decided that it was not cost-effective to build a station in that area. And here's a pleasant thought: traveling across the Nevada desert and not being able to find a fuel station for your AMC Pacer. Yikes.

Experiments in Project Management

So we find ourselves back at the example of the new job, where you're trying to convince your new manager that some kind of development methodology makes sense in the long run. For a lesson in standards, we need only go as far as your team project manager. Depending on where you work, this job function has been known to "manage" a wide assortment of tasks. Organizations such as the Project Management Institute (PMI) and methodologies such as Critical Path Analysis and Kepner-Tregoe Analysis have gained wide acceptance due to the multitude of conflicting and confusing standards being implemented across companies and industries in the name of project management. A unified methodology allows organizations to work together on large projects by offering a common framework from which to build.

With today's immensely complex, sophisticated software and hardware, "only demanding attention to detail and insistence on routines and standards make engineering design cost effective," comments Lowell W. Steele in his book *Managing Technology: The Strategic View* (McGraw-Hill, 1989). He continues:

> We are observing that phenomenon in software engineering—namely, the development of rules, concepts, and techniques for design, procedures for quality control, and measurements for writing software. Software programmers have been operating with few constraints on their personal idiosyncrasies and sense of elegance. The result has been vast duplication of effort and the creation of programs that cannot be maintained or modified, except by their creator, without a major investment in unscrambling them.

Look at the shifts in object-oriented software development over the past decade. The streamlining of modeling techniques, most notably the blending of notations by Booch, Jacobson, and Rumbaugh into UML, lends weight to the argument that people must learn how to standardize their software development practices through the use of repeatable modules and extensible packages. Tools must be rigid in their capabilities, but flexible in their application.

A History of Software Standards

Because software quality has been poor in the past, many companies have been trying to adopt industry standards—such as ISO 9000 from the International Organization for Standardization (ISO) and the Capability Maturity Model (CMM) from the Software Engineering Institute (SEI). Other companies have developed their own standards to help with product development. Companies take on these initiatives without a clear understanding of how much time and effort such projects will take to fully implement, much less to reap the benefits that these standards can provide. Many times these efforts fall short because there isn't a clear "captain of the ship"—without an evangelist for these standards, most implementations fail. Most of us have lived through such failures time and time again.

In more recent years, software standards have fragmented into several different aspects of software development: language, coding, analysis and design, quality assurance, product lifecycle, and configuration management are just some of the standards categories.

Language standards such as the American National Standards Institute's ANSI C have proliferated as code became more readily portable across compilers that followed the standard. This has not always been the case with language standards. For example, ANSI C++ took too long to standardize and several compiler vendors extended and fragmented the language. As a result, C++ has had its share of portability problems. (See Bjarne Stroustrup's page on the standard's approval, at http://www.research.att.com/~bs/iso_release.html, for more.)

Each language has an inherent coding standard, defined through its unique grammar. Languages, by and large, allow programmers to choose the names of the elements of the language. For this reason, coding standards are typically created for a development team so that the team can easily read each engineer's code. There are several well-documented coding standards out on the Web that are tailored for memory management, performance, readability, or portability. (For one example, see "The Path to Useful Coding Conventions," at http://www.macadamian.com/column/column_coding.html.)

As languages progressed and evolved inside the world of analysis and design, some structured and object-oriented standards developed. In the late 1990s, the object-oriented community adopted the UML as a standard object-oriented analysis and design language (http://www.omg.org/uml). Other standards have been developed to increase the quality and reliability of software. These standards include quality assurance, risk management, project management, configuration management, product lifecycle management, and several others. Some of the most prolific standards bodies have been ANSI, SEI, and ISO. Each standards body has focused on different aspects of software development, with some overlap. Literally hundreds of standards have been created over the years.

So how do you know what is best for your organization? You need to find the standard that fits your domain and the culture of your development team. For example, if your product is mission critical and has real-time constraints, you probably would look at the ISO standards for real-time systems. For other projects, standards are necessary due to industry constraints. For example, if you are creating a medical device with embedded software, you must follow the FDA software development standards. You need to make sure to follow the standards for all of the countries in which your product will be sold. With all of that said, don't overdo it. Make sure you pick those standards that increase the productivity of your organization (and don't choose a standard just to have a standard).

The Dawn of Configuration Management

So what is configuration management, anyway? Why is it important to have some kind of source-code management system on your project? Well, that's some of what we'll cover in future chapters. It is important to understand how configuration management fits into your company, and how the mechanics of version control, structured development, and parallel and distributed development should be adopted by your entire organization and used to guide your product development efforts.

Configuration management (CM) is in a unique position because these systems are typically the glue between engineering and the rest of the product development organization. The product cannot move unless the CM team coordinates with the build-and-release team and manufacturing. Since most groups depend on the CM team for information and guidance, the CM team members are the natural leaders to help enforce process across the teams. In fact, most configuration management tools have some kind of mechanism that allows for automation of software development processes. In ClearCase, these mechanisms are called *triggers*. Within most organizations, configuration management teams commonly handle the defect and enhancement tools, as well. These tools are designed for customized workflow and process management.

Most configuration management systems allow for the use of metadata with source-code control. The metadata concept is an important tool that configuration managers can use to help enforce process and standards. With each version of the file, additional information can be attached to the version. This provides an opportunity to attach several different types of data to the file, including the name of the person who changed the file, a reference to a test case, defect, requirement, and so forth. The possibilities are endless. Not only is metadata available within these configuration management systems, but also most defect-tracking systems allow for additional information per record in the database. Both systems are easily tied together using these techniques.

Metadata allows for the collection of additional information that a standard may require; however, most standards have some kind of process requirements. The process must be followed and documented. This is where event-driven add-ins or triggers can come in handy (covered in detail in Chapter 22, "Trigger-Happy"). Let's say that you want all source code to adhere to a coding standard. There are programs out there, such as Lint, which can check your source code for certain standards. You can register a trigger to run Lint before it allows a check-in. Other triggers can send notification to a group of code reviewers when code has been checked in so they can review the code before allowing it to be included in a build. The event-driven add-in technique can be found in most defect-tracking tools, as well.

There are some unwritten rules that you need to be aware of. Whenever possible, *do not* get in the way of development. If your triggers are slow and cumbersome, for example, software developers will complain, and as is their nature, most will do everything they can to subvert your unwieldy process. Ensure that your process improvement efforts focus on what is most important, and make sure performance is at the top of your list. The faster the better.

It's All in the Timing ...

A manager's dream is to start on a project at the beginning of the lifecycle, rolling out process and procedure at the inception phase of development. However, this is rarely the case. Whether you're a consultant hired to resurrect a twice "frozen" and now "critical" project that had been shelved and reshelved due to the fluctuations of funding priorities across your organization, or you are the victim of a rapid development initiative that hopes to break the time-to-market "sound barrier" of the software development cycle, configuration management can become a powerful asset for increasing communication, productivity, and quality through process automation and integration of the tools that most engineering groups use today. At any stage, implementing some kind of CM solution will organize your development efforts, and by helping your team prioritize and manage the development lifecycle, you are more apt to meet your customer's needs.

Changing jobs or starting on a new project is tough enough; working without tools and directives that guide you through the development process is not something you need to add to your troubles. While a narrow focus on process and standards can stifle creativity and add to bureaucracy, a lack of focus and development without guiding principles can also derail a project. A happy medium must be found. A wise man once said, "Standards are rules to live by, not rules to die by." Translation: Flexibility is the key. Configuration management can add structure and direction to your development efforts while allowing flexibility for change.

Welcome to the World of Configuration Management

Mom always said that nothing worth doing is easy. Sometimes getting a product (or even a software patch) out the door and into a customer's hands can be flat-out difficult—but the rewards can be great. Fortunately, configuration management can help manage the complex development efforts we face each day. To illustrate our point, let's analyze a common problem: a dog that needs a bath. So many ideas start out as "simple" solutions to everyday problems, but then there's that little issue of "implementation." The premise is that your dog is dirty. We recognize that soap and water clean things. Therefore, adding the dog to soap and water will clean the dog. Easy, right?

Not so fast, Mr. Software Developer. It's so easy to jump in there without thinking about all of the factors that go into washing a dog.

Planning for the event surfaces some issues that you might not have considered: Where do we wash the dog? How much water is needed? What kind of soap do we use? How do we dry the dog once he's clean?

Scheduling the big event reveals more issues: We can't use the good towels, and the beach towels are still in the clothes hamper. The downstairs bathroom is off-limits because the in-laws are visiting, and the spouse would not be thrilled if we messed up the master bathroom.

Implementation uncovers more unseen problems: There is no way to tie down the dog to keep him in the tub while cleaning him. The dog doesn't seem to like the water. The dog won't hold still while we try to wash him. The dog is having an allergic reaction to the liquid soap. Every time we try to rinse the dog, he shakes his fur and sprays water and soap all over the bathroom. The dog has escaped and is running through the house while soaking wet.

A Simple Idea Just Got Complicated

So what does any of this have to do with configuration management? Well, for one thing, it's all about managing the increasing complexity of a project. The preceding example illustrates how a series of tasks without management can quickly get out of hand. We've poked fun at the unforeseen complexities of an otherwise simple, everyday issue like washing a dog. But now let's take a look at something a bit more complicated: your current development project. How do you manage the complexities of an ever-growing list of customer demands, enhancements, and features?

In the world of software development, far too many engineers, analysts, and managers are tackling problems in much the same way as the aforementioned dog owner: they don't understand the scope of the project in front of them, and yet they jump right in. And it doesn't help that they're bombarded with books and articles and training classes promoting implementation as the key differentiator between projects and project teams that succeed and those that fail. The experts are only partly right. We're not saying that an artful and accurate (and speedy) execution is not critical to success (because it is), but we do insist that you cannot proceed down this path without a thoughtful and detailed design in place. Understanding this, how do you manage the complexities of your design, allowing your team to stay apprised of changes and enhancements, to focus on the tasks at hand, and to execute flawlessly?

Configuration Management Maturity

The last ten years have seen an increase in the use of source-code management systems, but there still remain numerous barriers to the widespread use of these products and systems. More and more companies are beginning to understand the need to version-control their code and protect their intellectual property. With this increased use of source-code control, the configuration manager has emerged. And because over the past few years we have seen an increase in functionality and complexity of these tools, configuration managers (especially those with ClearCase experience) are in high demand, and are demanding top dollar.

We will specifically address many of the different solutions available today, and how the software development industry has changed to accept these concepts.

Standards, and How CM Can Help

Because software quality has been poor in the past, several different companies have started developing their own standards to help with product development—everything from ISO 9000 to SEI's CMM. Companies take on these initiatives without a clear understanding of how much time and effort these projects will take to fully implement, much less reap the benefits that these standards can provide. Many times these efforts fall short because there isn't a clear "captain of the ship"—without an evangelist for these standards, most of these implementations fail. We've seen it time and time again.

Configuration Management is in a unique position because these systems are typically the glue between engineering and the rest of the product development organization. The product cannot move unless the CM team coordinates with the build-and-release team and manufacturing. Since most groups depend on the CM team for information and guidance, they are the natural leader to help the teams follow the process. In fact, most configuration management tools have some kind of mechanism that allows for automation of software development processes. In ClearCase, these mechanisms are called Triggers. You will also find that most configuration management teams are handling the defect and enhancement tools, as well. These tools are designed for customized workflow and process management.

Quality Starts with CM—Not the QA/QC Testing Process

It is a misconception that you can test quality into a product. The manufacturing industry has known for years that testing is an important aspect of product development, but it does not improve quality—it only quantifies the quality measures. Configuration management can play an important role in improving the quality of your product through process improvement and, hand in hand with the software architects' enforcement, improve your design and implementation practices. Many of these enforcements can be put into place by a good set of tools that prevent bad things from happening—some even automatically guide software engineers to follow good practices (using wizards and workflows).

Most of the quality problems that exist in product and software development are due to problems with process. Our answer to this is simple: If the process is wrong, fix it. Don't fall into the trap that so many companies fall into when they claim they don't have a process. Every company and development team has a process. You might not have it written down, or have a clear idea of the steps involved, or understand management expectations, but there are processes that evolve over time in every organization. Most of the time they are poorly conceived, duplicating much of the work that has already been done. Rework is the costliest of process errors and can only be corrected with a carefully enforced development methodology. Every time you get a new employee or an employee leaves the company, the process changes and adapts to the new participants. As you can imagine, this is not very productive, and quality suffers greatly.

Parallel and Distributed Development (Decreasing Time-to-Market)

What manufacturing has been doing for almost thirty years, the software industry has just begun in earnest: offshore or multiple-site development. The hope is to get cheaper, qualified employees into technology markets where it is virtually impossible to find the right people with the right skills. In the manufacturing industry, the problems with multiple locations have been identified and resolved for the most part, but the software industry presents a different set of challenges. Because the development schedules for software products have become extremely short, companies cannot afford to waste any time sending information back and forth between locations. The time adds up quickly. On an average project, entire weeks can be wasted.

While configuration management tools have made some leaps forward in allowing for replication of information to multiple locations, a solid plan still needs to be developed and followed to use these tools effectively. Some of the complexities of multi-site development can be solved through division of effort. If your code base is divided effectively, the dependencies between locations can be minimized and the "sync-ups" between sites can also be minimized. As a result, groups can work more independently. Since the CM team is typically responsible for the multi-site coordination and integration, it is important that they have some input into the architecture of the product.

Another of the issues that need to be addressed are the branching strategies that are used between the sites, and, potentially, at each site. Branching is used to isolate users from the work of others, it enables multiple releases of products to be developed at the same time, and is a basic requirement when working with multiple sites. For more information, see our chapter on Branches and Labeling.

"Consistency Is King" in multi-site development. Develop a branching strategy that does not get in the way of the developers, or they will not use it—believe us, they will subvert it. Once you have developed the branching strategy, you need to flat-out stick with it. When you have multiple locations in every corner of the world, it becomes a logistical nightmare to train everyone each time you have an epiphany and modify your branching philosophy. And continued education will be an important tool that you will need to use often to keep teams from stepping all over each other.

Traceability

Some of the first questions that we ask companies when working on their CM strategies surround their choice of defect-enhancement tool, and how their system coordinates with their source-code control. Many of the commercialized defect-tracking tools have hooks into source-code control tools. These hooks are typically defect-to-code check-in hooks. In Chapter 17, "Integrating Multi-site Teams in Your Spare Time," we address the use of defect/enhancement tools to aid in the estimation of effort for new development, selective feature builds, and full artifact traceability from requirements to code, and then to the delivered product.

Builds

One of the key responsibilities of most CM teams is the build and release of the product. The team is typically the gatekeeper between engineering QA/QC and manufacturing. Builds can become a nightmare if the build systems are not designed and maintained throughout the development process. Many of the issues that CM teams need to worry about include: frequency of builds, what gets built, are the builds repeatable, and which platforms need to be built. The key to all of this is that the planning of these activities needs to be done up front, before the software engineers start coding. Many times we have walked into software development companies that have had ad hoc build strategies and were disappointed when they could not integrate all of their code in a repeatable manner (what a shocker). These companies typically waste several months trying to recover from the disaster that they let happen.

Release and Distribution

You've completed your build and integrated all of your code—let's not overlook the need to actually release and distribute your product effectively. It does not do your company or your product any good if you cannot get it to your customers. This part of the process includes not only your product, but also the supplemental data that goes with your product, such as defect reports, user manuals, installation guides, and runtime requirements. One of the companies that we worked with had spent all of their time building and developing their product, and when the product was finally ready for distribution to their customer, it would not run on their customer's platform. Because the product did not include the appropriate documentation, no one realized until it was too late that the customer had moved to a new version of the operating system. Ouch.

In Chapter 6, "Ground-Level View of a Product Release," we cover different types of distribution including over the Internet, labeling your code and executables so there is traceability for customer support, defining runtime requirements, and several other internal release strategies.

Third-Party Libraries and Reuse

One of the traps that far too many companies fall into is the NIH syndrome (Not Invented Here), which is the idea that a tool, or a third-party library, that is created outside of the company is somehow less critical than one created within the company. Not factoring into the development plan all tools along the critical path can cause long delays in product releases and is generally acknowledged as a waste of valuable engineering time. The alternative does not come without effort. Third-party tools and libraries should be part of the development strategies that your CM team evaluates. A set of tests should be developed by your company to validate the functionality of these third-party libraries before they are released to your engineering teams. There is nothing worse than finding three months into development that a major part of your third-party tool does not work as advertised, and the previous version does not have the same API that your team has been using.

When using third-party products in the development of your product, you should treat them as part of your code: they need to be versioned and labeled. Having to go back to a previous release of your product to fix problems can be nearly impossible if the version of a compiler or some other third-party tool has changed.

And that's the long and short of it. Whether you're deploying ClearCase for the first time, or just trying to improve on your existing CM skills, there is always room for improvement. Quality is an iterative process, after all. But unlike the dog-washing experience, you won't necessarily end up out of breath and soaking wet.

4

Selling ClearCase into the Rest of Your Organization

There is a natural progression in the growth and development of a software development team or start-up. As the problems around your software and products become more and more complex, the tools you require to manage your solutions need to be able to handle these changes. What would software development be without change management? The two are inseparable. To successfully develop and deliver your software, you must put in place the tools and processes and knowledge required to successfully perform change management. Period.

If you look at the ClearCase value propositions included on the IBM Rational Software Web site, you'll find a short but sweet description of the solution:

IBM Rational Software can help you meet the challenges of managing software change with IBM Rational® ClearCase®, a robust software artifact management tool. ClearCase frees your team from the time-consuming tasks associated with software development, so they can do what they do best—write and test code.

IBM Rational ClearCase, when combined with IBM Rational ClearQuest®, a flexible defect and change tracking tool, is the market leading software configuration management solution that manages change and complexity. To software teams of all sizes, IBM Rational ClearCase offers tools and processes you can implement today and tailor as you grow. IBM Rational ClearCase provides a family of products that scale from small project workgroups to the distributed global enterprise, enabling you to:

- Accelerate release cycles by supporting unlimited parallel development
- Unify your change process across the software development lifecycle
- Scale from small teams to the enterprise without changing tools or processes

Software artifacts can include design models, documentation, test cases and source code. Software artifact management provides essential features like version control, build management, workspace management, and process configurability. A sophisticated software artifact management solution helps you ensure the accuracy of releases, develop and build software in parallel, isolate specific files relevant to given tasks, manage multiple workspaces and reproduce past releases. The IBM Rational ClearCase family of products helps you automate these error-prone, manual tasks.

—Reprinted by permission based on material from www.rational.net,
© Copyright 2001 IBM Corporation. All rights reserved.

Understanding the Components

What is configuration management (CM)? When people talk about CM, they are usually referring to the tools that manage source code. However, this is just one aspect of the solution. If you step back and look at all of the components, CM consists of many different pieces, including:

- **Identification.** Identifying components, structure

- **Control.** Controlling releases, visibility, and changes (for example, via branches)

- **Status.** Ability to report status, changes, and their impacts

- **Audit.** Ability to validate completeness and track changes (for example, history that is kept even after name changes)

- **Manufacture.** Ability to trace the process from the individual developer making a change through the release of the software

- **Process.** Ensuring that changes go through a particular lifecycle

- **Teamwork.** Ability to control team interactions at multiple levels

ClearCase is a tool that supports all of these components. And now that you understand the components, how do you convince your team of the importance of taking your change management practices to the next level? Where do you start? Well, it's always best to start at the beginning.

Change management is all about managing the increasing complexity of a project, plain and simple. Your team must understand how to manage the complexities of an ever-growing list of customer demands, enhancements, and features. And ClearCase is one of the most robust, versatile tools on the market to do just this.

Next, you need to understand how configuration management fits into your company, and how the mechanics of version control, structured development, and parallel and distributed development should be adopted by your entire organization. What are your current processes? How strictly are they adhered to? Why is it important to have some kind of source-code management system on your project?

A critical piece of change management is understanding all of the actors: Who needs access, and where are they located? You may all be centrally located in one office now, but what are your company's plans for growth? Have you considered using external, possibly foreign-based developers?

The actors will tell you who will use your CM system. Now you have to figure out how your system will be used. And how Rational's tool fits into your use model. The best way to figure this out is to model it. We suggest using business modeling with UML to get you started thinking about the components of your model.

Driving Standards, Improving Quality

Many companies take on large process or standards initiatives like this without having a clear understanding of how much time and effort these projects will take to fully implement—or how long it will take to reap the benefits that these initiatives can provide. Many times these efforts fall short because there isn't a clearly defined owner or evangelist. Without someone at the helm of the ship, driving standards for implementation, and monitoring how closely the new CM system adheres to company standards, most of these implementations fail. We've seen it time and time again.

Configuration Management tools, and ClearCase specifically, are in a unique position because these systems are the glue between engineering and the rest of the product development organization—the crux of your company's development standards efforts. The product cannot move unless the CM team coordinates with the build-and-release team and manufacturing.

Most organizations depend on the CM team for information and guidance. As a result, the rest of the company typically looks to the CM team to help drive process. Most configuration management tools have some kind of mechanism that allows for automation of software development processes. In ClearCase, these mechanisms are called triggers. You will also find that most configuration management teams are handling the defect and enhancement tools, as well. These tools are designed for customized workflow and process management—the driving force of standards in your organization.

Configuration management can play an important role in improving the quality of your products through process improvement, and, hand-in-hand with the software architects' enforcement, improve your overall design and implementation practices. Many of these enforcements can be put into place by a good set of tools that prevent bad things from happening—some even automatically guide software engineers to follow good practices using wizards and workflows (as in, for example, Unified Change Management or UCM).

You Know You Need ClearCase When ...

How do you know it's time to upgrade your CM system? It's amazing how far people will test the limits of their freeware and stretch the many manual processes supporting their hybrid, home-baked solutions before coming to the conclusion that they need a more robust, versatile solution for their software CM needs. We all recognize that there is a natural progression in the growth and development of a development team and its tools, but what are the leading indicators that your team is ready to roll out ClearCase?

Above and beyond the financial factors of implementing a new change management system—and all of the underlying implications for processes—it is not likely your management team will approve the funding of a ClearCase deployment without some fundamental needs. If your company or team is growing, you will eventually need to look at something more than the freeware or homegrown system put in place when the company was established. And more than likely, the problems you will experience (or are currently experiencing) are defined below.

Here are the top ten signs that your organization needs to deploy ClearCase:

- **You have recently expanded your development organization by opening a regional office in another country.**
  In an increasingly global development community, multi-site development capability has become critical to many companies due to offshore development teams, outsourced components, and mergers and acquisitions of complementary

products and services. Although many CM systems allow their users to FTP source code out of a central repository, this capability does not enable true multi-site development. Moving data back and forth is just one aspect of the equation. Most teams need to move information between sites several times a day, with everyone at each site working in parallel and accessing the same data. ClearCase MultiSite is a great tool for synchronous and asynchronous file sharing. Multiple geographical locations can work together very closely—and depending on your multi-site needs, you can sync the sites at any frequency, as needed.

- **You spend more time adding features to CVS than building and testing your product.**
  Do you find yourself navigating a vast web of scripts and homegrown add-ons to make up for the lack of onboard functionality in your current tool set? ClearCase is a commercial product and has several features that your typical freeware just cannot support. For those of you thinking that your freeware offers comparable features, check out the downloads and add-ons that have been developed for ClearCase at IBM Rational's main Web site, or on the Rational Developer Network at http://www-136.ibm.com/developerworks/rational. There is a reason why these tools provide links over to ClearCase—they cannot duplicate the functionality.

- **A software developer asks you to find a version of a file he cannot locate in the source tree.**
  As the number and complexity of your development projects grow, file (artifact) management becomes increasingly difficult. ClearCase provides capabilities vital to artifact management, helping you to better track and organize what is going on within your development team. Because activities are never outside of your control with ClearCase, you have a much better audit trail than with the freeware tools—and even most other commercial products.

- **You lost three weeks of work because the machine on which you were developing "bit the dust."**

Unlike several other CM systems that actually copy the data out of a repository onto your local file space, ClearCase uses dynamic views that can be accessed from any machine. Views allow users to see the code, modify the code, and to check it in for integration. Setting up ClearCase using Unified Change Management (UCM) or basic branching mechanisms also allows users to check in their code without affecting other people on the system. This also ensures that the code is in a centralized location, allowing for proper backup.

- **Software developers are constantly stepping on each other's source code when they check in.**
  Most other CM systems have no concept of the number of people who are currently working on a single piece of code. When engineers decide it is time to check their code back into the system, they typically see several merge conflicts. Because ClearCase allows users to see any code they want and to check out only the code they need to change, keeping track of who is working on what is very easy. ClearCase can provide visibility for a developer, allowing him or her to see all of the other people working on a particular piece of code.

- **Your build cycle is too long. Every time you build your product, it takes two days.**
  The typical "make" system has build avoidance through a well-defined dependency tree. But that only works in the developer workspace. Can you imagine sharing derived objects (.o, .a, .so, .class, and so on) between everyone in your development team? ClearCase automatically "winks" in derived objects from everyone working on your project. Your two days of compilation before debugging a problem can be as quick as it takes to copy the derived objects from ClearCase. The best part is—it happens just by typing "clearmake".

- **Your largest customer says they found a bug in your product that is three years old, and they need a fix in a week.**
  You may be asking yourself, "How can ClearCase help in this situation?" Actually, ClearCase has several features that can help out in this predicament. ClearCase allows for labeling of

all of your code with a tag that can be accessed at a later time. It also allows users to see all of the code checked in on a specific date and time. But that's not all. Because ClearCase has a built-in make system within the CM system, build auditing can be used to verify that what the customer was shipped can be duplicated exactly. It can even duplicate a product three years after it was originally released. Very cool stuff.

- **You need to control the content of your product. You have several rogue software engineers that like to put flight simulators or other "Easter eggs" in your product, wasting time, memory, and valuable resources.**
  OK, this is a sore spot for us—and for many software companies. To meet this requirement, ClearCase includes an integration with defect/change management systems, such as Rational's ClearQuest. But there are several defect-management tools that are supported both by IBM Rational and third-party companies, all of which provide some important functionality. For example, change requests can be tied to specific versions of source code checked in by your engineers. These integrations also help project managers control the content that gets into the product releases. So, if you have a change request that says something like "Fix the horizontal stabilizer on the F18" and your product is a spreadsheet program, you'll probably know you have something else going on.

- **You cannot seem to find the source code from the software engineer they just escorted out of the company for running a gambling site on the company's computers.**
  The point is, sometimes people leave your company—and not always on the best of terms. With ClearCase, your engineers work directly in ClearCase views, not in their home directories—or at least they should be. The system is flexible, but it gives you better control of what is going on in your organization. All of your code can be found in the same place, instead of scattered across several different computers. We have even used ClearCase to control our documentation, marketing information, and product releases. This way, we can re-create any artifact that was created for the product.

- **Your IT budget was just increased, and it's "spend it or lose it."** On occasion, you have the opportunity to step back and look at your organizational needs and make decisions based purely on anticipated growth and future requirements. When considering expanding your development organization, think about all of the problems we've addressed in this chapter, and plan your own systems accordingly. Your tool must be versatile, flexible, and scalable, and it must provide visibility. ClearCase will provide your team with the functionality you need to meet the demands of a growing, changing, and geographically diverse development organization.

Although not the only reasons why you might consider ClearCase, these ten reasons reflect the major considerations of the typical development team.

There are tools other than ClearCase that can be used to achieve these same results, but these tools can require thousands of lines of specialized scripts to accomplish the same things that can be done with a single command in ClearCase. The following list shows the key benefits of ClearCase over its competitors:

- Process control (UCM)

- GUI interface (for one, the version tree is fabulous)

- Multiple levels of parallel development

- Enables rapid development cycles

- Extensive query abilities

- Metadata

- Version extended pathing (that is, the ability to differentiate against a version in another view)

This chapter provides a snapshot of some of the factors leading teams toward ClearCase, but we invite you to continue reading to see detail on the issues surrounding the rollout and best use of this change management solution.

If you have identified with one or more of the items from our top ten list, you may be looking for more information on how to convince your management team to provide funding for the effort. In subsequent chapters, we outline the core components of ClearCase, and we explain the major benefits of deploying the tool to free up your team from all of the repetitive and time-consuming tasks that keep your team from being productive. And we answer the basic question "Where is the value proposition?"

Chapter 26, "What to Do When Things Go Wrong," is an invaluable guide to some of our administrative recommendations for minimizing problems with ClearCase, from finding the appropriate logs using the ClearCase GUI administration browser, to the steps you need to consider prior to contacting customer support. Although we don't attempt to handle every known issue, this chapter will help you avoid some of the common pitfalls for new ClearCase administrators, and get you thinking about how to properly architect your solution.

Once the decision is made to roll out ClearCase, this book will help your team understand your existing change management system and its uses, including branching, build, and test strategies, as well as ways to optimize your overall product development processes. Before switching systems, you need to have a clear understanding of your current tools and processes to help facilitate a clean switch. Later chapters will provide a number of valuable recommendations, such as moving to ClearCase in several steps, including an offline conversion to test moving a small part of the system, an offline conversion to test moving the entire system, and a beta test with some of your developers/testers to ensure that the test system works as planned (including builds, branching, and so on). We also recommend that after implementing the conversion, you keep the old system around in case of any compatibility issues.

Moving from Other Tools

On that note, unless you are forming a new company or a new development team, you are probably not starting out with ClearCase from scratch. Your company has a tool, a process, and a development methodology. CVS and VSS are popular tools. These tools, with your existing processes, may not be working very well for your team—which is probably why you are considering ClearCase in the first place—but you still must take this system into account. Not only do you need to consider the current system, but you also need to look at the types of artifacts that your team will produce. Artifacts can include document files, images, marketing collateral, source code, and even executables. You will need all of this information to put together some kind of value proposition to persuade people to move from their current system to ClearCase. To do this, you will need to know the strengths of ClearCase versus the other tools that are out there.

Here are a few items that are good selling points for ClearCase over other tools:

- **Very fast workspace, view, and creation.** Most other tools require a complete "checkout" in order to see files in your project. With ClearCase, you can start working with views right away. This decreases the time engineers need to wait to start working.

- **Build avoidance and derived object sharing.** If you have a large project that takes time to build, you can take advantage of ClearCase's derived object mechanism for "making" the product. This prevents files from being compiled or linked again before they are used by your engineers. This further decreases the amount of time it takes to get an engineer working on a problem.

- **Connecting additional data to elements.** There always seems to be additional information that we need to store about the project, file, or directory. ClearCase has a simple interface for adding information to a ClearCase element or version. This data can be queried, modified, and removed. This feature prevents the scattering of information about the project, which typically happens over time.

- **Directory versioning.** Believe it or not, several CM tools do not have directory versioning—they only version files. This may seem like a trivial thing, but watch out for this feature when converting people to ClearCase. Your developers probably will not be used to it.

- **Multiple artifact merge capabilities.** ClearCase allows many different types of files and directories to be versioned and controlled. This includes merging of artifacts—which can be very important. For example, merging Microsoft Word documents can be very difficult in other source-code management systems, but ClearCase has several built-in integrations with different artifact types.

- **Multi-site development.** ClearCase has a good multi-site development tool that allows people in multiple locations to work on the same code at the same time. It has the advantage over most other tools because it moves only changes across the net. It is highly customizable and by far the best solution for multi-site development out there.

Most configuration management systems allow for the use of metadata with source-code control. The metadata concept is an important tool that configuration managers can use to help enforce process and standards. With each version of the file, additional information can be attached to the version. This provides an opportunity to attach several different types of data to the file including the name of the person that changed the file, a reference to a test case, defect, requirement, and so forth. The possibilities are endless. Not only is metadata available within these configuration management systems, but also most defect-tracking systems allow for additional information per record in the database. Both systems are easily tied together using these techniques.

Impact on Current Projects

As the need grows for things that are faster, smaller, and more efficient, arguably, technology projects are becoming more complex. Luckily, configuration management systems are available to aid in your development efforts. They can be a powerful asset for increasing communication, productivity, and quality through process automation and integration of the tools that most engineering groups use today. Implementing some kind of CM solution will organize your development efforts around solid and repeatable processes—and by helping your team prioritize and manage the development lifecycle, you are more likely to meet your customers' needs.

One big concern of every development organization is the impact of adding a new tool or process to the existing workload and development schedule. It's not as though one can flip a switch and suddenly have a robust CM solution. These things don't happen in a vacuum. Just as one common management dream is to start on a project at the beginning of the lifecycle, rolling out process and procedure at the inception phase of development, the CM architect's dream is to join a project or company at the beginning and design the support tools and CM infrastructure the right way, at the beginning. However, this is rarely the case.

Most organizations will require some kind of phased deployment of any new CM systems. This includes finding one project that is generally not in a critical path of your overall development activities and trying things out on this project before rolling ClearCase out to the larger organization. When all of the bugs are worked out of the system, then another project can be added. And if all goes well, you can plan out the deployment to the rest of the organization. Most installations involve building the system in parallel, and slowly phasing out legacy tools and processes. You will run into some common issues when taking a phased-in approach, such as the following:

- **Conflicting use models can confuse your engineers.** Be careful: as your use models diverge, it can confuse your engineers and potentially cost you hours or days of clean-up work when someone makes a mistake. If you have two completely different use models, you will probably have to come up with a strategy on migration of the use model in addition to the tools.

- **Duplication of effort.** More than likely, you will have to maintain duplication of files for a period of time during the migration. If you can avoid this, do so. But if you can't, try to come up with a well-documented process or mechanism to handle the two file repositories. The danger here is loss of information. Using some automated scripts to keep things periodically in sync is advised.

- **Decreased productivity**. Make sure you let the project management and executive management teams know that there will be an impact to the schedule. To think otherwise is just fooling yourself, and if you aren't realistic about the impact, your management team will be. With good planning, dry runs ahead of time, and adequate training for your engineers, you can decrease the impact of the change—but don't believe that it can be completely eliminated.

If you're thinking about rolling out ClearCase, we recommend you first take a look at Chapter 5 for ideas on how to properly plan for this system. In that chapter, we present many of the questions you need to understand before embarking on a ClearCase deployment, including:

- How big do you think the project will be?

- How many people will be involved in the product development?

- At how many locations will the product be developed, tested, and deployed?

- Is the product internal or external?

- What third-party tools will you be using?

- What is the development cycle of the product?

- How do your current development methodologies fit into your tool plans?

- Are any key roles missing from your team?

- Do you have the hardware you need?

- Do you have the infrastructure ready to support your plans?

Preparation is the key to successful deployment of ClearCase. In other words, if you ask the right questions, gather the right requirements, and take into consideration all of the tools and processes your team currently uses or requires—you will be successful.

The Management Squeeze

To understand the best way to sell change management, you need to understand the key players. Who will sign the check? Who will implement your change? And who might resist the change that will result from adding Rational tools? Typically, you can look across your organization and find three groups of people that affect change:

- **The Executive**—The one who signs the checks

- **The Worker Bees**—The ones who just want to get their work done quickly

- **The Middle Manager**—The one whose schedule will be impacted

The Executive

Before approaching a member of your executive team about funding a ClearCase deployment, you need to first understand what motivates the executive. In most cases, the bottom line is the biggest factor. This is especially true if you work for a public company. The fact is that tools cost money—and if you have a large organization with multiple locations, they can cost a substantial amount of money. To help the executive make the decision to sponsor your choice of tools, you need to show the cost benefits with an actual return on investment (ROI). You cannot get away with selling tools into senior management simply by referring to them as "cool technology" and "cutting edge." Do your homework, and understand how these tools will affect your company financially. Be realistic with your numbers. Executives today are much more conservative than before the dot-com bust. Some of the things that help show ROI are increased productivity, decreased development cycle time, reliability, and decreased staffing costs.

The Worker Bees

The worker bees want to get their work done. They will typically accept change as long as it does not get in their way. Altering their work habits will involve some process change and, to be perfectly honest, some short-term pain. You need to make sure that you include the worker bees in helping you develop the best use model for the Rational tools. If you include the engineers, they will feel like they participated in the process—and will more likely accept the decision to replace the old system. They will probably want to use the new tools instead of resisting the change. Even if the executive decision maker dictates change, nothing will happen if the engineers reject it. They are the ones that will make or break the use of these tools. Get them on board early, and the project will go that much more smoothly.

The Middle Manager

The middle manager is mostly concerned with power. Some people may snicker or disagree with this assessment, but middle management has the greatest responsibility over day-to-day business decision-making. They have power over schedules and over some resources. The key to middle management is to obtain more power. You need to make sure that your adoption of the tools does not impede middle managers' thrusts for more power. They can obtain power from meeting their schedules, increasing the efficiency of their organization, or by increasing resources for their organization. You will need middle management to help effect the change, as it will impact schedules. If you cannot get middle management's support, use the executives to apply some pressure down to them—and the worker bees to push change up the ladder. This squeeze play can work, but you need to make sure you have sold the idea completely to the executive and the worker bee. If not, the whole thing will backfire.

In an ideal situation, you make your pitch to all three groups, and all three are sold on the concept. The reality is that at least one of the groups will resist. Just remember that you need to address the concerns of each group individually. Find out what motivates your key decision makers and tailor a presentation for that audience. We know this sounds obvious, but we have sat in presentations where this precept was not understood, and as a result, good ideas fell flat on their faces. Remember, you are the salesman (or saleswoman) for your idea.

The Glue That Binds

The demands on the software development organization are always growing, and both the problems and the solutions are getting more complex. Tools such as ClearCase free up your team from all of the time-consuming and repetitive tasks that take time away from what is really important: developing products and services. No matter what the size of your project team, or how you are geographically dispersed, employing the help of ClearCase will improve the accuracy of your project releases, automate those repetitive tasks, and help manage your team across multiple workspaces.

As we stated before, source-code management tools really are the glue between engineering and the rest of the product development organization—and the crux of your company's development efforts. Your main task in selling a solution into your organization is making everyone understand this fact. That's the hard part. Once they recognize that truth, you need to be ready with a solution. And with the Rational family of products, demonstrating value and ROI is easy.

5

Mapping the Manufacturing Process

Software engineering and project management share many parallels, but nothing stands out as clearly as how to integrate the activities of numerous teams or individuals or projects and still deliver a consistent product. Developing software is a complex world of ever-changing requirements and fine-tuning code—and so you'd think more time would be spent ensuring the system has been designed efficiently. In a perfect world, each effort would leverage key learnings from past projects, combine the skills and critical input from the vast array of cross-functional team members, and act as a template for future projects. Oh, that we lived in a perfect world . . . .

More than likely the scenario goes something like this: A requirement from Customer X that has been lingering in the system for a couple of months gets reassigned to you, and suddenly some VP decides that Customer X's request is critical. The request is marked urgent, made your main priority, and sent to the top of the management team's daily status report. Not the kind of attention you want from management. So you quickly craft a solution, move it through the test queue, and shake the dust off your shoes. You've just thrown your code "over the wall."

Where does ClearCase fit into all of this, you ask? Whether you're in the process of deploying ClearCase, or have it up and running and are now focusing on how you can better utilize your tools and processes to increase project efficiencies, everyone within the development organization should understand the manufacturing process.

Sizing Up the Wall: The Manufacturing Process

No one ever wants to think of himself as guilty of throwing a project or code "over the wall," and yet by not thinking about how our work integrates into the project as a whole, that's what we are doing. Think about your current development processes: How do they integrate into the processes of your coworkers? Your project team? Your company as a whole? Our guess is that there is room for improvement. It's common to find developers working in silos: focusing almost entirely on specific features and not thinking about how their work plays into the larger picture. System integration and the processes around manufacturing are typically overlooked and rarely planned effectively. So let's talk about that perfect world: You build the feature set. You package it with the other parts in the system, and with the results of your team's development. You test the components as a whole and make adjustments. You release the product.

The steps it takes to design a piece of code (your manufacturing process) should be scalable. At the macro level, it is the coordination of projects, work teams, and company resources to deliver that product to the customer. On a micro level, the heart of your system design is the outline of the integration, packaging, and delivery of the product. The purpose of this chapter is not to get into development methodologies, but there are fundamental steps that all projects must undergo. Whether developing code or managing the development of a product across multiple teams, there are four steps to this process: build, package, test, and release.

Build

You need to create processes that allow you to compile the system effectively and efficiently. These processes should be scalable and repeatable, and they should take into account the key learnings of your team. Here are some things to watch out for during the build process:

Circular Dependencies Between Libraries Compiled

The largest problem with circular dependencies is deciding which library to build first. Time after time you'll find yourself building one of the libraries twice. This can be avoided by either creating a third library that both libraries depend on or combining both libraries into one library. It is very difficult to find this circular dependency when more than two libraries are involved. This is where the benefits of visual modeling surface: circular dependencies can be seen graphically very quickly.

Complex Dependencies for Compilation

The more complex the dependencies are, the less likely it is that you will be able to build components in parallel. Again, graphical representation is the only way to really see what is going on. You can easily see in a component diagram the dependencies between components (libraries and binaries) and try to minimize them by consolidating libraries or by breaking into smaller libraries those that are heavily used. The key is to minimize the number of dependencies between classes. This will decrease compile time and make for a more repeatable build process.

Generation of Secondary and Tertiary Derived Objects for Compilation

The Interface Definition Language (IDL) generates header files and source code. Header files are used in libraries of other components to generate object files to be put into libraries. With the expanded use of IDL, we have another problem we need to worry about. Typically, IDL compilers will generate client and server implementation header files that other libraries depend on before they can be built. As shown in Figure 5.1, UML has the ability to define those interfaces to libraries, and they can be described using component diagrams. If described in the model, the makefile and build system can easily recognize what is happening within the system.

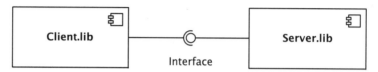

Figure 5.1   *UML Interfaces to Libraries*

Package

Every good designer recognizes that presentation can be as important as the design itself. The same is true for software development. Take the time to optimize your presentation, and preserve the integrity of your project requirements. Ask yourself: Now that I have built all of the libraries and binaries for the system, where will they reside when I install the system? Do all of the binaries go into one directory? Do they run at start-up? Where do dynamic libraries dwell? Is there more than one machine in the system? Where does each component reside?

Test

Let's face it: in the majority of projects, the testing of the product will require additional compilation of code and a rehash of requirements over software and hardware particulars above and beyond the target platform. We know that this happens, so it's important to be prepared for it. A well-planned testing environment can save precious time typically wasted trying to figure out if the problem is a real bug or just some kind of setup or environmental issue. There is nothing more frustrating than having a bug move back and forth in an endless cycle of "fixed" and "unresolved" due to a problem with an environment.

Release

Details, details, details. The key to successful release is in your ability to master the details. When completing your product or project, remember that there are important bits of information that the end customer requires—and which make all the difference in the successful release of your work. Ask yourself some fundamental questions about the customer experience: What are the machine requirements for the product? Does the user need Windows or UNIX? What version of the operating system is necessary? How much memory does the product require to install and to run?

You can see how these questions could be critical to the successful launch of a program, but how do they apply to turnkey solutions? In this case, it is even more imperative to scrutinize every aspect of the customer experience. Chances are that a team of manufacturing engineers will need to physically build the system before it gets shipped to the customer. An even more sensitive customer relationship involves the field service rep walking through the installation process on site, and in front of the customer. Add complexity to your customer experience, and the details surrounding delivery grow exponentially. Will the product be shipped on a CD or over the Internet? Will it be packaged with something else or by itself? Is your product ready for this kind of encounter? Have you thought about how your code fits into this process?

Scaling the Wall: UML Implementation Diagrams

The first step to building your manufacturing processes is to establish a naming convention for file names in your source-code tree. Most compilers help with this task by requiring file name suffixes in order to compile. A consistent naming convention will pay off in the long run when new people are added to your team. By starting this habit now, you'll save them from hours of searching for a particular implementation for a class. And by using Rational Rose (or some other visual modeling application), you can get the added benefit of jumping directly to the source through the component diagram.

The next step is to take a look at your component diagrams. Should they contain the whole source-code directory hierarchy? It all depends on you. Some people need to show all of the individual files in the component diagrams, while others just show the components (libraries and binaries) and the interfaces within the system.

What Is Compiled?

For those of you from the UNIX world, much of your development probably takes place on more than one platform. We suggest using makefiles as your method of compilation. In the UML, component diagrams show you the dependencies between components. Utilizing this information, you can write the dependency rules of your system easily in your makefiles from the component diagram. Figure 5.2 illustrates a simple example.

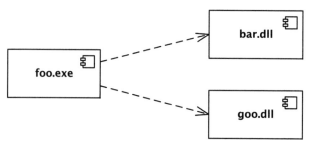

Figure 5.2 *Sample Component Diagram*

Notice that the component foo.exe is dependent on the libraries bar.dll and goo.dll. The corresponding makefile would be something like this:

```
Foo.exe : bar.dll goo.dll
```

Where Will It Be Installed?

For those of you who have worked as a build-and-release engineer, you've probably heard everything from "Hey, it worked on my machine" to "Didn't you install this new library?" We often completely ignore the fact that our products need to be installed and run on multiple machines and multiple operating systems. We need to define the directory structure of the installation, including documentation, library binaries, help files, and examples.

At the top-level component diagram, you would typically define an installation package. The installation package defines the directory hierarchy of the installation of the product. Create packages for each platform onto which the product will be installed. Inside each platform package, create directory hierarchies using packages and represent libraries and binaries by the component model element. Ancillary files, such as help files and examples, are included as components within these diagrams.

The component diagrams illustrate where each of the libraries is to be positioned on each machine, but they do not show the requirements for each machine or how the machines will communicate. Deployment diagrams can be used to display the connections between machines, their individual and shared requirements, and their individual processes.

Each machine is shown as a processor in your model. The connections between machines are connections between the processors. One thing to remember is naming the type of connection between machines: Is it HTTP? CORBA? NFS? Remember that other developers should be able to review your design and build the necessary machines to run your product. In the specification window for a processor, you can include multiple characteristics. Use this feature to describe the operating system requirements, memory requirements, third-party tool requirements, and so on.

How Will It Run?

We're almost there. The product has been built, compiled, and tested on numerous systems within your lab setting. But what about a test run on your customer's system? How often do you come across a customer machine that has not been fine-tuned—even worse, the user has applied numerous operating system patches over the last few months to get her system compliant with the latest OS version. Some libraries that you expect to have installed—aren't. Or the latest version of a .dll has been installed, but it is not compatible with your product. These types of problems are difficult to diagnose and fix.

The deployment diagrams, as shown in Figure 5.3, demonstrate how machines will communicate, but they do a poor job of showing how processes communicate. In the past we have borrowed a modeling trick from the book *Writing Effective Use Cases,* by Alistair Cockburn (Addison-Wesley, 2003).

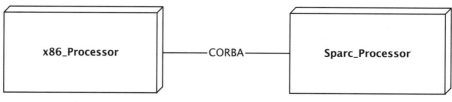

Figure 5.3 *Sample Deployment Diagram*

Create a package named "Process View" at the top-level logical view package. Next, create the hierarchy for process class definition shown in Figure 5.4.

For each process in the system, create a class. For each process, create a class diagram, as shown in Figure 5.5. For each process, assign interfaces that each process can handle.

In scenario diagrams, as shown in Figure 5.6, show the communication between processes by using color and objects that represent boundaries.

Choosing the Right Tools

Now that you have designed your manufacturing process for your product, it is time to map this design to something useful. The most common next step is creating makefiles. ClearCase has a great tool, called clearmake, that can take advantage of the ClearCase database to help with build avoidance, auditing, and shared object files. The

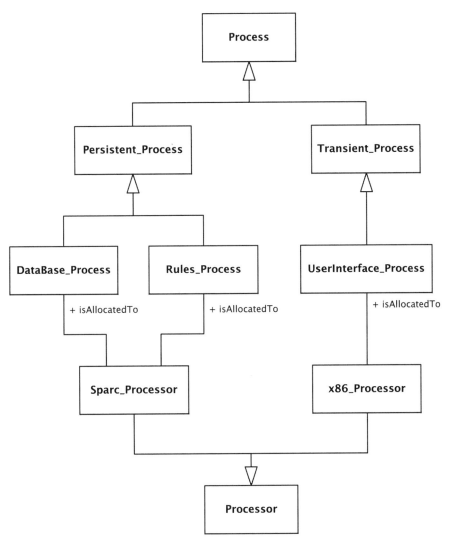

Figure 5.4 *Process Class Definition Hierarchy*

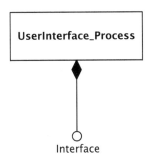

Figure 5.5 *Sample Class Diagram*

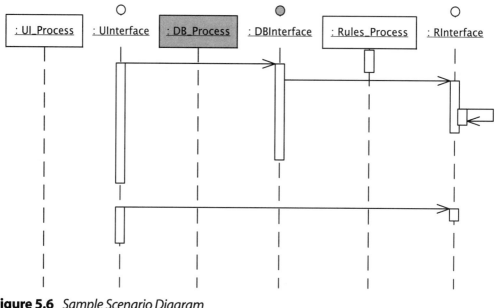

Figure 5.6 *Sample Scenario Diagram*

clearmake command is a very powerful tool that can save you hundreds of hours otherwise spent waiting around for builds to complete.

Before getting started with clearmake, it is best that you understand some basic concepts:

- **Configuration lookup.** Most make systems use a standard timestamp scheme to avoid building files over again. clearmake is more sophisticated than the standard scheme. Because ClearCase stores metadata with artifacts in the system, it can know what files were used the last time something was built and automatically set a dependency on that file during build time—even if the makefile does not show the dependency.

- **Derived object sharing.** A derived object is any file or directory that is created as a result of running commands specified in the makefile target. In ClearCase, derived objects can be shared between developers working in different views. This is commonly known as "winking in files" and can dramatically decrease build time for developers. Instead of the build recompiling the file, it basically copies the file from the already built file.

- **Creation of configuration records.** Configuration records show a so-called software "bill of materials" for each derived object in the system. You can look at the configuration record for a binary built with `clearmake` and see all of the versions of all of the files that went into creating the binary. It also includes parameters passed to the commands to build the derived objects. This is very handy if you need to re-create a specific build, or if you feel a build is suspect.

Using `clearmake` has some pretty big benefits over many of the other makefile systems floating around out there. But that does not mean you can avoid the previous step of planning things out. A poorly planned build system will still perform poorly, no matter what the tool. The benefit of `clearmake` is that you now have an audit trail telling you where you went wrong.

The Wall Comes Tumblin' Down

The end result is an efficient and effective design system that integrates the many parts of your system. Within the life of one feature set, planning ahead can stop you from wasting several days of development time. As systems become more complex, the lack of supporting designs for build-and-release systems can be paralyzing. Modeling provides the mechanisms for describing the system and helps system integrators manage change and complexity.

6

Ground-Level View of a Product Release

The word launch means different things to different people. To some, it means the time when the product has completed the technical development phase and is ready to test. To others, it means the kickoff point for the beginning of a new product development cycle. And to still others, it refers to a high-profile advertising event that announces the product to the external world. Most often, however, launch refers to the process of preparing the market for your product and putting all of the vehicles and infrastructure in place to get it to market.

—*From* High Tech Product Launch, *by Catherine Kitcho (Pele Publications, 1998). http://www.launchdoctor.com. Portions quoted in this chapter reprinted with permission.*

Analyzing the Product Road Map

When MapQuest.com came online years ago, it was fantastic. In the early days of the Internet boom, it was new and relevant. Some of the major portals and search engines also offered mapping tools, but

MapQuest was the biggest and the best. Arguably, one of the biggest benefits of MapQuest was the ability to look at your destination from a street-level perspective—and then zoom out and look at it again from a broader, more regional perspective.

There is an old Chinese proverb that says, "Climb mountains to see lowlands." In other words, to get a good view of your product or your product road map, you sometimes need to get a different perspective. It can be difficult to look at a product or project objectively when your nose is down in it and you're working hard toward a new release. The problem is that it can be very difficult to release your product if all you have is a street-level perspective.

Some engineers never see outside of their own development areas—they don't see all of the steps involved with launching a product from start to finish. By the time the end product has been delivered by Marketing to QA, you should have already gathered a substantial amount of information about your customer, the market, your strategy, and your messaging. This late stage in the product release cycle is not the time to start developing the vehicles that will carry your messages into the market.

Gaining a Broader Perspective

Plato once remarked, "The beginning is the most important part of the work." This message holds true in product development, and it certainly applies to the rollout of a new system. The first step, of course, is the product concept. But let's take a step back: take a look at the process with a broader perspective. The first step in the product launch is preparing the market for your product.[1] It is at this initial stage that many of the communication vehicles and materials—or marketing programs—are developed and used to prepare the marketplace.

According to Catherine Kitcho, there are two kinds of marketing programs: *external marketing programs* are directed at customers and the outside world. These generally include print collateral, data

---

1. *High Tech Product Launch*, p. 3.

sheets, press releases, white papers, brochures, direct mail, Web content, trade shows, seminars, product demos, product packaging, and sales training tools. *Internal marketing programs*, on the other hand, are focused more on educating your sales force, employees, and sometimes your channel partners. These include sales training, sales kits, memos, corporate announcements, presentations, newsletters, data sheets, and advanced press releases, as well as other tools.[2] Together, these internal and external programs can be quite complex, communicating information about the product being launched and the overall marketing strategy. (Kitcho)

You cannot successfully launch a product without addressing both of these areas, no matter what the project. How do you expect to sell your product if your customers do not know about it? On the flip side, how do you expect to sell and support your project (ClearCase) without educating your users and the support team who will maintain the system? Without internal and external marketing programs, you will have little hope in selling your ideas.

Catherine Kitcho, in her book *High Tech Product Launch,* provided a solid outline for the product launch process, which we reproduce here, with some added detail.

First, Understand (Assess) Your Product and Market
Product Definition
It is amazing how many products get off the shop floor without a thorough product definition. It should come as no surprise, then, when a poorly defined product has to undergo major reconstruction when it is discovered that the customer wanted something slightly different. Or something entirely different. By documenting the product definition and getting team and customer feedback, you are more apt to build the right product or solution.

Strategic Objectives
How does the product fit into your product or company objectives? Where does this new version fit into the industry or commodity lifecycle? Understanding the strategic objectives can affect how you

---

2. *High Tech Product Launch,* pp. 111–124, 139–148.

build, deploy, or support a product. It also helps you prioritize your time, resources, and financial commitments if you can see the big picture.

The Customer
If you know your customer, it stands to reason that you'll better understand how to prioritize your product features and support mechanisms. Why would your customer choose your product over your competitor's? What specific pain points are you addressing? What specific customer demographic or psychographic areas are you addressing?

The Market
Where does your product or product genre fall in the market cycle? Is it still a fairly new innovation, a follower being spun out to match a competitor's offering, or is it a cash-cow commodity in decline? How much of the marketplace are you targeting, what are the cyclical buying habits of your core customer group, and where does your company already touch the customer? In an information economy, you cannot enter any market blindly. There is not a single market in which there is not competition. Understanding your market and the competitive forces within it is essential.

Competition
Who else builds this kind of product, and how do your features compare to theirs? Speaking of comparisons, how do you compare in pricing? In features? In design? In market size? How do your company's direction and strategies compare to theirs?[3] Are you in head-to-head competition, or do you have very few areas of overlap? You can learn a lot about how to build and manage your products by looking at what others have done and what they are currently doing.

Channel Marketing
Do you have partnerships in place, and are you planning to use them to extend your marketing reach and sales capacity? Few things are

---

3. *High Tech Product Launch,* pp. 68–72.

more powerful than to find compatible technologies and build relationships—especially if you can build linkages to established products or companies. Build out multiple channels as a way of reaching your customer faster—and by linking your offering to other products or services, you'll generate better ROI for your customer.

Second, Develop Your Marketing Strategy

Positioning

Where does your product or service fit into the marketplace? How does it fit against your existing or future product plans? You can understand your market and customer, but you must also correctly position your product within that market, and in a way that encourages, compels your customer to buy.

Messaging

It is one thing to create something that people want, but it is quite another to help your customers recognize value when it comes to parting with their money. Whether it be a commercial or a consumer product, messaging is critical to helping people understand the benefits of your product.

External Marketing Programs

Since you've taken the time to understand your customer, you have probably also figured out your external marketing strategies. Whether it is through trade magazine ads, conventions, commercials, or press releases, you must have some kind of orchestrated strategy for disseminating your message. This includes public relations and advertising activities.

Internal Marketing Programs

As we mentioned previously, to support your new product or service, you need to train your team and put the proper support mechanisms in place. Plan out all of the necessary collateral and brochure-ware, for both internal and external distribution.

The Marketing Plan

Once you have defined all of the parts, you'll need to organize your efforts and build a high-level plan for executing your strategy. This will allow you to track your resources, your progress, and your finances as you roll out each step of the plan.

Third, Plan and Implement Your Product Launch

The Launch Team

This is the team responsible for coordinating and implementing all of your product and marketing plans. This might include members of product management and engineering, marketing, operations, and the executive branch.

The Launch Plan

Unlike your marketing plan, which outlines all of the high-level internal and external marketing initiatives, the launch plan is much more tactical and low level. This plan details the day-to-day steps necessary to move your product to delivery, with each of its key deliverables and milestones clearly identified.

Managing the Launch

Whether your company follows a detailed launch methodology or you are simply guiding your team via a Microsoft Project template, it is important to manage the launch process, making sure that issues are captured, alternative solutions are implemented when needed, and progress is gained.

It's amazing how readily you can address problems when you plan properly. Problems always pop up: A build fails, pushing back an important milestone. A last-minute customer enhancement request causes you to reprioritize certain product features, requiring changes to the architecture and documentation. Packaging delays cause the team to scramble and find alternate vendors before a big trade show. But by understanding every aspect of the product launch, you can better prepare for the unexpected, and build better contingency plans.

Getting a Ground-Level View

So how does all of this apply to deploying a software configuration management system? Well, now that you have an understanding of the bigger picture and where your product fits into your company's overall strategic objectives, let's jump back down to ground level and look at specific launch activities from the perspective of a configuration management administrator.

Although these activities don't seamlessly align with the marketing and management activities we've just outlined, how you set up your CM processes and move a product through to production is critical to a successful launch plan. Besides, before you can plan for a product launch, you need to make sure your product itself is on track for release.

Here are some practical steps that apply directly to the CM role in a new product launch.

External Launch

Let's first take a look at preparations for an external release:

- What delivery mechanism are you going to use? Are you burning a CD? Will it be an Internet download?

- Are you supplying a service?

- Can you use a VOB to control your releases?

- How often do you need to release the product to the customer?

- Is the product mission-critical for your customers?

You might think, "What does configuration management have to do with the release of a product to the marketplace?" Every time you release a product, you are changing the perception of your customer, either good or bad. We can't tell you how many times we've seen

QA/QC groups who have tested a product but then accidentally released a previous version—or even worse, a new version that their build and release team just built that has not yet been properly tested. With solid CM processes and procedures, these kinds of mistakes can be eliminated.

First, use your software configuration management solution not just to store your code, but also to manage your release. That's what it's there for. Each time you release the product, an image is created—either for burning a CD or for Internet distribution. This image can consist of one file (.exe, .zip, .tar, and so on) or an entire set of files—it doesn't really matter. What is important is that all of the files for the image are together. We recommend creating a release VOB for this purpose.

OK, we're going to take a quick tour through the more advanced subject of VOBs. But don't worry; there'll be more about VOBs in upcoming chapters. A simple VOB structure might look like Figure 6.1.

In this example, we're dividing the software code to be released into separate source, test, and release VOBs to keep things organized. Because all of the VOBs for the product have the same administration VOB, the source, test, and release can be labeled using the same

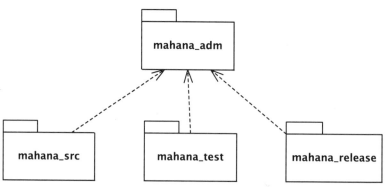

Figure 6.1 *Sample Versioned Object Base Structure*

label. This will allow you to go back to the exact image that you released to your customer.

How do you know what you have released to your customer? Make sure that each version of your product has a reference to the label that you have placed on the elements in your VOB.

```
# mahana -version
Version: mahana 3.1 b 3425
```

As you can see, the version is 3.1, build 3425. This should be directly referenced in the VOB by a label, as shown in Figure 6.2.

This same label should be placed on all of the elements in your VOBs. This will allow you to go back to a previously released image and access any and all custom code and tests that went into producing the image.

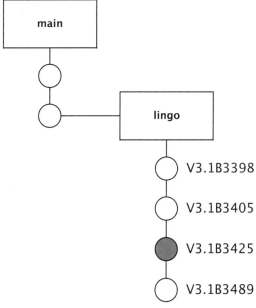

Figure 6.2 *Sample Build Label*

Internal Launch

When a product release is internal, you typically have to deal with internal integration problems in addition to the normal external customer problems:

- Are other teams going to use your project to develop their product?

- Are they using ClearCase? (In a perfect world, everyone is using ClearCase.)

- How often can they get releases from your team?

- What kind of coordination do you need to provide?

Naturally, releasing a product internally should be very similar to releasing it externally. You should treat your internal customers just as you would your external customers. One difference, however: a release VOB should be used, but you may consider releasing files instead of an image. In large software houses, there tend to be groups of developers that release libraries to other groups in the company. To decrease the amount of coordination between these groups, release VOBs can be used to access libraries or files directly instead of through installation of the released tools.

Here is how it works: Let's say that a group, Madajaju, develops libraries that the group Mahana requires to complete their work. Madajaju has their own release schedule driven by the needs of their customer, Mahana. Mahana then uses these released libraries in the development of their product. Take a look at the illustration in Figure 6.3.

In ClearCase, a configuration specification, called a *config spec* for short, needs to be written to select the specific versions of the artifacts for the user to see. By placing the MAHANA_PUG_BASE label on the madajaju_release, the config spec for the Mahana development team can be simple and easy to manage. The following is an example of a config spec. (Config specs are covered in more detail in Chapter 12, "Understanding Branching and Labeling.")

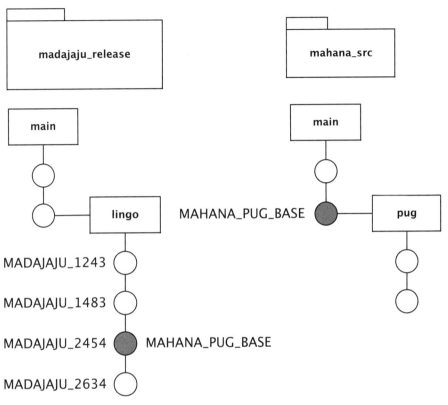

Figure 6.3 *Sample VOB Library*

```
element * CHECKEDOUT
element * MAHANA_PUG_BASE
element * . . . /pug/LATEST
element * /main/LATEST
```

This same config spec can be used when the Mahana group needs a different version of the Madajaju libraries. Just move the MAHANA_PUG_BASE label to the new version, and every view in the Mahana development will automatically see the new libraries. This strategy does not work as effectively when not everyone in your organization is using ClearCase. Look for mixed strategies in later chapters.

The Big Picture

> Probably the most critical ingredient in successful technology development projects is achieving successful participation from all functions, but especially engineering, manufacturing, and marketing. What do we mean by effective participation? It is the kind of participation that results from a sense of ownership in a project; it is not just somebody else's project for which you are providing some inputs.
>
> —*From* Managing Technology: The Strategic View, *by Lowell W. Steele (McGraw-Hill, 1989)*

Developing a product launch plan is difficult enough without having all of your different teams wondering how it all fits together. As with our MapQuest example at the beginning of this chapter, you need both a ground-level or tactical view of the product launch activities—how you, as a configuration manager, will handle the actual release of your product to an external customer—and a broader, high-level perspective on how the product and timing of the release fit into your company's overall strategy.

As part of the CM team, you play an important role in how your company organizes its launch strategy. As we mentioned, some engineers never see outside of their own development areas—they don't see all of the steps involved in launching a product from start to finish. By helping to enforce the process around how a product is built and released, you have a unique window into the product launch process. The key is to guide the process, to help your organization achieve successful participation from all functions, and to seamlessly execute against that launch plan.

7

Planning Your ClearCase Deployment

How often do you visit fortune-tellers? Not many of us make a habit of visiting the local palm reader before making major software decisions. But how much different is a visit to the friendly neighborhood soothsayer compared to many of the "shoot from the hip" decisions we make? If you're about to implement a very large ClearCase solution, you might find yourself cutting corners in the name of time. How different is corner-cutting from fortune-telling? Let's hear the rationalizations: You manage a team of smart, competent people who should know exactly what they're doing, right? The software comes with full documentation, and the default install process is fairly simple, right? The new software should plug right into your team's existing infrastructure and development processes, right?

Since we're leaving so much of your future to fate, let's look at your options from a fortune-teller's perspective: Down one path we see pain, misfortune, and possibly failure. This might equate to poorly defined requirements, improperly defined handoffs and procedures, and a nonscalable architecture. Down another path, we see hard work but smart management of your intellectual property assets and, ultimately, success.

Designing and building a software configuration management solution is much like following the counsel of a palm or tarot card reader if you don't plan for it: without proper planning, you're letting fate decide your success. Remember the old adage, "If you fail to plan, you plan to fail."

Gosh, that always sounded so hokey when our parents or teachers threw it into a lecture or reprimand—and yet we've seen firsthand how poor planning has affected far too many teams and projects, usually with the justification of shaving a few man-hours from the schedule.

Here's another way to think about it: You're getting ready to take a long trip overseas. Do you just grab a backpack, throw in some odds and ends, and head for the airport? For most of us, of course not. You think about what you'll need, maybe you jot down a list of items to bring along. You do some planning, think about how many days you'll be gone, which clients you'll see and in what social settings, the weather at your destination, and the extracurricular activities you might partake in. Yes, you could throw into your bag an extra pair of shoes, some socks, and a few pairs of underwear and probably make it for a few days. But is skipping some planning steps up front really worth all of the trouble? Four days down the road, you don't want to be stuck in a meeting with clients in Singapore wearing the same outfit you wore on the plane, without fresh socks and underwear . . . metaphorically speaking, of course.

Planning to Plan

It's quite simple: you need to plan. Here's a start: think about all of the actors. Understand their relationships. Build your use cases. Apply them to your business rules for validation. And then build your plan. It all begins with a few targeted questions. But do you even know which questions to ask?

The questions posed here are nothing but a starting point to building a system and tool set that meet your organization's long-term development needs. We all suffer from "writer's block" from time to time, so think of this list as a tool to help grease the wheels in your brain. Here's where we recommend you start.

How Big Do You Think the Project Will Be?

This is an interesting question and oftentimes difficult to answer. How do you determine the size of the project? Do you use lines of code (LOC), number of classes, function points, or what? In most cases, the LOC is a good start for determining the size of the project. You can use several different methods to project the LOC for a project. Check out *A Discipline for Software Engineering,* by Watts Humphrey (Addison-Wesley, 1995), for some ideas.

How Many People Will Be Involved in the Product Development?

The size of the project is determined not only by the amount of code you will produce, but also by the number of people on your development team. Many times you can "guesstimate" the number of people that you will need on the team. When doing this, don't forget about the supporting roles of software development: QA, project managers, technical writers, and even managers. These people need to access the code and can therefore benefit from using ClearCase just as much as—if not more than—the software engineers.

Some might say, "We don't need to worry about the size of our VOBs because the new ClearCase architecture allows us to have really large VOBs." Just because you can have *huge* versioned object bases (VOBs) does not mean you should have them. Let's not forget that segmentation and the use of multiple VOBs have their benefits.

At How Many Locations Will the Product Be Developed, Tested, and Deployed?

If your first inclination is to answer, "Well, we're only here at the one location," or that your team can just telnet into the central office to do their work, then your project is either really small or you are not thinking big enough. With the expansion of broadband communications throughout the world, more companies are looking for cheaper ways to get teams to work together. It is expensive to move your whole team to the Silicon Valley when you can just as easily put a VOB server in each employee group's geographical location. Or maybe the product is being tested or developed overseas. The number of locations and the work that each location is performing will play an important role in your VOB architecture, triggers, and integration with third-party tools.

Is the Product External or Internal?

If the product is external, what delivery mechanism are you going to use? Are you burning a CD, are you providing an Internet download, or are you supplying a service? Can you use a VOB to control your releases? How often do you need to release the product to the customer? Is the product mission-critical for your customers?

When a product is internal, you typically have to deal with internal integration problems in addition to the normal external customer problems. Are other teams going to use your project to develop their product? Are they using ClearCase? (In a perfect world, everyone is using ClearCase.) How often can they get releases from your team? And what kind of coordination do you need to provide?

What Third-Party Tools Will You Be Using?

How many third-party tools do you plan to use? Make a list of all of the third-party tools that your development team (that is, your expanded team, as mentioned previously) is using. Don't forget about project management, testing, and technical writers. It makes sense to have some kind of VOB strategy for these tools. This includes things such as OS patches, compilers, Quantify, Purify, FrameMaker, MSWord, and so forth. There is nothing worse than having to spend weeks patching a mission-critical product that is over five years old, and you don't have access to all the tools you need to build, test, and document the thing.

What Is the Development Cycle of the Product?

Are you using a traditional waterfall method to develop your product? Is your cycle time Internet-fast (three months) or telecom-slow (seven years)? This can play an important part in the way you lay out your VOBs. You want to make sure your VOBs and ClearCase are not getting in your way, and actually help you get your job done faster. If you have a plan, you can use triggers to help enforce policy and automate things that are typically done by hand.

If you cannot answer this question about development cycle, let us point you to the Rational Unified Process. It is a good place to start for those in need of some direction.

How Do Your Current Development Methodologies Fit into Your Tool Plans?

We have seen far too many groups change their process to fit their tool set. This can be a dangerous exercise in bureaucracy. You might find processes that nobody can remember instituting, or that have no defined purpose. We have even seen processes created in an effort to circumvent the original process that no one could remember creating or instituting. Most of the time, we view these as shortcomings of the tools your team uses. It's important to find the right tools to fit your methodologies. Most today are very flexible and customizable and can handle whatever processes you might come up with.

Are Any Key Roles Missing from Your Team?

Make sure you have included everyone in the development team you need. Think through several scenarios. Were you asked recently for information about the project from someone who you don't have on your list as a key player in the development of the product? What was his or her role, and should your team be expanded to include this individual? If you are working with more than one location, who is the person responsible for coordinating meetings with all locations? Who is your multi-site administrator? Does your customer need access to ClearCase release VOBs? Make sure you have everyone written down.

What Are the Security Issues?

Don't fall into the trap of believing that just because you are behind a firewall your project is automatically secure. There are several issues that could pop up which you might not have considered. For example, you may have customers that want you to test your product against their proprietary systems, or some other protected intellectual property. You may need to restrict access to parts of your data while keeping other parts open between the customer and your development team. Another consideration: how can you protect your code from theft by a former employee? These are questions you need to ask.

What Types of Artifacts Are You Creating?

If your answer is, "I produce code—nothing else," then you are actually in the very small minority. Most products include documentation, binaries, project plans, images, and various marketing collateral. Map out all of the types of artifacts you need to version. A good rule of thumb is this: anything that is shipped or consumed by the end customer should be put in the source control system.

Do You Have the Hardware You Need?

It is really hard to deploy a development environment and ClearCase without hardware. Although it can be done, there is nothing worse than putting your VOB server on someone's desktop machine. You never know when you will have a janitor turning machines off in the middle of the night to save energy or, more commonly, have the air conditioning in your office turned off on the weekends to save money. That one is always fun. Make sure you have the hardware that you'll need up front. It is much easier to do it right the first time than to try and fix things later.

Do You Have the Infrastructure Ready to Support Your Plans?

Another item that people often forget is the infrastructure to support their development plans. Air conditioning, power, floor space, and networking are important to ensure you have a successful development environment. For instance, if you have to boot your machines in a specific order so you don't throw circuit breakers, you definitely need to get more power. If the $12.99 "blue light special" fan from Kmart keeps your computer from overheating, you need more A/C. Another thing to consider: if you are developing in multiple locations, you will need to make sure that you have connectivity to all locations (it's the little things—like connectivity—that always come back to haunt you). The hardest part, of course, is convincing someone who has the money to make the investment. If you do the work up front and have your project properly planned, it will be much easier to convince the senior executives to support these kinds of expenditures.

Preparation is the key to successful deployment of ClearCase, pure and simple. Ask the right questions, gather the right requirements, connect to all of the necessary tools and processes—and you've got it made.

Now You Know ... and Knowing Is Half the Battle

Planning how to set up your VOBs and ClearCase environment can seem like you're trying to peer into the future, because you need to predict the future of the product. But unlike the telephone fortune-tellers who make baseless recommendations on how to live your life, you need to start asking questions—and making some key decisions based on the answers you get. Many efforts start out as if they're relying on fortunetellers, but as you slowly start answering these questions, your project will become a self-fulfilling prophecy. By properly planning things, you rely less on "predictions" and greatly reduce the risk.

Smart deployment is all about risk management—planning reduces risk. And properly planning for a strong source-code management system will roll over into other practices. With a strong set of tools and processes driving your development machine, you'll find your team planning their development efforts with more rigor and logic. The resulting products will be . . . well, better.

Think of it this way: when you were growing up, did you ever notice the difference between doing homework in a messy room versus one that was clean, from top to bottom? Clinical research shows that students in a clean and orderly environment excel over those in a messy environment. So how different is this from your work environment?

How clean is your room?

8

Modeling Your Configuration Management System

Bridging the CM Gaps

Building a bridge is one of the most fundamental ascents of mankind over nature. Few endeavors over the last 100 years have posed such risk while also providing such great utility, linking regions and communities otherwise locked away behind distance, and usually water. Without the vast systems of roads and bridges, humans would be forced to travel less efficiently, and society would be disjointed.

In the United States, for example, the development and success of two major geographic regions came about largely due to the building of bridges.

The island of Manhattan is surrounded by major waterways, including the East River, the Hudson River, New York Harbor, and the Harlem River. Before the development of our modern modes of transportation, travelers depended on boat and ferry service—but this could be unreliable and even dangerous, particularly in winter, when weather often prevented boats of any size from crossing between Manhattan Island and the mainland. In these early days, the construction of a bridge was a major event, allowing remote communities to expand and extend themselves across an entire region. For Manhattan, the Brooklyn Bridge was the first major connector to the island, and it was quickly followed by a system of bridges.[1]

On the opposite side of the country, the communities of San Francisco and those in the North Bay shared the century-long dream of spanning the Golden Gate Strait, which is the entrance to the San Francisco Bay from the Pacific Ocean. The strait, a treacherous body of water with currents ranging from 4.5 to 7.5 knots, is approximately three miles long by one mile wide. Construction of the Golden Gate Bridge commenced on January 5, 1933, with the bridge opening on May 28, 1937.[2]

Bridge over Troubled Waters

There are bridges in software development, as well. Building a configuration management system can be a daunting task for any organization. Yet many teams, in the rush to solve immediate problems and focus their time on "billable" development activities, will push some kind of CM solution out the door without properly analyzing the organization's needs, short term and long term.

As we're sure you've all seen, far too many teams are tackling problems without understanding the full scope of the project in front of them. And yet, time after time, that's how projects get under way—with arbitrary deadlines—and usually behind schedule from the start. Customer demands and project deliverables require a speedy implementation. But a speedy deployment and a well-planned and well-developed system do not have to be mutually exclusive.

---

1. http://users.commkey.net/Daniel/bridge.htm
2. http://www.goldengatebridge.org

One common management dream is to start on a project at the beginning of the lifecycle, rolling out process and procedure at the inception phase of development. However, this is rarely the case. Luckily, configuration management systems are available to aid in your development efforts. They can be a powerful asset for increasing communication, productivity, and quality through process automation and integration of the tools that most engineering groups use today. You could call CM the "bridge" that links your company's development teams. Implementing some kind of CM solution will organize your development efforts around solid and repeatable processes—and by helping your team prioritize and manage the development lifecycle, you are more likely to meet your customers' needs.

As we've stated previously, configuration management and the teams that manage these tools are in a unique position because they are the glue between engineering and the rest of the product development structure in your organization. The product cannot move forward in a timely manner unless the CM team coordinates with the build-and-release teams and, generally, manufacturing. And unless your project is proceeding quickly, it's a safe bet that your customers are not happy.

Now . . . back to the steps that lead you to the solution. The process of determining the path and structure of the system as it is applied to your organization is called *business modeling*. The purpose of business modeling is to determine who and what the customer is—but not necessarily the requirements of the project. The point is to seek to understand the client's perspective, and not make any judgments about possible solutions or what the customer thinks he or she needs.

The purpose of this chapter is not to walk through the dos and don'ts of business modeling—there are plenty of chapters available on the Rational Developer Network on the subject.[3] It's probably safe to say

---

3. For an excellent review of the whys and hows of business modeling, we recommend "Business Modeling with UML," by Bryon Baker. It's available online at http://www-106.ibm.com/developerworks/rational/library/content/RationalEdge/dec01/BusinessModelingwithUMLDec01.pdf

that business modeling is the most undervalued part of the software development process. With that said, we feel it is important to remind everyone that we are not trying to identify the requirements at this stage. The business model is the "problem domain" while the requirements are the "solution domain," which we address later in the development process. Instead, it is critical to know what you are building and why.

> Models help a software development project team visualize the system they need to build that will satisfy the various requirements imposed by the project's stakeholders. The aphorism "A picture is worth a thousand words" holds especially true when it comes to work involved in developing software: much of what's interesting about a given system lends itself to visual modeling better than plan test does. The UML is specifically designed to facilitate communication among participants in a project.
> —*From* UML Explained, *by Kendall Scott (Addison-Wesley, 2001)*

Identifying Actors

When analyzing a system, we first like to draw a box around it, to define the boundaries of that system. This is best done by defining the actors—the people, software, hardware, and others— that interact with the system. In the configuration management world, we can usually write down a list of actors that participate in a CM system fairly quickly. Remember: think of the CM system as a black box. Just make sure you define all of the outside parts of the black box.

Figure 8.1 is a diagram of the actors within a basic CM system, along with a brief description of each.

Software Engineer

The software engineer is responsible for the design and development of the software that makes up your product. The software engineer will use the configuration management system to store designs, code, and sometimes tests, so that they can be integrated into a releasable product.

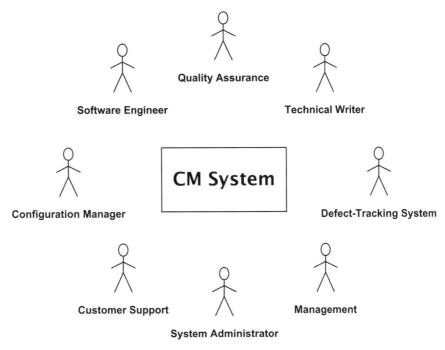

Figure 8.1 *Actors*

Configuration Manager

Those of us who come from the CM world might consider the config-uration manager as the most important actor in any CM system. It is typically the CM manager's job to control the "crown jewels" of the company: the source code. We typically see the CM people not only administrating ClearCase and the process of software development, but also performing the builds and releases of the product as well. This is especially true in smaller organizations, where resources are tight.

Quality Assurance (Product Validation)

We prefer the term *product validation* to *quality assurance,* because these individuals do much more than check the product to find bugs the software engineers created. These teams play a very important role as the final validation of the product use cases before going to the customer. They will use the CM system to store their tests and test suites, and to get controlled release of the product from the configuration manager.

Management

Whether we like it or not, management is a necessary evil. We deal with management on a daily basis (some days better than others), and as the providers of the company's CM solution, they recognize that we supply them with the information they need to make decisions about product direction and strategy. The CM system contains the information that management needs, but it is our job to present the data in a manner that is useful to them.

Customer Support, or a CRM System

Another necessary actor is the customer support organization. Customers just might have problems with your software—no matter how well it was designed—and you need to be able to give information to your customer support organization about product releases, customer requests, and bugs that have been fixed in product releases. This information can either flow directly to the support team or be tracked within a CRM solution.

Defect-Tracking System

This can be part of the system or not. If you do not define this as an actor, you should at least be ready to include it in your system later down the road. If you are not integrating your CM solution with a defect-tracking system, you should seriously consider this option. Joining the defect data with the source code can help you make improvements in project management and the overall quality of your product.

Technical Writer

Make sure you include everyone who will develop artifacts for your product. There is nothing worse than getting documentation that is two versions behind the shipped software. If your tech writers are not using ClearCase, then teach them how to use it. If it is too hard, then write the scripts that they can use to make their jobs easier. Everything will run much more smoothly if they at least know the basics. Just keep it simple.

System Administrator

Your configuration manager is not a system administrator. Of course, in a small organization they could be the same person, but these roles are very different. The system administrator is there as a support for your hardware and, potentially, software problems. He or she should be making sure that the systems are configured according to product specifications and fine-tuned to the requirements of the CM team.

Use Cases

Now you need to look at how the actors use the system. As shown in Figure 8.2, for each actor, write down how the actor will use the system—or how the system will use the actor. Draw an arrow in the direction of information flow. Don't forget the administration use cases, such as "Backup the Source Code," "Restore from Backup," and so on. Don't include use cases that do not involve the CM system. For example, "Reboot Machine" is probably not a good use case, because it does not directly involve the CM system.

Pick the most used use cases and start working from there. Look at how the actor will use the system and how the system will guide the user. The CM world has some well-defined scenarios, so try to focus on what is different about what your team does compared to other teams.

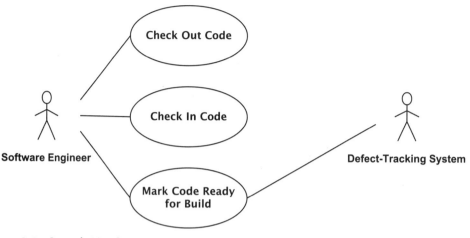

Figure 8.2 *Sample Use Case*

Activity Diagrams

The next step is to look at activity diagrams and process analysis. The first thing you will find out is that your organization most likely already has some process in place (whether you like it or not). Whether or not there are formal guidelines for development, people typically work the same way over and over again. They get into a mode of working so they don't have to think about what comes next. They would rather spend their time working on new things instead of worrying about what is the next step in the process. What you need to do is figure out what your team is currently doing and model it. Then you can find ways to optimize it.

Don't fall into the trap that process engineers run into time and time again: "I am going to develop a new process that will make everyone more productive." In reality, it usually has nothing to do with the team culture or habits, and it hinders more than helps the organization. First, find out what your team is doing and then try to change with little steps of improvement.

Figure 8.3 is an example of an activity flow of a typical CM system.

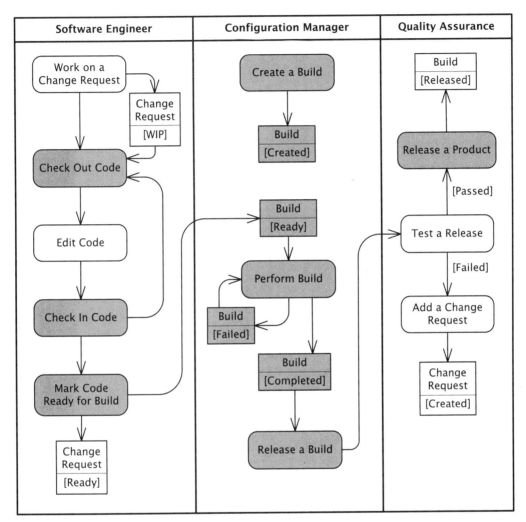

Figure 8.3 *Sample Activity Diagram*

Component Diagrams

One often-overlooked aspect of designing a configuration management system is the definition of components. Although you won't
know what all of the components of your system are at the beginning,
with your knowledge of the system you should still be able to group

things pretty well. You should also consider the actors of your CM system when defining components. Don't forget about the product's supporting files, such as licenses, documentation, releases, and so forth.

Consider the following small project named "Kish," as illustrated in Figure 8.4:

- kish_adm—Administration VOB for labels, branches, triggers, and supporting CM scripts.

- kish_process—This is a process VOB. UCM likes to use this to store information about the project in the VOB.

- kish_doc—Documentation VOB. Your technical writers need a place to put their information.

- kish_src—Most products have some kind of source that gets compiled.

- kish_release—We prefer to store the releases in a separate VOB from the source. It gives us the opportunity to multi-site the VOBs separately and scrub them differently.

- kish_test—Most test harnesses become larger than the code base itself. This is great again for multi-site purposes.

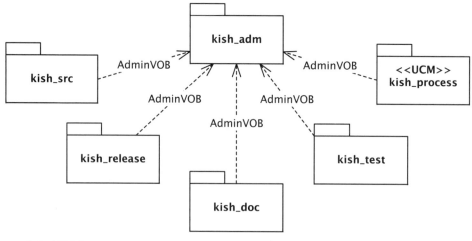

Figure 8.4 *VOB Layout*

These VOBs can be broken down into more VOBs, according to the project size. We will talk about that in the next chapter.

Deployment Diagrams

For the context of this CM effort, deployment diagrams, as shown in Figure 8.5, can be used for three things:

1. To show the different machines you need to support the size of your team: VOB servers, view servers, build machines, test machines, and workstations.

2. To show the different platforms that you need to support. This is overlooked far too many times, and it can have an impact on the way you set up your VOB structure and your multi-site strategy.

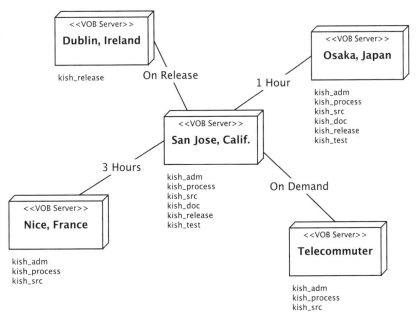

Figure 8.5 *Sample Deployment Diagram*

3. To show the different locations that will be working on the product and the VOBs that they need. This helps you with your multi-site strategy dramatically.

Bridge Building

Well, we've attempted to illustrate clearly the steps to designing your new CM solution, and hopefully you've figured out how to get started on this planning phase. As outlined in their book *Use Case Driven Object Modeling with UML* (Addison-Wesley, 1999), Doug Rosenberg and Kendall Scott summarized the goals of use case modeling:

* You've built use cases that together account for all of the desired functionality of the system.

* You've produced clear and concise written descriptions of the basic course of action, along with appropriate alternate courses of action, for each use case.

* You've factored out scenarios common to more than one use case.

Once you have accomplished these things, you should be ready to design the next stage of your CM system.

Remember: bridges don't just happen. They take years of planning, followed by systematic implementation. The result is a resource that can improve the lives of those who use it. The same can be said for a solid configuration management system.

Our next few chapters will continue to explore the different aspects of configuration management deployment, including VOB architecture, security and data integrity, integration of other back-office applications, and customer-facing deployment strategies, such as training and support.

9

Using Configuration Management to Control Process

Ixnay on the Oliticspay

Political battles always seem to take center stage, making it easy to see how one political skirmish can affect everything around us. While all but the most severely brain damaged among us would reject the notion that our companies are managed purely through political maneuvering, most of us have learned to expect some kind of subjective posturing in our workplaces—and have learned to live with it. In fact, many of us recognize that, within some organizations, there can be a constant barrage between certain teams or business units. Now, understanding that political environment, try making a change to your company's software development practices.

Because configuration management teams typically end up in the middle of the development process, they see their fair share of politics—especially when new process initiatives get pushed down from standards boards, executives, or even customers. In this chapter, we will take a lesson from American politics and learn what to watch out for when deploying a new development process in your company, and the important role that configuration management plays.

Let's start by describing each of the players.

First, there's the *legislative* branch. They make the laws or create the processes that need to be followed to obtain an acceptable outcome. There are several different legislative bodies that affect the development processes in your company, including standards boards, executive teams, business process teams, and so forth. There are all different types of regulatory boards out there to aid you in building your development processes. There are business quality standards such as ISO 9000. There are software development standards such as SEI's CMM. Both standards can be used as a good starting point to understand your development teams' processes. There are also corporate quality boards, which, aside from adding weeks (and often months) onto the schedule of your innocent and unsuspecting project, maintain consistency across all company initiatives. That's right—what looks like a nameless executive team's efforts to crush your progress might actually be an effort to ensure all initiatives hold to the corporate goals and shareholder expectations. Who would have thought?

The second branch is the *judicial*. The ultimate judges of the quality and worthiness of a product, of course, are the customers and the market. However, there are additional judges who need to be appeased, as well. Most standards groups have auditors who certify that the correct processes and procedures are being followed. In most cases, internal auditors (the lower courts) are used to prepare a company for a more formal audit. The most important part of an audit is documentation: What did you say you were going to do? Did you do what you said you were going to do? If you didn't do what you said you were going to do, why not?

Simple enough, right?

Again, configuration management can play an important role in preparing for internal or external audits. No matter how detailed your steps or automated your process, you need to keep track of the progress and the process that was followed. If not adequately captured, the details will get you every time.

Finally, we have the *executive* branch—which is essentially configuration management. While the company president and the board of directors may decide the overall company direction, it is configuration management sitting at the center of the software development hierarchy. Configuration management is the key actor in the executive function of the process (laws) that the legislative branch has developed. Typically, the executive branch of company politics is ignored. Few companies are lacking in legislative and judicial oversight. While there are always plenty of people to create processes, and there are always more than enough standards to follow, executing and managing the process is what falls through the cracks. Because configuration management teams sit at the center of communication for the whole team, it is the ideal location to control process and procedure.

Now that we have clearly defined the software development hierarchy, let us dig down into the legislation that sits before us.

Process Automation

Before you start automating, you should first analyze your process. Map it out. Find out what kind of enforcement will be allowed by the development team. It is the job of the configuration manager to decide what parts of the process to automate or control—and what parts will increase the quality of the product the most. You must take into account more than the wants and needs of the legislative branch; you must also realize that the common citizen, the coder, may need several exceptions to the law. Much like the English language, there are typically more exceptions than rules. Make sure that your automation can accommodate the changing needs and ideas of the engineering team. Failure to do so could result in creative engineers subverting your automation efforts. Once you have determined the strategic processes to automate, there are several options.

In ClearCase, software developers can be guided to follow process through triggers. Triggers are scripts that are called before (pre-op) and after (post-op) a specific ClearCase operation (check in, check out, make element). For any operation that requires some kind of control, you first need to determine whether it is a pre-trigger or a post-trigger. Here's an easy rule of thumb: Pre-triggers are typically used to enforce process or disallow the operation from occurring if certain conditions are not met.

Try to avoid triggers that prompt the user. This can become annoying when engineers perform mass check-ins. Nothing will drive your engineers crazier than having to hit the Return key for each check-in. If you need user input, make sure you can get the information from an environment variable or file. The prompt should be a backup input mechanism. Another option would be to prompt once and use the information for the rest of the triggers that are called.

Running post-triggers in the background will decrease the operation completion time. This is not a big deal for checking in one or two files, but checking in hundreds of files can waste a developer's time.

Be careful about speed. Nothing is more frustrating than a slow check-in of a file. The engineers will quickly develop the bad habit of not checking in files if this step takes a long time. This can lead to engineers forgetting to check in a file for a build later on.

Post-triggers are great for tool integration. If you have any integration with other tools, this should probably be done in the post-triggers of operations.

> **Remember: process automation should help engineers, not hamper them.**

Several areas of the software development process benefit from automation. The following areas bring the largest return on investment: defect and enhancement tracking, build and release management, and reporting.

Defect and Enhancement Tracking

Another important aspect of configuration management is handling defect and enhancement tracking. Over the last five or six years, the software development community discovered defect tracking to be critical to overall project quality. In recent years, software tool vendors have delivered *some* integration with the most popular source-code control and defect-tracking systems, but there is still much that can be improved. When evaluating multiple tools—and the integration between them—it is important to consider first how they will best serve your development processes. A thorough look at your software development culture will uncover volumes. Due to your technology decisions and political controls, you will have either more flexible or more rigid integration between these tools. (Profound, isn't it?). Whatever you do, don't let the tool get in the way of the productivity of your developers. If your developers are spending valuable time entering duplicate information into multiple tools in an effort to keep them coordinated, you are going to hear about it. Always look for the simple solution.

One of the simplest solutions is to purchase a fully integrated CM package from one vendor. For example, purchasing ClearQuest and ClearCase may be the way to go. The benefits of a single-vendor, integrated solution are huge compared to doing the integration yourself. Maintaining your own integration is very similar to maintaining a product, but much worse. Anytime there is a new release of one of the tools that you integrated into your system, you'll need to go through and recheck the integration. When all of the tools in your system come from one vendor, you leave this nightmare behind (for the most part—the reality is that with most software, quality is job 1.1, and any new version promises at least a few bugs). Additionally, most single-vendor tools have higher quality than your run-of-the-mill homegrown integrations.

Build-and-Release Automation

One major benefit of the integration of defect-tracking and source-code control is the ability to selectively pick source code that will go into a build. The only requirement in the integration is some kind of mechanism to determine what source code has been changed to fix a specific defect. Here are some options.

Labels or Metadata Tags

In this paradigm of build-and-release automation, when developers work on a defect, they connect a label or an attribute to the file when they check it in. Within ClearCase, this can be enforced through the deployment of pre-check-in triggers. The trigger should at least ask the developer for the defect ID of the specific check-in. However, as you probably know all too well, this technique can become overbearing for a developer who works on several files. One way to decrease the interaction with the developer is to write wrapper scripts to set environment variables that the trigger will read, and then it will set the label or attribute of the version appropriately.

Another option is to keep the extended version path name in the defect-tracking tool with the defect. That way, ClearCase is not bogged down with loads of metadata. Again, the trigger can be used to do this. Be careful that your triggers are not too sluggish: if they are, they will invariably slow down development, and your software engineers will find any way they can to get around that pesky trigger.

To determine what source goes into a build, a list of defects will be selected and the corresponding code will be labeled with one specific for the build. Then a configuration specification will be created with the label for the build and the previous build. What this means is that the view the build has performed will contain all of the source code according to the defect list. Although this appears to be a good mechanism—it works in most cases—you should still be careful. If you have more than one engineer working on the same file, there is potential difficulty in deciding what version of the file to select for the build. If you need to modify the change set at all, you will need to

ensure that all of the files in the change set are checked for any version conflicts. This method of automated build-and-release has
some drawbacks. It should be considered only if your team is small
and code ownership is enforced.

Branching and Integration Branches

With this technique, all work is performed on defect branches. Simply put, for each defect in the defect-tracking system, a branch is
created. All work to fix the defect is performed on that predefined
branch. About this time, it's probably wise to write some kind of automated defect view creator script, because most software engineers
don't care for changing their configuration specifications. Occasionally, you have a highly educated, ClearCase-savvy software development team capable of changing view configuration specifications,
potentially decreasing the number of scripts you need to write. After
the developers have finished working on the defect, they can simply
mark the defect as completed in the defect-tracking system.

To determine what source file goes into a build, a list of defects
should be selected for the corresponding defect branches to be
merged into an integration branch. The build on the integration
branch will be performed with the same configuration specification
as always. In general, this is the way Unified Change Management
from IBM Rational Software works. Although UCM and the defect-
branching mechanism appear to be a clean approach, to make it
work properly, there are some problems you will need to overcome.

First, merges are not always nontrivial. This can cause problems if
the build is held up due to a nontrivial merge. If there is a nontrivial
merge, you will need to make sure that all merges from the defect
branch are not committed. The defect-tracking system will need to
be able to monitor integrated defects.

Second, using these mechanisms requires several branches, and the
version trees of these files can become difficult to follow. Pruning the
version trees of aged and integrated defect branches can help

decrease confusion in the version tree. See the command `cleartool lock -obsolete` on how to obsolete branches.

Third, a good view creation script and a view aging script are also a must. Without these scripts in place, many errors can occur in code branch management. There is nothing worse than trying to untangle a rat's nest of branches late in the game. Another thing to watch out for is the plethora of views that will be created. An increase in views will slow down your ClearCase performance.

Reporting Progress

To appease the judicial bodies that will surely audit your company, you will need to show them that your process is being followed. An automated reporting system should be part of any automated process. There are two main benefits: (1) you never have to worry about the location of the documentation, and (2) it will also decrease the amount of extra paperwork necessary when the auditors come to check your department. Remember, the whole purpose of reporting information is to let the appropriate people know what is currently going on, what has gone on over the course of the project, or what will go on in future development.

One of the areas most positively affected by reporting is the build-and-release cycle. The build-and-release cycle occurs when all of the work from the engineers comes together. The integration of all of the code can take a long time—and it is exacerbated when integrating code from a multi-site development team that spans the globe. Reporting the build-and-release status in an accurate, real-time system (via the Web) is an important tool to get everyone working together to resolve problems. But don't just throw everything into a monolithic log file on the Web site. You need to make the reporting usable and easy to determine what is going on and where the problems are. Try breaking up the build-and-release reporting hierarchically. If there is a problem, (it wouldn't be unheard of) this structure will make it easier to find, and easier to fix.

And so, we end our lesson on the politics of software development. There are no political action committees, no rogue Supreme Court justices, and no whining electorate. Just pure clean, chad-free coding fun.

10

Planning for the Rational Unified Process

Orchestrating Your Software Opus

As member of the product development organization, configuration management engineers should take pride in the work they do in helping to get products out the door. To accomplish the great task of a product launch, the team must have a plan—or adhere to some guidelines that help steer your team toward delivery of that great opus of your software team. IBM's Rational Unified Process (RUP) is a good starting point for building such a plan.

Overview of RUP

To be perfectly honest, to fully understand RUP, you'll need several books and time. Although many books are available, better than any book is to go out and get some good old-fashioned experience with RUP itself. IBM's Rational Unified Process is a set of processes, best practices, document templates, and workflow for developing software products.

RUP breaks the software process into basic phases, iterations, and disciplines. The diagram in Figure 10.1 shows an overview.

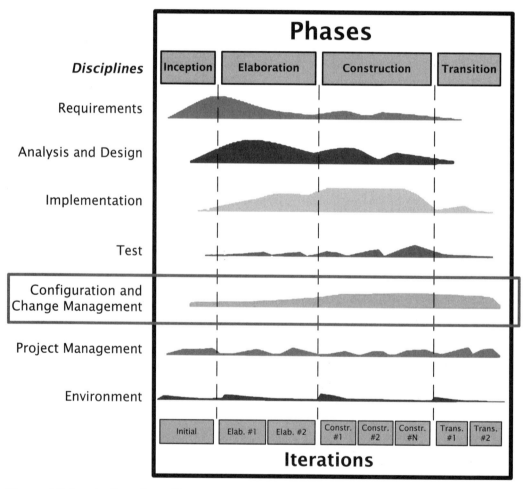

Figure 10.1   *An Overview of RUP*

The Roles of CM in RUP

Just like the conductor of an orchestra, performing your great musical opus requires you to understand how all of the instruments come together in harmony. It is important for you to understand the different roles involved in the development process. Since we are most interested in how configuration management fits into the process, our focus will be on the discipline called Configuration and Change Management. RUP describes the different roles that individuals play throughout the software development process. Although there is a configuration manager role, in many places the CM team covers several roles described in the process, namely:

- The *change control manager* (CCM) oversees the change control process.

- The *process engineer* is responsible for providing efficient and streamlined development processes.

- The *project manager* manages the resources, demands, and time of the product team.

- The *integrator* plans and performs the integration of elements to produce builds.

- The *configuration manager* is responsible for the overall CM infrastructure and environment for the development team.

Granted, most CM teams will not perform all of these duties, but it is important to understand where other roles, individuals, or teams intersect. Also, if you are in a small organization, chances are that you will perform several duties defined by these roles.

The Change Control Manager

The change control manager is primarily responsible for change requests for the product. This typically includes reviewing change requests (CRs) or bugs and cleaning up duplicate or rejected change requests. If you have a small development team, more than likely you are the change control manager. You may or may not know that you are, but if you are often stuck "cleaning up" CRs, believe us—you are the change control manager.

There are several tools available to track change requests. Many organizations have some kind of defect/enhancement-tracking system, either homegrown or commercial. IBM's Rational ClearQuest has been tailored to fit RUP, and vice versa.

There are a couple of things that change control managers can do to make the development move forward. First, they schedule and hold change control board (CCB) meetings. Second, they maintain the list of CRs and ensure they are void of poorly written descriptions, erroneous information, and duplication.

Managing the Change Control Board

When holding CCB meetings, it is important to have attendance from the key people from all teams in the development organization. This should include the project manager, the CM manager, the test manager, various product line or development managers, and at times, customer support. If you, as the change control manager, are the only person to attend these meetings, don't just count yourself lucky and take an extra-long lunch break. Without the key players from all of the necessary organizations, you will not have the "buy-in" to make decisions about specific CRs.

Everyone hates meetings, and having meetings too often can make many of these sessions seem irrelevant. On the flip side, when meetings don't happen often enough, the result is one long, extremely painful and boring meeting to make up for not having many short meetings. The net-net is that the frequency of these CCB meetings is important. As your product moves through iterations in the development process, you will find that these CCBs become more frequent as the product moves from development through alpha and beta. In most cases, weekly meetings probably make sense during the alpha phase of development, but they are overkill during development, when the team needs to focus without all the interruptions. The beta phase, on the other hand, may require meetings more than once a week, as this stage usually requires much more management oversight in the decision-making process.

Make these meetings working sessions, walking through each of the open change requests and the disposition of each for the team. This regular session allows for valuable input from every section of the organization, all of which can be seen and added to the change request during the meeting.

Cleaning CRs

To make the CCB run smoothly, it is best that the CCM "scrub" the list of CRs. The things to look for in cleaning up CRs are duplicates, poorly written CRs, and CRs that are not applicable to the product. In the case of poorly written CRs, ask the submitter to add more information—or to completely void the CR. Although the entire CCB can resolve these items (and often do so when something slips past the CCM), it is best to handle these outside of the normal CCB meetings to keep this session efficient and focused on issues that require decisions.

The Process Engineer

In some organizations, the process engineer is not a part of the development team. Instead, this part of the process just *happens*. This is really unfortunate, because a sound foundation in process can decrease the time and effort of developing a product. Simply asking your development team to follow the principles of RUP is not good enough. RUP is more or less a collection of guidelines, not a set of static processes that can be followed step by step. There are portions of RUP that may not apply to your organization or your current project. This is where a process engineer can really enhance your team. In smaller organizations, someone may find himself or herself in the roles of both process engineer and configuration manager.

For those interested in expanding their roles, there are many resources available for the upstart process engineer. The downside is that there is far too much information to learn in a single afternoon, and it will take some effort to fill this position. Not only must you learn about team development techniques, but you may also need to learn additional tools to be integrated into your solution in order to support your processes. If you can locate an experienced process engineer who is familiar with the tools your company uses—or who can provide a set of tools to supplant or support your existing tools—pay this individual anything he or she asks for. With experienced resources and tool sets, your development processes will run more smoothly, your end product will be higher quality, and you will be much more likely to deliver your product on time. OK, we can't guarantee *all* of these things will happen, but your chance for success is much greater *with* than *without*.

So after you have learned all you can about process engineers, let's look at what tasks they typically perform during product development:

1. **Define the Scope of the Process.** Not all of RUP is going to be useful to your organization. You need to evaluate the team, the tools, and the product to be developed.

2. **Extend the Process Framework.** Depending on the analysis done in the previous step, you may need to extend the RUP framework to cover areas that are not sufficiently covered.

3. **Prepare the Process for the Project**. This normally includes working with the process engineer to integrate tools and the defined process.

4. **Introduce the Process to the Team.** In other words, train the team on the process and the tools they will be using. Without training, the process is basically worthless.

5. **Maintain the Process.** Not only does the process need to be defined, but also you will become the "process policeman." You will also find that throughout the process, you will need

to make adjustments—which is perfectly normal. In fact, if you never make adjustments, you may need to pay closer attention to your product teams and release schedules to find ways of making the process more efficient.

The Project Manager

If you don't have a project manager and you end up playing the role yourself, the list of activities will likely scare you. Not because they are particularly complex or difficult to accomplish, but because of the vast *number* of tasks that need to be managed. It can be intimidating, and it requires a well-organized and focused person to fill this role. We will not go into the details of each task but highlight the ones that affect configuration management.

Scheduling and Assigning Work

In the ideal world—and of course that is what we all strive for—all work assigned in a project plan would have a change request associated with it. This means integration between a project management tool (such as Microsoft Project) and a change request management tool (such as ClearQuest). In fact, if done correctly, this can decrease the amount of "babysitting" that project managers perform over the course of a project. If you have a good integration between these two systems, project managers can be left to focus on their primary responsibility: managing resource and task issues, not spending an inordinate amount of their time following up with team members, asking what tasks have been completed. (It's a tender subject for anyone who has ever been a project manager.)

Developing the Iteration Plan

The goal of the iteration plan is to produce a detailed breakdown of work tasks and the resources required to perform the tasks throughout the iteration. This is basically the initial project plan. In addition to determining what needs to be done, milestones and deliverables are created. Deliverables that affect configuration management are typically build-and-release deliverables. The frequency of builds and releases should be determined during this stage, as well.

Not only are the CM deliverables important in the iteration plan, but also key features or functionality added to the product may need special or planned integration. This can affect the branching strategy, frequency of builds, and integration points for the CM team. It is important that the CM team is involved throughout this step.

The Integrator

Some organizations refer to the integrator by several names: build-and-release engineer, build master, and sometimes "the reason the product is delayed." In some cases, the CM team is assigned to both builds and integrations. The key to a good integration is to have a good strategy; with proper planning, many integrations can be automated. The integration build plan is the most important document you can produce, saving you time and plenty of unnecessary headaches.

Creating the Integration Build Plan

This is the key document produced by the integrator. It should be generated from input from the architecture of the product, the iteration project plan, and feedback from the development and test teams. The integration build plan should include at least the following sections:

- **Timing.** This is the frequency in which the build is performed. The timing may change depending on the phase of development, which should be noted in this section. For example, during development, the number of official builds will probably be less frequent than during alpha.

- **Subsystems.** The subsystems and their dependencies should be easily obtained from the architecture document. The key is to keep the architect document up to date.

- **Integration Points.** After identifying subsystems and the timing desired for building the software, it is important to plan out when the different subsystems will be integrated. The key with integration is early and often. Keep that in mind.

- **Reporting.** You should identify how and what you need to report from the individual builds and integration points.

Planning the Subsystem Integration

If your product is sufficiently complex, you will have multiple subsystems that need to be integrated. It is much easier first to plan the integration of each subsystem separately, and then to devise your system integration later on. Things that should be considered include how the subsystem should be built and tested and what elements should be contained in the build. This is also where you define the subsystem dependencies to other subsystems. This plan will be used to help determine system integrations farther down the road.

Integrating the Subsystems

Pull out and dust off any *makefile* books that have been sitting on the shelf in your office. Most serious software development projects use some kind of make system available in an IDE, or with good old-fashioned makefiles. Whatever the tool, builds have to be done. One point that is often missed is the reporting of build status. Web-based build status reporting tools can be an excellent resource.

Planning the System Integration

If you have properly planned the subsystem integration and their dependencies, then the system integration plan should be fairly straightforward. The key in this plan is to identify all of the subsystems needed to deliver a product. If your product is sufficiently complex, you may need to define build sets that include several groups of subsystems, possibly from different locations. In some cases, the integration of the complete product can happen incrementally over time. Make sure you spend time looking at the system integration. This can easily become the bottleneck of the development process if things are not properly planned and staged. Are you starting to see a trend here? Planning can make your life much easier.

Integrating the System

There are two major steps in integrating the system: integrating the subsystems and promoting baselines. Integrating the subsystems usually consists of gathering subsystem builds from several locations in a multi-site implementation and then packaging them together in one consistent, repeatable manner. This is a great place to automate, increasing the reliability and quality of the product. Once a system has been integrated, the development team typically wants to use a stable base from which they can continue new work. This is called *promoting baselines,* which we discuss later in this section. There are several different ways to do this, depending on your ClearCase use model.

The Configuration Manager

Now let's look at what is left for the configuration manager to do. If you are thinking that everything you've read about up to this point is exactly what you already do, chances are that your multiple-hat-wearing activities have caused you to overlook some details. It's quite common for one person to fill many roles—which is how most of the common mistakes are made. Some of these steps are things that need to be done up front, while others are day-to-day activities.

Setting Up the CM Environment

Setting up the CM environment cannot be described in brief. This set of tasks consists of everything that we have been discussing in this book, including general planning, training, hardware setup, implementation, and day-to-day management.

Mapping the Architecture to the Repository

To successfully organize your VOB layout, replication strategy, and component definitions, you really need to understand the software architecture. In fact, the CM team should participate in the architectural decisions made by the software development team. The goal is to decrease the number of dependencies between VOBs. In most systems, architectural subsystems can be divided into their own VOBs.

Creating the Initial Baseline

If you are starting a new product from scratch, the initial baseline will consist of all version 0 (zero) elements. Since most software projects typically start from an existing product or set of code, you will need to create a baseline that consists of the versions of the elements for a starting point. Basically, there are two ways to accomplish this in ClearCase: using UCM and using labels. In UCM, create a baseline using the `mkbl` command. In simple ClearCase, the combination of `mklbtype` and `mklabel` can be used.

Defining Baseline Promotion Levels

Periodically, your development teams will need to rebase their views or development streams. Most engineers want to work from a "stable" baseline that has been verified as being "tested." Depending on your ClearCase use model, this can be done in UCM directly, or through labels and rebasing branches. See Chapter 12, "Understanding Branching and Labeling," and Chapter 15, "ClearCase UCM Integration," for more information.

Practicing Your Scales (Day-to-Day Stuff)

Reading through RUP, you might think that your job is complete when you have planned out your team's working schedule. And why not? Most of your deliverables are tied to planning activities. But this can be deceiving. There are several day-to-day tasks that need to be done. Each role has major recurring activities, which, if left undone, can slowly but surely cause your project to spiral out of control.

Just like individual musicians, repeating your scales helps you learn your instrument. Playing music day in and day out enhances your skills even more. And when each musician knows his or her part and has perfected his or her art, you can build a world-class orchestra. So your job is to learn what the scales are and to do them daily. It will be different for each organization, but there are some common threads that all groups need to tend to:

- Integrate and build code often.
- Monitor the process and make sure things are moving along.
- Scrub your CRs to remove duplicate or erroneous bugs.

And don't forget the details.

11

Build-and-Release Basics

Skiing the Back Slopes of Software

Oh, the joy of starting new projects. At the beginning, it's all about the design and the code—no worries yet about integration with other projects, testing, or customers—just the purity of working on the code. It's much like being the first person down a snow-powdered slope after a big storm: clean, peaceful, and without the distractions of other people. A huge white canvas on which to carve your own path, and make your own creations. If only software engineering could be as great as that.

The reality is that there are always many other people involved in your software project; it's more like an overcrowded ski slope. And the slopes tend to get messy over time. By the end of the day, the slopes—and your project—are a carved-up mess, with few patches of nice, soft powder, replaced with slush and hard, icy sections where the shadow of the hill hides from the rays of the sun. It makes it difficult to ski, and painful to code. Gone with the overcrowded ski hill is the joy of the virgin slope—and for your project, without some control and communication, you are doomed. The skiing analogy really does apply to managing your software projects: a crowded ski park can only be enjoyed if the lines to the lifts are maintained and the flow of skiers down the mountain is watched and managed. The same can be said of your project.

As you quickly move from a solo project to something that needs to be delivered to customers, you need to bring all of your code together in the form of a build. When sufficient testing and integration has been done, your customer (you know, the guy who pays the bills) releases the product you have created. You may be thinking that you don't need a build or a release, that your project is simple—you may not even have a real customer, or it may be just a one-time thing. That could be the case, but make sure you think twice about your project being isolated. For example, when you are in school and a professor asks for a simple program to show some new algorithm or data structure, that's an isolated project. But 99 percent of projects include the involvement of other people and customers. You may have fresh powder in front of you, but there is a steady stream of skiers to your flanks and behind you, so it's best to figure out how to ski with them.

Builds

OK, we have mentioned the terms *build* and *release,* so let's explain what we mean. These might seem obvious for languages that require compilation and then linking of object files or libraries into an executable, but what about interpretive languages such as Perl, Python, Lisp, and so forth? Although there is no compilation with these languages, you may still need to organize things together so that the project can be exercised. Even in the interpretive languages, using some type of lint program or "run with warnings" is important to finding problems.

Builds should consist of everything needed to execute and test the program. Builds are primarily for the engineering and testing organizations, and they can be used to find bugs through testing and debugging efforts. Builds typically consist of much more than just the libraries and executables—there are several types of compilation or links that are created in a single build, as shown in Figure 11.1.

The first step in the build process is usually gathering code. If you are using a branch-based CM system such as ClearCase, then you will probably need to merge code from development or change request branches to an integration branch, so that the code can be compiled and linked together. Also, notice in this build cycle that purification and quantification are performed so that testing can also be done to find timing and memory leak problems. With this complexity, imagine now building on multiple platforms, and you see how very quickly this can become a nightmare to manage.

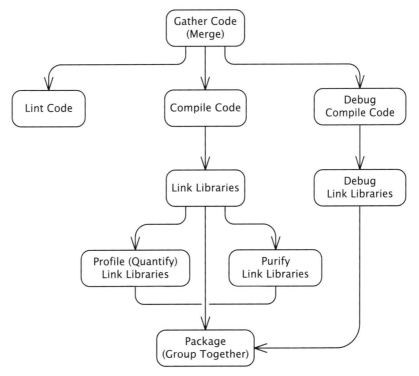

Figure 11.1   *Build Dependencies*

Releases

Now that you have built the product, your testing and engineering teams quickly and seamlessly qualify the product as being ready to release, right? Okay, it's not usually that easy. Most projects encounter numerous battles over the product to determine whether or not it is ready for customers. But once the determination is made that the product is ready, you need to release the product to the customer. This typically requires packaging up nondebug and nonpurified executables of the product. But executables are not enough. Your release should contain everything that the customer needs, including executables, documentation, examples, demos, and more.

Frequency

Now that you have some concept of builds and releases, it is important to understand how often to build and to release the product. If you have ever been to a ski resort that does not believe in grooming their hills, you quickly learn that the hill becomes choppy and inconsistent, unless you get some new snow all of a sudden.

Build Frequency

Your product can also become choppy and inconsistent if you do not integrate and build often. You can introduce bugs and merge conflicts that will be hard to resolve. The key is to integrate and build often. A good rule of thumb, in fact, is to build once a day. Although that cannot always be done, it should be your goal. Of course, if your build time is averaging 20 hours, nightly builds may not be very useful. There are other strategies that can be used to decrease build and test times, which are covered in Chapter 11 and, more specifically, Chapters 24 and 25.

If you are working between several different locations, you may adjust your build times to accommodate the multiple builds in a 24-hour period. On the other hand, if your builds are really short, you may want to build several times a day.

Release Frequency

Releases are a different story completely. Releases depend on the successful testing of a build and on customer requirements. This is where politics comes in. What does it mean to be successful in testing your product? When 100 percent of the tests pass and 100 percent of the code has been covered? Numerous books have been written on the topic, so we will not even try to address this question now. But you need to be concerned with how often your customer can access these new releases. In some cases, releases can happen as often as builds; other times, customers cannot handle new products until their own development cycle is ready for change. The key is to stay close to your customers and to understand their needs.

Uniquely Identifying a Build

Because "to err is human" and computers can show your errors faster than you can type, there will be bugs—and after any release, your customers will be calling on the phone about bug fixes. So how in the world do you know what version of the product the customer is calling about? How do you know if you need to fix a problem, or if the problem has already been fixed by the next release? You need to label or identify your releases to your customers. Every time you release the product, you need to automatically assign a name to the release. This way the customer can reference this release number when they call your customer support with a problem.

But a release number is not enough most of the time. It is important to identify your builds, as well. Testing organizations need to identify the build that they are testing just as much as, if not more than, the customer. This gives traceability between testers and engineers. There are several different naming schemes for builds. The most popular has a three-number name for each build and release:

Version.Release.Build

- **Version.** Also known as the major release of the product, this is the version that the customer is used to seeing. It denotes major changes in functionality or upgrades required.

- **Release.** Typically incremented every time the product is released to customers, this denotes small changes to the product, including bug fixes and minor enhancements.

- **Build.** The build number should be incremented every time it is run, ensuring builds can be uniquely identified.

You don't need to follow this numbering scheme, but you should at least have some numbering scheme that uniquely identifies each build. Now that you have a numbering scheme, you need to somehow label or mark the code with the build number. There are two steps to marking the code:

1. Mark the files that went into building the product. This can be done with most CM systems through a "labeling" or "tagging" method. All of the source code, and many times all of the executables and libraries, should be labeled with the build identifier.

2. Mark the executables so the customers or testing team can know what version, release, and build of the product they are using. There are several ways to accomplish this, but it usually requires putting the build identifier in a header file or some other file that is included during the build.

The build identifier should be automatically generated, to prevent errors in changing the build number each time. A good practice is to make this part of the build process—in fact, make it the first step of the build process. The build ID should be kept in some sort of database so that it is stored persistently and can be accessed at any time.

Automation

If you are still building and releasing your product by hand, you need to use the tools that are readily available to automate your process. Think of this as taking a shovel and a rake and trying to groom an entire ski slope. Yes, you can do it, but you'll freeze to death in the process. They have this really cool machine called a Sno-Cat that will do the work in hours instead of days. They still have to drive the Sno-Cat, but the machine does most of the work. Your build-and-release process should work the same way.

There are a number of reasons for automating your builds. The first is consistency. If you do not build your product the same way every time, how do you know what is a real bug and what is a false bug? Nothing can slow down your development cycle more than an inconsistent build process. You can easily spend days chasing your tail trying to figure out if the bug you are seeing is a build problem or a real code problem.

The second is repeatability. Many times your development team is working on the next release and a customer identifies bugs on a previous release through using the product. In these cases, changes to the code need to be made on a previous release, and those previous releases need to be rebuilt and released. If you do not have the build automated, this can be a very tedious and error-prone process.

Last, builds should have the ability to be distributed across several resources in a computation or data grid. This will decrease build and test cycle time and increase the quality and productivity of your team.

Communication

Because there is normally more than one person on a development team, communication among team members is very important. There are two major types of communication that you need to consider when developing your build-and-release system: *immediate notification* and *historical information*.

Immediate notification requires a build engineer or release engineer to be notified when the build has problems, or when it is successfully run. E-mail seems to be the best method for performing immediate notification. Make sure that you don't go overboard with the automatic e-mail messages that get sent from a build. Your build system can quickly become a spam generator with several messages a day, and most people will just ignore these e-mails over time.

Historical information gives the complete team information about the builds that have run. The amount of information you show the team about the build completely depends on your organization. Typically, a Web site is best used for this type of communication. The following is a list of things that can be obtained for each build and test cycle:

- Compilation warnings and errors
- Purify warnings and errors
- Test results passed/failed
- Lint results
- Log files for different steps in the process
- Timing information
- Platforms and machines

Now remember, this list is not all-inclusive. You need to figure out what is best for your organization, making sure that your Web site stores more information than just the latest build. You should have a calendar or list of builds that have been performed. This will help you look for trends in building statistics, and it will give your engineers and testers some context to work from.

A Full Build-and-Release Cycle

In this chapter, we have focused primarily on just the build side of things. But there is much more to getting a product to the customer than building the product. The process shown in Figure 11.2 is a very common full build-test-release cycle. Not every cycle will be the same, but Figure 11.2 will give you an idea of what can be done.

Notice that the testing comes after the build, and the release comes after the testing is completed. Also notice that the release includes documentation, examples, and demos so that the customer has a complete set of artifacts.

Speeding Up Builds with Grid Strategies

One of the hottest buzzwords in technology today is "grids." So how can you take advantage of grid technology and ClearCase? Though the answer is not that easy, clearmake has a few basic primitives that

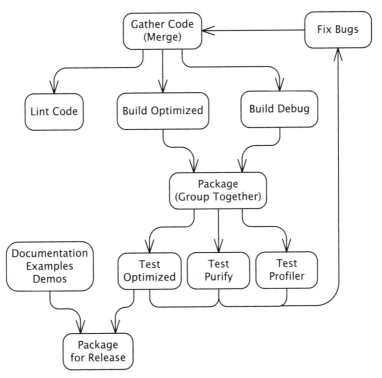

Figure 11.2   *Dependency Graph for Cycle Time Reduction*

can be used to get some distribution out of your builds—but it does require some setup. First, you need to make sure you have all the machines you want available to build your software in the same ClearCase region. Next, you need to call clearmake with some command line options.

```
clearmake -J 100 -B bldhost.file
```

The bldhost.file contains a list of machines from which to distribute the compiles. In this example, clearmake will run at most 100 compiles at the same time. For more information about using clearmake -J, see the IBM Rational ClearCase manual.

Skiing the Black Diamonds

Although you are not quite ready to ski the black diamonds after reading this introduction to builds and releases, you should be able to stop and turn enough that you can probably get down the hill. You've seen the basics you will need to start analyzing your build-and-release system, and to make a plan that will help you create a successful build-and-release system. Just like any determined skier trying to improve his or her skills, you may hurt a little at first—and you may even eat snow a couple of times—but just remember the basics, and you will be fine.

12

Understanding Branching and Labeling

Living in a World of Labels

Managing your code can be a complex task. Few companies excel at this activity, most companies find it to be a constant battle, and some fail miserably. There is always room for improvement, even for those with a handle on things. Depending on your software background, you have likely seen a number of different strategies for using code branches and labeling—some very elegant and some not so elegant. In our experience, a good strategy is to have an appreciation for what others have done first. It's always better to learn from others' mistakes instead of making them yourself.

Labeling and Branching Basics

So . . . what is a label, or tag, and what is a branch? In a nutshell, a label allows you to "tag" a version of code by associating the version with a unique name. This unique name can be used to identify all derivative versions of the file and related directories at a later date. Labeling lets you mark code that is in a consistent state before doing something that introduces instability. It is also great for keeping track of code released to customers by marking code before a platform upgrade. The list of different ways to use labels is innumerable. The key idea is that it basically allows you to identify versions of a file or a directory with a common name, as illustrated in Figure 12.1.

Branches also allow you to uniquely define your code, but unlike labels, they do not allow you to tag versions of files and directories. Instead, they give you a parallel version tree of files and elements. Branches basically allow you to maintain several different streams of development on the same segment of code. Branches can be used for very simple tasks, such as isolating work from other development activities, to very complex multi-site, multi-stream development, such as two separate teams developing different product versions.

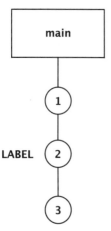

Figure 12.1   *Sample Label*

Most branches start from a root version of a file or directory. A label, as shown in Figure 12.2, is generally used to specify the root of a branch. Though it is not necessary to branch from a label, this is the common practice—and for good reason. It's just a good way to track a branch's origin.

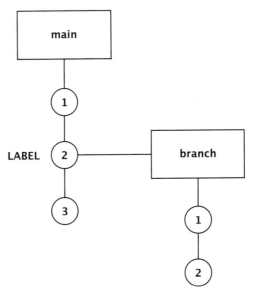

Figure 12.2   *Sample Branch and Label*

Naming Schemes

ClearCase does not enforce any naming scheme on branches and labels. This means that you need to come up with a naming scheme and enforce it. There are some common conventions that most ClearCase deployments follow:

- All branch names are lowercase (such as kish_dev, pcr12345)

- All label names are uppercase (such as KISH_BASE, KISH_DB_READY)

These are simple guidelines, and they really don't give you much information about the type of branch or label that is being used. When you are designing your branching and labeling scheme, the key here is to come up with a naming convention and stick to it.

Branch Naming

Branches are typically named after an effort of development. For example, this could be a major release, a maintenance release, simple defect changes, or a special project. Naming the branch should reflect what is actually being done on that branch of development. The following are some examples of branch names and their purposes:

- kish-v04-dev—Main development branch for the product kish release 4.

- kish-v04-maint—Maintenance branch for the product kish release 4.

- pcr12453—Product change request that corresponds with the defect number 12453.

- darrenp_dev—The user darrenp has his own development branch.

There is one branch name that you cannot use in ClearCase: "main". The name "main" is reserved, and ClearCase will not allow you to use it—so try to be a little more creative.

Label Naming

Labels are placed on versions of artifacts to mark them for use later down the line. Labels can be put on versions of elements that went into a build, marking versions to be used later, for other users to look at, or to specify a common branch point for a development branch.

- KISH_V04_BASE—Base label for the change on the branch kish-v04.

- BLD_V04_01_6346—Build label on the version 4.01 build 6346

- DARRENP_DEV_READY—The user darrenp has code that is ready to be integrated.

There are label names that are reserved by ClearCase as well:

- CHECKEDOUT—This points to the checked-out version of an element in the current view.

- LATEST—This is the last version of the element on the branch specified.

Things to Remember

Before we go into some of the more complex aspects of using branches and labels, it might be helpful to understand some of the "gotchas" of using them. Not all configuration management systems behave the same, so you need to watch out for these problems in whatever system you use. Some of these mistakes can waste a serious amount of valuable cycle time if you are not aware of them.

Labels and Branches Are Metadata

First you must create the label and branch type, and then you can actually apply it to versions of a file or directory. Just because you create a label or branch type does not mean it has been used anywhere. After you create it, you must apply it to the appropriate versions.

Watch for Moving Labels

Most CM systems allow users to create views, which look at the particular versions of the files. Labels can be used to configure the view. This gives engineers the ability to see specific versions that are related. If you move the label that your views are using to locate specific versions of an object, you may actually move the version out from underneath someone. That would be bad, and it could potentially cause ill feelings between you and the rest of your development team. In Figure 12.3, a static or snapshot view was used. As you can see, when the label is moved, the engineer does not see the change.

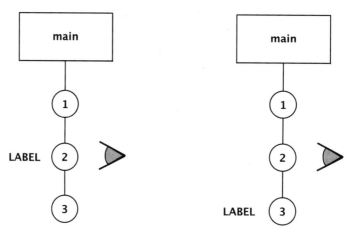

Figure 12.3 *Static or Snapshot Views*

If you are using a CM system such as ClearCase, which allows for dynamic views, as shown in Figure 12.4, then the behavior is different. The engineer sees the update because the configuration of the view has the label attached.

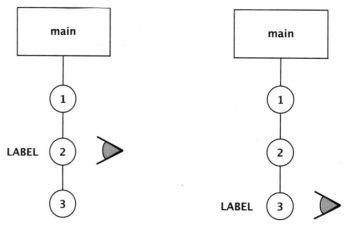

Figure 12.4 *Dynamic Views*

Moving labels can be very beneficial—just make sure that you understand the ramifications of moving each label. When using dynamic views, all of your engineers will automatically see the new version of a file. This can decrease problems that occur at integration, but it does have the nasty little side effect of changing code underneath the engineers. Just remember that engineers are our friends. Be nice to engineers.

Hey, What Happened to My Changes? Or, Working on Branches

Sometime in the future, you may be minding your own business, moving files around on your CM system, when an engineer approaches you asking, "Where are my changes to that file?" or "Why didn't my changes get put into the build last night?" or "I can see the file changes in my work area, but nobody else can. Why is that?" If he doesn't accept your "gremlins" theory, education on branching is something your engineer may need. Remember that branches isolate the work that one engineer is doing from another. If the engineer has made changes to a file, a branch of the file is automatically created and the engineer becomes isolated from everyone else. Of course this changes if you have multiple people working on the same branch, as shown in Figure 12.5. Any changes made by other people will not be seen by the first engineer until they are integrated into a common base branch.

In this example, two engineers are working on the same file in different branches. The result is that each person's changes will not be seen by the other until the changes are merged into the common base branch. For example, when the engineer working on branch1 merges her code into the integration branch, the result is shown in Figure 12.6.

Once the work has been merged, other engineers can now see the changes. But be careful here: the engineer working on branch2 still will not see the changes if the other engineers start working on the

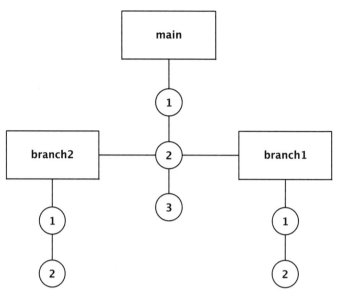

Figure 12.5   *Working in Two Branches*

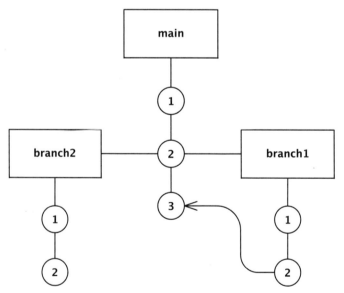

Figure 12.6   *Merging a Branch*

file right away. As long as they don't begin working on the file, everyone will see the changes, because the file would not yet have created for it a branch2.

There are two common ways to allow the engineer on branch2 to see the changes from branch1, as shown in Figure 12.7: merge from branch1 to branch2, or merge from the integration branch to branch2.

The latter method gives the engineer on branch2 all of the changes from branch1 and potentially changes from other branches.

Note: As illustrated in Figure 12.8, *do not* merge from branch1 to branch2. This is a common mistake with merging, and it can result in missed updates from other branches, lost time as the team backtracks to fix the mistake, and a loss of hair and other stress-related health problems on the part of your CM manager.

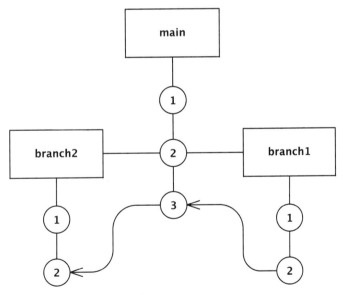

Figure 12.7   *Merging from branch1 to branch2*

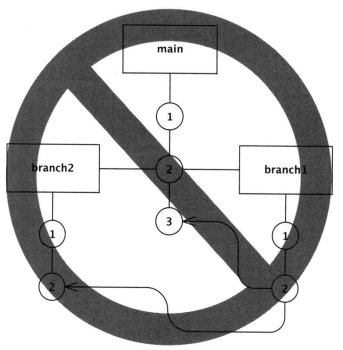

Figure 12.8   *Incorrect Merge*

Another thing to watch out for is that branches are created only when someone checks out a file to work on the branch. If no file is checked out, no branches are created—it's as simple as that. This is important to remember because it means that if an engineer does not make changes to a file, and the file from another branch is integrated into the main code base, the engineer will see it as a change. So don't be surprised if you do not see branches on files or directories when you look at the version tree. Just remember that branches are created only when files or directories are checked out, and then you won't be surprised.

Versioned Directories

You need to figure out if your CM system versions or does not version your directories. Surprisingly, most do not. Some engineers consider this a good thing because it makes the system easier to manage. Others require directory versioning. Directory versioning can be tricky at times, so here are a couple of things to remember: First, remember that directories are versioned. OK, we know that sounds simple, but sometimes you forget the little stuff, and that's what catches you—especially when you're in the middle of a crisis, trying to figure out what happened to some critical files, or why a file does not contain the information you think it should.

In Figure 12.9, two engineers are working on the same directory. If you are doing something similar to this, then you probably need to do a better job at architecting or dividing work—but to be honest, it happens all of the time. A scenario you want to avoid is when a new file needs to be created and the engineers are working on different branches.

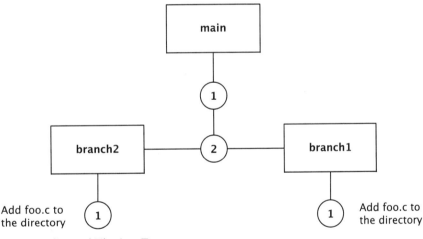

Figure 12.9   *Uncoordinated Files in a Tree*

In Figure 12.10, both engineers have created files with the same name, but in different versions of the directory. These files are not coordinated at all—they are separate and unique files. This is the crux of the problem. When the engineers are done working on their changes, they typically merge their changes to the main branch or some integration branch. You can see what happens in Figure 12.11.

Version Tree of a Directory

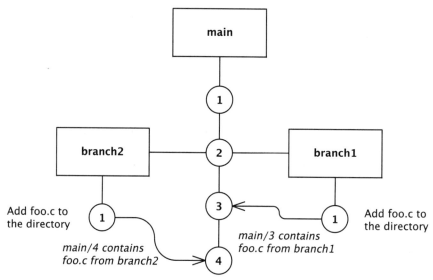

Figure 12.10   *Coordinated Files in a Tree.*
The foo.c from branch1 is no longer referenced in main/4.

There is nothing more frustrating than finding that a file which contained certain information yesterday has something completely different in it today (except maybe your CM manager trying to blame things on the presence of gremlins). Most of the time, look at the version tree for the individual file, as shown in Figure 12.11.

OK, why in the world are they different? They are the same file, right? *No, they are different files.* Remember that, gremlins aside, the engineers created these files independent of each other. Your CM system still sees these as different and unrelated files.

All right, you know the issue, but how do you fix this? First, find out if one of the engineers is willing to change his file name. If not, and the files actually need to be merged, you need to merge by hand the changes from the second engineer, and then remove the element from branch2 in the directory. Why remove it? You do not want this to come back and bite you again.

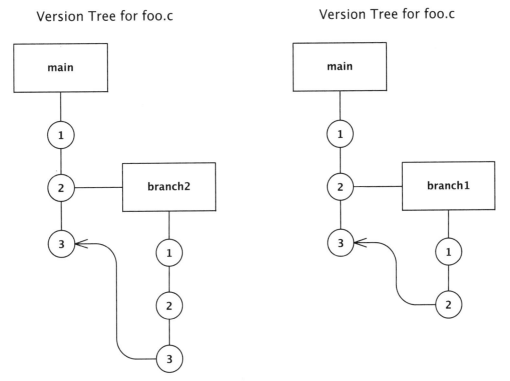

Figure 12.11 *Managing Different Files in the Tree*

Finally, remember that if you cannot see a file that was there yesterday, look at the version tree of the directory. Chances are that someone has made a change that removed a file, or had a merge problem that is causing you grief.

Config Specs

Config specs are used to filter versions of elements for a view. There are ordered rules that help define the versions that show up in the view. When a view is created, it is created with the default config spec.

```
element * CHECKEDOUT
element * /main/LATEST
```

This config spec allows users to see the last version of elements on the main branch. In addition, users can see the last version of any file or directory that is checked out by this view.

Config specs can have branches, labels, and time stamps to specify what versions are selected.

```
element * CHECKEDOUT
element * ../kish-dev/LATEST
mkbranch kish-dev
element * KISH_BASE
element * /main/LATEST
```

In this example, the view will select versions that are checked out first, and then it will get the latest versions on the kish-dev branch. If there are no versions on the kish-dev branch, then the version labeled KISH_BASE will be used. And if the user checks out the file, then a branch for that file will be created. If KISH_BASE is not on a version, then the latest version on a branch will be used, and if the user checks out the file, a kish-dev branch will be created for the file.

In this next example, a time stamp is used to select versions of files on a specific branch according to the time specified.

```
element * CHECKEDOUT
element * ../kish-dev/LATEST
mkbranch kish-dev
element * KISH_BASE
element * /main/LATEST -time 10-Jul.19:00
```

Only the version that was on the main branch on July 10 at 7:00 p.m. will be used and put on the kish-dev branch if previous rules cannot find a version that matches.

A whole book can be written about config specs and different approaches to writing and maintaining them. For more information, see the ClearCase man page config_spec.

Now What Do You Do?

This is a lot of information to swallow in one chapter, especially if you're relatively new to ClearCase. But hopefully this will serve as a reference for you, and give you a grounding in branches and labeling. Remembering these basic and simple rules can make your debugging and planning easier, and much more productive. Now you have to plan out your branching strategy, and this is the hard part of your task. The import thing to remember is to analyze what you want to do first, and then come up with a branching strategy. And try to ignore the gremlins.

13

Deploying ClearCase

Boxes, Packing Tape, and Some Heavy Lifting: Moving to ClearCase

One of the best examples of Murphy's Law in motion involves moving to a new house. Whatever can go wrong will go wrong. You may spend weeks preparing, boxing, and labeling your belongings from each room in the house, throwing out the old junk, cataloging everything, taking care to package fragile items with the utmost care—and yet, somehow, things get lost, broken, or damaged. Sometimes the best way to deal with change is to be prepared for the dent in the table, the spot on the couch—and have a plan for dealing with these issues once you are established in the new house.

If you want to make your move from one of the free configuration management systems to ClearCase as seamless as possible for your development team—basically, to the point where they don't see a difference at all—you are dreaming. Conversion to a new configuration management system can be a life-altering experience for some of your engineers. It requires them to think differently about their development. In essence, you will be affecting life as they now know it.

Software developers are very much tied to the way they do things. We don't know how many times we have heard someone claim, "I have been developing code for 25 years, so why do I need to change?" Don't get us started on the whole "quality of software" problem. When considering a change of CM systems, remember that you are going to have to deal with people who do not like change—and you are really going to change the way they work.

Before you get started, two pieces of advice:

Avoid the temptation to write scripts to make ClearCase look like the previous CM system. This typically results in a complex set of scripts that need to be managed and will quickly become a legacy issue in and of themselves. The scripts will also create a large number of complaints about how the system runs slow or is too cumbersome. So just steer clear of this route.

If you move to ClearCase, use ClearCase the way it was designed. It sounds simple enough, but so many people try to make modifications right from the start. Don't dress this giraffe to look like an elephant. It is still a giraffe no matter how much gray paint you use. Understand how it works before you get started, and make the necessary process changes with your engineers to fit the tool.

Planning the Move

Understanding Your Current CM System

All righty then: your bags are packed, you've sold your house, and the car is gassed and ready to go—you've made the decision to switch to ClearCase. No matter what you do, there is going to be a paradigm shift for your developers. They are used to doing things a different way. For example, the command set will be different. It is best to understand how these systems work, how they map to your current processes, and how their limitations will affect your team before moving to ClearCase.

Here are some things to consider.

File System—No Version Control

This is the worst way to manage configuration management for a team, but it is sometimes seen as the best method for an individual developer trying to push something through quickly. If you are just using the file system to store your code, you are not taking full advantage of your CM functionality. This is not necessarily a bad thing, because the training for your team will actually be easier. People who have very few expectations tend to more readily accept system upgrades. However, the problem is that you not only need to train your engineers about ClearCase, you will also need to train them on some of the fundamentals of configuration management.

Source-Code Control System

Your source-code control system (SCCS) usually comes with the operating system, and it is the starting point for version control on UNIX operating systems. The command set is extensive and, to many engineers, much harder to use than a revision control system (RCS, which is discussed next). This tool is typically used for smaller projects, and it does not allow for multiple developers working on the same file. Your migration from this tool will include teaching several new commands and the concept of views, instead of working directly with the file system. SCCS also has no directory versioning.

Revision Control System

RCS is considered easier to use than SCCS, but it has many of the same limitations, such as single-user access to the same file. It is easy to set up and easy to work around if needed. And here will be the most difficult thing for your engineers to get used to: they will want to go directly into the view storage and VOB storage directory to change around things that they neglected to modify earlier. This is how it is done in RCS. Be careful of this engineering urge.

Concurrent Versioning System

The concurrent versioning system (CVS) sits on top of RCS and has added features to allow for labeling all of the code, as well as concurrent access to a single file. This tool is much closer to ClearCase, but the users are not able to use dynamic views. In all of these systems, developers cannot see the changes of others until they check out the files. In ClearCase, however, the changes are seen in real time. Again, there is no versioning of directories.

SourceSafe

Developed by Microsoft for use with its Visual Studio and other compiler products, SourceSafe does not support many of the features found in ClearCase. Typically, migrating from SourceSafe has many of the same issues as converting from CVS, but for Windows users instead of UNIX users.

Choosing a Use Model

Now that you have an idea of the main difference between these CM tools, it's time to think about process. In short, your use mode is going to change. Depending on your previous CM system, your changes may be small or they may be large. There are some things you can do to help see what needs to be done before switching from your current system to something new.

First, understand how you are currently using your CM system. Always a smart move is to use UML to model your current processes and understand all of your actors, use cases, and relationships within your system.

Second, learn about the different ClearCase use models. There are several to choose from. UCM comes right out of the box with ClearCase, and they have off-the-shelf integrations to several other Rational tools that you will probably be using.

Next, select your use model. We recommend that you use UML again. If you think that you are going to use UCM out of the box with no modifications to the process, you are probably mistaken. Model out how you will work, and see which use model works best for your organization. Your goal should be to optimize the productivity of your development team, so keep that focus.

Last, start building out a migration plan. You will need to keep several things in mind when looking at your migration plan. The following sections describe some of these considerations.

Hardware Requirements

Disk Space

When you move from any system over to ClearCase, don't forget that you will need plenty of disk space to perform the conversion. A good rule of thumb is to make available at least 2.5 times your current CM system's disk space for the swap. This should allow enough room for your current system, the conversion files, and the new ClearCase data. Plus, you'll need to leave some disk space for all of those illegal MP3s you downloaded off Kazaa.

CPU

Remember that things in ClearCase are different from most other systems. ClearCase is a client/server application, and it requires more CPU power than most comparable systems—so plan accordingly. The ClearCase manuals have good information about the hardware requirements for VOB servers, view servers, and your team's desktops. Make sure you understand the differences between the requirements of these servers and allocate your resources appropriately.

I/O Bandwidth

Ah, the crippling effects of system latency. You can have incredibly fast machines as your VOB and view servers and still experience very slow ClearCase performance. Investigation of these issues usually reveals poor disk I/O, or more commonly, the network bandwidth is simply not sufficient to provide the desired performance. Your VOB server should have the biggest network pipe you can afford. Your view servers should have the next biggest. *Do not* let your network switch autonegotiate network bandwidth. This solution usually defaults to the slowest speed possible. Lock down your network throttle to the fastest setting that both the switch and the network interface in your server can handle.

Build and Test System Scripts

How much is your build or test system tied to your CM system? Before you say none at all, make sure you understand that a build and test system is more than just compiling your code and running tests against it. There are a number of other functions that these systems perform:

- Gather code from developers through a merge mechanism
- Label code for a build
- Package binaries and libraries after they are built
- Notify users about build progress
- Run test suites
- Produce quality metrics
- Possibly much more

Don't forget that when you change your CM system, you are modifying the tool and process foundation that your development team relies on day in and day out.

Defect/Enhancement System Integrations

Does your CM system integrate with a CRM system? What about defect and enhancement tracking? If you had integrations with these types of systems with your old component object model (COM) system, are your integration points going to be the same, or are they going to change? In most cases, the way you use these systems will be different when you change your CM system. If the use model changes, your integration will probably change as well. Make sure you schedule time in your plan to update these integrations.

Downtime

So now that you have your new use model and a project plan, you'll see that you will probably need a couple of months to complete the change. Unfortunately, you cannot ask management to stop development for two months while you change CM systems. Ask for this, and your sanity may be questioned. Instead, management gives you the weekend maintenance window—or if you are lucky, there is a three- or four-day weekend coming up. So, instead of eating Thanksgiving dinner, you may be spending your holiday season converting CVS to ClearCase.

This is why planning is so critical. Try and do as much work ahead of time in a "shadow mode" with your current development processes. This will give you the ability to try out the new system before you make it live to your developers. Remember, you will typically have three to four days to get the new system up and running. So planning ahead and trying it out are critical to your success, and probably to your job.

Training Your People

Don't make any assumptions about the education level of your team: everyone should go through some level of training on the new system, regardless of experience. Someone with seven years of ClearCase experience could have been working on a highly modified version, and he or she will still need some training (albeit less than people new to the program) on your specific installation.

And make sure you involve the key change agents in your development organization when you develop your new use model. They need to be your cheerleaders when you roll this out to the rest of development. It will make the transition much easier for you and the developers.

This change to your CM system will probably have the greatest impact on your developers. People do not like change, but if they are informed, they tend to handle it better. So about a week before you switch over from your old system to the new one, train everyone on the concepts of ClearCase, the differences between the old system and the new one, and the new use model. But don't do the training too far in advance. People are busy, they have a lot on their minds, and they tend to lose most of the benefits of training if they cannot quickly apply this new learning. One best practice is to follow up with your team shortly after the new CM system is in place for constructive feedback and any additional training needs. Plan for this additional training; don't just let it happen by people wandering into your cube and asking endless questions. You will never get anything done.

Changing Your Scripts

Although we have already mentioned the danger of migrating your current development scripts over to your newly deployed ClearCase environment, it's worth repeating. Basically, if you try to use ClearCase just like RCS, you are going to fail. It would be like using your mom's butter knife as a screwdriver—inevitably, you always end up bending the butter knife. And if you thought dealing with your angry mother over a bent butter knife was bad, try dealing with a team of developers and your boss when the new source-code management system goes down.

Scripts are a great way to automate, but make sure they don't hide ClearCase completely. It is better to train your developers properly than to have them think that ClearCase is a big black box that only the magical ClearCase administrator knows anything about. Some people are inclined to believe that there is job security in writing and maintaining these scripts. Believe us, you don't want that kind of job security. It includes 20-hour days and the kind of constant attention that you don't really want.

Keep it simple, and make sure that you follow the use model you designed.

Moving the Data

Starting with ClearCase 4.1, Rational added several migration scripts to help you move from one CM system to another. It involves two basic steps:

1. Exporting from the current CM system using `clearexport_*`
2. Importing into ClearCase using `clearimport`

See the ClearCase Reference Manual for details on both of these scripts.

What to Export

Before you start packing your house, you need to figure out what to throw away, what to put into each new room, and how many boxes you'll need. Likewise, before exporting information, you need to decide what information you want to store in ClearCase:

- Do you export a complete history of your files into ClearCase?
- Do you want to store a snapshot of the latest information into ClearCase?

These two questions can lead you down two very different paths. If you want to store the history, your export and import will be longer, and not all of the information may be compatible with ClearCase. Each exporter has different limitations; see the man page for the exporter you plan to use. You will need to spend some time verifying that the information was imported correctly. Depending on how much history you plan to move, this can take a substantial amount of time.

Before you give up on storing the complete history, there are downsides to storing just a snapshot of the latest information from your old CM system. For starters, if you just store a snapshot, you are going to have to keep both systems for some time. And more than likely, you will probably have to keep both systems active to provide your engineers with some transition time. We do not recommend this option unless you are at a point in development when you don't have to support previous versions, or when you are moving from a prototype to your first product release.

Exporting the Data

ClearCase supports the following exporters with ClearCase 5.x. Note that these exporters do not actually perform the import of information into a VOB; they create a data file that can be passed into the `clearimport` command:

- **`clearexport_ccase`**—Exports from one ClearCase VOB to another. This is good for splitting a VOB.

- **`clearexport_cvs`**—Exports CVS information to a ClearCase VOB. This handles most CVS symbols and converts them to branches and labels.

- **`clearexport_pvcs`**—Exports PVCS information to a ClearCase VOB. This converts PVCS symbols to labels and branches, but there are some restrictions.

- **`clearexport_rcs`**—Exports RCS information to a ClearCase VOB. This handles the RCS symbols and converts them to branches and labels.

- **`clearexport_sccs`**—Exports SCCS information to a ClearCase VOB. This handles SCCS symbols and converts them to branches.

- **`clearexport_ssafe`**—Exports SourceSafe information to a VOB.

For each of these exporters, see the corresponding ClearCase man page for more information.

In all of these cases, a data file is created. The data file is used to import information into a ClearCase VOB. The data file can be analyzed and modified to fit your conversion needs.

Test It First

Before moving the entire system, try converting a small directory hierarchy from your old system to ClearCase. Make sure the conversion meets your expected results. Remember: if you don't get the results you expect, you can always make changes to the data file before doing the import. In fact, it is best to try this several times before you convert the complete system. You will also be able to estimate how much time things will take based on these small tests.

Burning It In

Now that you have tested each component, it's time to make sure that the complete system flows properly. Your end-to-end testing needs to be done without disrupting the current development process. Be prepared to run your staging system in "shadow" mode—in parallel with the production system—from time to time. Pick a couple of developers to try things out during your "burn-in" phase and put it through some rigorous testing. There is nothing worse than turning on a new system and having only part of it working. Not only is it embarrassing and destructive to productivity, but a failed product and process release can cost you your job. Make sure that you run every scenario and test case that your current system can handle, including development work, builds, tests, and release procedures. In fact, do everything you can to test the durability of the system. Whatever doesn't melt the hardware will only make it stronger.

Heavy Lifting

There will be complaints. Get used to that fact. People don't like change, period. Be prepared for it, and plan time for additional training and delays into your schedule. From our experience, plan to spend up to 50 percent of your time during the actual deployment just handling complaints. Remember: education should be your priority. Don't try to develop a script to handle each and every user complaint.

Inevitably, some people will be uncomfortable with the new system. Don't ignore them, but make sure that they understand that this is the way things will now operate, and that they will need to adjust to this change. Stand your ground. There will be pressure from all levels to alter, tweak, adjust, or modify the new system—all so it looks and feels more like the old system. Again, make education your first recourse for handling these complaints. Once people see that you are standing firm on your commitment to the new system, things will quiet down, and people will begin to appreciate the system improvements and expansion of functionality.

Moving from one source-code management system to another is never an easy task. But like moving across town or across state, with proper planning and preparation, any team can handle the change—with minimal loss of life.

14

ClearCase Integration Analysis

Progress has not followed a straight ascending line, but a spiral with
rhythms of progress and retrogression, of evolution and dissolution.
—*Johann Wolfgang von Goethe*

Cooking Up an Integration

One of the common corporate practices these days is to shell out a
ton of cash for tool integrations. Not too long ago in the tool evolu-
tionary process, the rule of the day was to break apart the large and
complex systems—usually developed along proprietary infrastruc-
tures—into their core functions and components, using the "best of
breed" applications from several different vendors, versus relying on
a single vendor's solution set. Now it seems that we're heading toward a combination of both solutions: users want a single, unified
solution, but the engineers and administrators want flexibility in the
vendors they select.

It is highly unlikely that you will find a single software vendor that can handle all of your development tool and data manipulation needs, but it is increasingly important that the front end looks and feels as if users are plugging into a single solution. Whatever your back-end requirements or approach for pulling together disparate systems and tools, there is a recipe for ensuring that your project provides value to your company and ultimately meets your users' needs. In two words: proper planning. We're not trying to trivialize the effort behind something as massive and far reaching a project as integrating tools into ClearCase, but it's amazing how many projects get under way without following some basic scope and sizing exercises.

Let's review a few basic guidelines for any system or tool integration effort, which also apply to any ClearCase integration. Ask yourself the following questions.

Is the User Group Well Defined and Informed?

If you're getting ready to undergo an integration project of any size, hopefully you've already thoroughly defined your user group and their specific requirements. Having an organized user base—to share experiences, good practices, tips, and tricks—is invaluable in heightening the ROI of the project.

Is the Solution Scalable?

Replacing point-to-point interfaces with a tool becomes senseless if the tool can only easily manage a small percentage of those interfaces. It is critical to understand all of the actors within the scope of your solution.

Does the Solution Impact Performance?

The tool must have a high throughput of data and, at the very least, must provide users with the same level of performance as they have today. The coolest tool will be dead in a week if a user spends too much time sitting and tapping his fingers while waiting to access his files.

Does Security Meet Company Standards?

Support for various security standards is required. Make sure your solution does not break any standards. And if your solution requires new technology or the adoption of new standards, make sure your plan includes your company's formal review process.

Is Deployment Relatively Easy?

The ability to fine-tune the system or change certain parameters is essential. Make sure that when you design your solution, keep in mind that someone has to actually install and test the thing. Adhere as best you can to common practices and protocols.

Is Administration Straightforward and Centralized?

Ideally, interfaces must be able to be administered automatically and from a central place. Think about how users will be added to and removed from the system, and where errors and acknowledgments will be tracked.

Does the Solution Include User Training?

The better the training program, the quicker the enterprise will realize its return on investment. If you document the solution as you go, this process will be much easier.

Is the Proper Support in Place?

A good, tiered support function (offering up to 24/7 telephone support and a knowledge base of frequently asked questions) will help alleviate the inevitable problems that come with integration efforts. The best thing is to be prepared.

Analyze Your Ingredients

Over the course of your career, how many projects have you managed or contributed to that were successful? Before you answer, think about your definition of a successful project. To be successful, we believe a project must be completed on time, under budget, and within scope. And lest we forget: the customer should probably also be pleased with the process and the results. Can't forget that critical ingredient.

There's nothing new about these concepts. We should all know this stuff. Chapter 13, "Deploying ClearCase," outlines the simple steps to planning, including identifying the actors within your project, their relationships to each other, the use cases involved, and how everything applies to your business rules. Once you have all that figured out, it's just a matter of planning. Piece of cake, right?

As with your initial ClearCase deployment, the first step in any integration effort is the identification of the actors. This simple step will help you keep things in perspective and keep the project scope in check. During this planning process, it is a good rule of thumb to include all possible actors in the system, present or future. Look at it this way: it's always easier to cut back on scope later, but it's difficult to build a system properly (such as buying more hardware, getting more software licenses, rounding up more technical resources) that has not been adequately sized up front. In fact, this is common project management fare; build an optimistic plan up front, then as issues and risks present themselves, make decisions on scope and adjust later. You always want to allow yourself the option to make a decision later. By limiting the scope up front, you limit your decision-making ability over the long term.

When defining your actors, don't forget to include products you want to integrate with. Hey, isn't that the point of this project? And don't forget ClearCase as one of the main actors. This is key. ClearCase is not part of your system—unless you are going to rewrite ClearCase, which is a bad idea.

One important use case to keep in mind when scoping your project is that of system administration. This includes all of the common administrative tasks that you will need to manage the integrated system you are developing, including licensing, system maintenance, monitoring, configuration, and more. (For more information on system analysis, see Chapter 13.)

Do You Want Sauce on That?

The next step in making informed decisions about your system is understanding the different types of integration that are typically seen with ClearCase.

Artifact-Generation Tools

Tools that are used to generate artifacts such as documents, project plans, code, tests, and executables are considered *artifact-generation tools*. Most of your employees' time is spent using these tools to perform their work. They range from word processors to compilers, and for as many different types of tools there are out there, there are an equal number of integration possibilities. These tools can be broken down into some general categories.

Software Development Tools

These are your typical integrated development environments. They allow software engineers to perform some basic ClearCase operations from menus to key-mapped macros. Consider Figure 14.1, on the next page.

Additional operations that an integration with this type of tool might include are:

- Undo checkout

- Remove from source code control

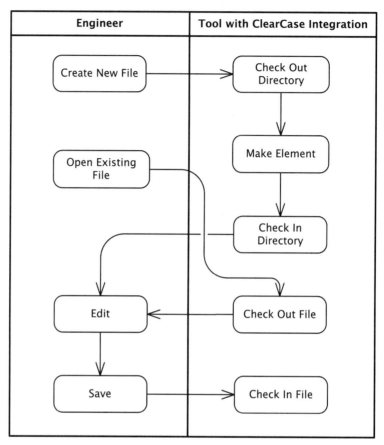

Figure 14.1   *Activity Diagram*

- Show the difference between versions
- Look at the version tree of a file or directory
- Start the ClearCase Explorer application

There might also be a number of UCM-type operations dealing with streams.

There are several tool integrations available off the shelf. Most of them focus on the basic operations, which is all you'll need about 80 percent of the time. Examples of these integrations include:

- Visual Studio

- Vi

- Emacs

- SNiFF+

Authoring Tools

We separated out the category of authoring tools because users of authoring tools are different from those of other artifact-generation tools. And it's more than the funny hats they wear. Most authoring tools are used by technical writers or business process managers—in other words, not your typical ClearCase users. These integrations are usually more complex, and they hide a good portion of ClearCase from the end users. Additionally, many of these tools create more than one ClearCase element for a given artifact on which a user is working. For example, Microsoft FrontPage creates several files that are hidden from the user, but they are generated by the tools to store information about the Web. These files, as well as the individual Web pages, need to be version-controlled. The same is true for most of the other tools that fit into this category:

- FrontPage

- Word

- PowerPoint

- FrameMaker

Most of these integrations can be purchased or downloaded for free from Rational Software, or from the vendor that supplies the tool. If you're so inclined, you can even write your own integration for these. However, remember that you might have to deal with multiple ClearCase elements for a single artifact, and that the majority of your users will not be ClearCase users, so hide as much of the complexity as you can.

Transaction-Tracking Tools

ClearCase can be used with several different transaction-tracking systems. Some of these systems you may think have nothing to do with ClearCase. In one case, ClearCase was used as the back-end database to monitor the stock-trading transactions of stockbrokers. The integration possibilities are endless.

Storage Integration

Source-Code Management Integration

Occasionally, ClearCase deployments include some kind of migration from existing source-code management systems into ClearCase. These integrations are typically a one-off integration to convert from one system to another, but there are always exceptions. For example, there was one company (which will remain nameless) that wanted to please all of its engineers yet still build itself a robust configuration management system. Instead of making the software engineers move to ClearCase, they spent time and a "heckuva-lotta" money (look that one up) working on an integration with CVS and RCS. This integration converted changes that the engineers made into ClearCase commands and stored things in the ClearCase VOBs appropriately. At first glance, the problems with this solution seemed trivial, but there were exceptions. And then they started to pile up. And those pesky exceptions started to cause problems. Go figure. The original purpose of the integration was not to disrupt the software engineers. It had the opposite effect. Instead of doing it right in the first place, taking the one-time hit on training the engineers but decreasing the number of configuration management systems and the overall system complexity, the project became bogged down in complex procedures and code that seemed to fall apart every time something unusual happened. Which, not surprisingly, was fairly often.

Workflow and Shared Information Integration

Workflow and shared information integration usually includes some kind of defect-tracking or change-request management system, project management system, or build-and-release system. The most common integration is with a defect-tracking system, which ClearCase supplies with ClearQuest and ClearCase UCM integration.

Defect and Change Management Systems

Most of these integrations can be boiled down into the primary scenario in Figure 14.2.

In this scenario, the defect-tracking system can handle the automatic creation of ClearCase views when a defect is being worked on by the developer. The view is removed when the defect is closed. Also notice that a typical post-exec trigger is used to check in code, or any other mechanism used to connect changed files to the defect. This information can be used later for the build-and-release section.

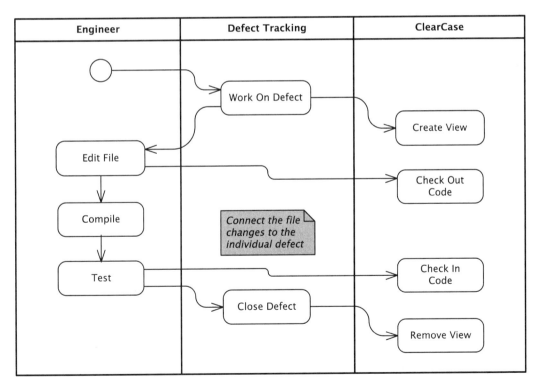

Figure 14.2   *Primary Scenario*

Project Management Systems

Several project management systems can drive software development through ClearCase. Here are some representative examples of how such systems might be used:

- Automatically create UCM streams that fit the project management schedule.

- Automate workflow to follow project management schedules. For example, certain triggers can be turned on during different phases of development, or depending on the project schedule requirements.

- Automate build-and-release content according to the project schedule.

These types of integrations are typically not found very often, but they can help control your product development schedules.

Build-and-Release Management Systems

These systems are rarely tied only to ClearCase. They typically connect with project management and defect-tracking tools as well. Some vendors refer to these solutions as *content management systems,* and if implemented right, they can control the build, test, and release of products more reliably. Here are some common ways in which these systems integrate.

- **Perform builds according to "closed" defects in the defect-tracking system.** This can be done with several different mechanisms, such as branching, labeling, or metadata. Everyone has his or her own way of doing it. This chapter will illustrate some of the secrets and pitfalls of the different approaches.

- **Automatically generate release notes from defect-tracking systems.** If you train your engineers to put comments in the defect-tracking system, these comments can be used to automatically generate release notes for a build.

- **Gather statistics about code changed per build and release.**
  By asking your project change request (PCR) system to list the
  files that have changed, the system can ask ClearCase for the
  differences between the version selected and the previous
  build's version. Again, there are several different options for
  getting this information, which we will address in Chapters 23
  and 24.

Caveats (Think Really Bad Fruitcake)

Hopefully we have all learned the lessons of source-code migration
integrations (similar to what was outlined previously). In short, when
it comes to workflow and shared information integration, we need to
tread lightly. Several man-years can be wasted writing integrations
for workflow and ClearCase. Here are some rules that may help when
working with workflow management systems.

Make Sure You Are Doing What You *Need* to Do

While keeping busy passes the time, your company probably expects
you to provide actual value. (Hey, it's not unheard of.) Impress your
friends and amaze family members by doing your use case analysis
up front. And when asked to add yet another feature to the integration (it's inevitable), point the requestor back to the use case model
that you meticulously built with the input and approval of your engineers and management, and let her justify the change. Remind her
that it could easily get out of proportion, and like the famed Christ-
mas fruitcake that is passed around the family circle without ever
being consumed, so will this project never cease. If you find that you
cannot reason with her, fall to your knees and sob like a child. Sometimes it works.

Pick a Place for Your Golden Data

Many tools store duplicate information or data. Try to avoid this,
even when you think you are caching things for quicker access.

When you have data stored in different tools, the data can quickly become stale or just plain wrong. Limit the amount of duplicate data between your tools. Almost every tool allows for some kind of extension to the database or repository. Use this power wisely, and pick the location where the data will be used the most. Some of you may be thinking, "Hey, I'll just write a cron job that will sync up the data between all of the tools every thirty minutes." Avoid this as much as possible. You never know when a machine will go down. And if you have your tools spread all over the place, you're going to have problems. If you have no other choice but to spread your tools between different machines, pick which source is the "golden" source, write to it in real time, and use it to sync the other tools.

Use Published APIs; Don't Use Back Doors

Oh, the temptation to skip through the recipe and ignore directions is great. Especially when cooking up an integration. The results are usually disastrous. Use the published API; don't use hidden back doors or unpublished hints from user groups. You never know how long those doors are going to be there. Another thing to avoid is accessing the database directory of a tool. Although you may think you are using the API of the correct tool database, believing it is a published API, you are just one customer. And unless you represent a large portion of the ClearCase licenses in the world (or have pictures of ClearCase developers in compromising situations), someone can (and at some point probably will) change the database on you. If not ClearCase, it will be one of the other tools in your integration solution. It's just not worth the headache.

Let the Tools Do the Work for You

Why are you doing the integration in the first place? Isn't your goal to empower your team through better automation? So why not apply that philosophy to your integration effort? Let the selected tools do the work for you. Don't think that you have the time or know-how to equal the development team of the product you are using. While it is widely accepted among our readers that CM people are the brightest and fastest coders in the world, unless you are the Wolfgang Puck of software development and configuration management, don't try it. Or even if you are that good, spend your time on more pressing issues. Buy or download from freeware everything you can—including the integrations themselves.

Now that we've walked you through the basic recipe for ClearCase integrations, let's delve deeper into specific integration concepts and tips.

Integration Design and Implementation

Remember that old Saturday morning cartoon educational series "Schoolhouse Rock"? For many of us who grew up in the 1970s, those brief musical interludes were a memorable part of our adolescence. We came to know most of the songs and storylines, and we were sometimes even able to apply them to our schoolwork. Each of the cartoons was only a couple of minutes long, but each contained an important message—from conjugating a verb, to the ins and outs of multiplication, to the legislative process of moving a bill through the U.S. Congress—and each episode drove home that message with a catchy (albeit sometimes irritating) song.

That's how we like to present these chapters: a little repetition, some light humor, and a solid message that you can retain and, hopefully, apply to your current—and future—projects.

The goal of the Schoolhouse Rock cartoons was to provide a foundation in the basic components of grammar, math, and science. Think of these lessons as points of integration into the larger subject matter—APIs, if you will. Through these educational snapshots, and by learning the basic protocols of each subject, we were able to make the connection to the larger data set and the wealth of learning opportunities behind them.

Well, ClearCase software does not come with any cute cartoon characters singing and dancing (although I'm sure it has passed through the mind of someone on Rational's marketing team), but it does offer a variety of points of entry into the tool. In fact, ClearCase, as we're sure you've come to realize, offers an enormous array of options and configurations. In Chapter 7, we talked about the different integration points for ClearCase and other tools. We've tried to demonstrate many of the different tools available in your tool chest—from the "no-brainers" to the more complex/less deployed tools—all of which can be integrated and configured to your heart's content. It's all about building the "perfect system," right?

For those purists who are on the path to ClearCase enlightenment, there are really just two implementation approaches that can be used when integrating tools into your perfect system. And though we are not providing music to which our readers can sing along (we had trouble coming up with rhymes for things like "Perl module" and "`ClearCase::CtCmd::exec`"), we hope the integration message we share will come in handy down the road.

Selecting Your Approach

The messages were so simple back then, but memorable. Although ClearCase is slightly more complex than identifying a noun or an adverb, there are really just two approaches to implementation: wrapper scripts and triggers. And hey! "Wrapper" is both an adjective and a noun! (Sorry.) Included next are brief overviews of each approach, followed by a detailed view of how to implement your scenarios using command line, Perl, and COM, including the benefits, limitations, and an example of each. Feel free to sing along.

Wrapper Scripts

This approach replaces the common commands that actors of your system use to get work done. This approach is commonly known as *helper scripts,* and we have seen every kind imaginable: everything from a simple view creation script that makes sure that view storage is always placed in the same area, to very complex defect-tracking ClearCase integrations that use data from several different tools to automatically create views for users.

Wrapper scripts are great for helping users get their work done more effectively. However, they're not as useful when you're dealing with curious (that is, control-freak) engineers who can't keep their hands off the hardware. This type of engineer is constantly cruising through "`cleartool man`" to find out *all* of the commands that you, the configuration management lead, have tried to hide from him by providing scripts to do everything. You just can't make some people happy.

One way of controlling the curious engineers is to train them on the basics of ClearCase, and, more important, on the use model and philosophy of using ClearCase in your organization (a point typically forgotten, even among the most experienced CM managers). If they know why you are doing things, they are more apt to respect process and your management role.

Triggers

Another way to control engineers within the ClearCase environment is through triggers. In Chapter 22, we discuss in detail the different types of triggers and how they can be used to control process and enforce the use model that you want your actors to follow.

Triggers can also be used to coordinate information between multiple tools. Most of the coordination between tools should be handled with post-exec triggers, unless, of course, the behavior of a particular ClearCase command depends on the output of commands from another tool, such as those used in a defect-tracking system. For more details on the many different types of triggers and their uses, check out Chapter 22, "Trigger-Happy."

Implementation Options

Once you've finished mapping all of the use cases within your system to one or both of these implementation approaches, it is time to make another decision: how to implement your scenarios.

Your first thought might be just to write the ClearCase commands using shell scripts or Windows batch scripts. But before you jump, let's review the different options available for implementing your design: ClearCase command line interface, ClearCase Perl module (CtCmd), and the ClearCase Automation Library (CAL).

ClearCase Command Line

The ClearCase command line interface is robust, and it allows any operation you can imagine with your ClearCase VOBs and views. Most systems have several scripts that use the command line interface to integrate systems together. Basically, if the user can type it on the command line, you can put it into a script. In addition, you can choose any scripting language you wish—but be sure to choose a language that works on all of the platforms within your system. Perl tends to be the most popular scripting language for multiplatform system integrations.

Benefits
The benefit of using this approach is that it is simple and straightforward. You can quickly prototype your script by first typing it on the command line. Most of the time you'll find that scripts are written by individual users for those repetitive tasks that have to be done day in and day out.

With this option:

- All ClearCase operations are available.
- The scripts are easy to prototype.
- The approach mimics the user's calls to ClearCase commands.

Limitations
Although there are many benefits to writing scripts that just call command line interfaces, there are also some downsides to using the command line:

- Command line interfaces can and likely will change.
- Error handling is basically pass or fail.

- Reasons for failure must be parsed from the stderr and stdout. This can change from one release to another.

- Querying for information from ClearCase requires some parsing of stdout and stderr.

Example: Issuing a ClearTool Command (cleartool)

```
$theResults = 'cleartool lsview';
if($!) {
     die("cleartool returned error: $@\n" . $theResults);
}
print $theResults, "\n";
```

In this simple example, the stdout and stderr are both in $theResults. To separate them, you have to set up file descriptors to handle the different streams of information. It is better handled using the ClearCase Perl module, which separates these out for you.

ClearCase Perl Module (CtCmd)

Rational Software recently released a ClearCase Perl module that can be downloaded from Rational or from http://www.cpan.org. The module allows Perl script writers to access the ClearCase commands directory, and it gives better access to error codes and error handling.

The Perl module basically consists of one subroutine to allow scripts to call ClearTool commands—ClearCase::CtCmd::exec(). The ClearCase::CtCmd::exec() subroutine takes either a string or a list as an input argument and returns a three-element Perl array as output.

The first output element is a status bit containing 0 on success, 1 on failure. The second output element is a scalar string corresponding to stdout, if any. The third element contains any error message corresponding to output on stderr.

Benefits
If you are already focused on multiplatform solutions, or if you are already using Perl as your scripting language, this module handles the error handling more efficiently for you.

- Handles most of the ClearTool command options.

- Simplifies error handling over the standard calling ClearCase commands.

- Easy to prototype, much like the ClearTool command line option. You can write the exact command that the user will enter in the string passed to exec().

Limitations

The limitations of this option are very similar to those of the ClearTool command option. However, because of the implementation of the Perl module, there are some additional limitations:

- You cannot use the -ver and -verall options on any commands.

- All single characters preceded by a hyphen must be quoted.

- Other Perl characters, such as %,@, and $, must be quoted.

- The output still needs to be parsed to get the data that was queried.

Example: Issuing a ClearTool Command

Taken from examples in the CtCmd documentation.[1]

```
use ClearCase::CtCmd;

@aa=ClearCase::CtCmd::exec("lsview");
my $status_now = $aa[0];
my $stdout = $aa[1];
my $error = $aa[2];
die("Cleartool returned error: ", $error, "\n")
if($status);
print $stdout, "\n";
```

---

1. Reprinted by permission, based on material from *ClearCase Administrator's Manual,* © 2001 IBM Corporation. All rights reserved.

ClearCase Automation Library COM Interface

Finally, the ClearCase Automation Library is a COM interface that allows you to access and manipulate ClearCase data *on Windows platforms only*. This will not work on UNIX platforms, so make sure that the scripts you write with CAL need to run only on Windows machines. You can use CAL to write scripts, standalone programs, or macros embedded in other applications.

The CAL approach does not deal with the command line interface at all, and it gives you access to objects in the VOB. Thus, you can manipulate ClearCase in ways that the command line may not readily allow. This can decrease the execution time to run your programs, and it gives you better control of your data. For a great introduction to this interface, take a look at Mark McLaughlin's article on the Rational Developer Network, "Saying Hello to CAL."

Benefits
- Error checking is more exact.

- No need to parse the output of stdout or stderr. You can work with the objects directly.

- Queries can be more exact and decrease the amount of time to run.

- Integration with other tools that run on Windows boxes can be tightened.

- Multiple languages can be used to implement solutions.

- Single commands can be written that would normally take several command line commands.

- Scripts don't need to change as the outputs of commands change. It is less likely that the API will change and more likely that the output of running the commands will do so.

Limitations
- Windows platform only!

- Common commands may require more code than just calling the ClearTool command.

- There is definitely a learning curve. The object model is much harder to get your head around than the ClearTool command set and options.

- CAL runs as an in-process COM server; it is not a DCOM application.

- It does not provide access to all ClearCase functionality. For example, with CAL:

  - You cannot create VOBs.

  - You cannot access build capabilities.

  - You cannot access view profiles.

  - You cannot get properties or perform operations on symbolic links or derived objects.

  - You are limited to operations that ClearTool and the ClearCase GUI can perform.

Example: Issuing a ClearTool Command (Perl)
Taken from the CAL documentation.

```
# The syntax used here was compatible with ActiveState
build 522.
use Win32::OLE;
# Connect to the top-level ClearTool object
my $ct = Win32::OLE->new('ClearCase.ClearTool')
    or die "Could not create ClearTool object\n";
$output = $ct->CmdExec("pwvlsview")
    or die("Cleartool returned error: ",
           Win32::OLE->LastError(), "\n");
print $output;
```

Example: Displaying Information about All Branches Sprouting from a Version (Perl)
Taken from the CAL documentation.

```
use Win32::OLE;
# Connect to the top-level ClearCase object
my $cc = Win32::OLE->new('ClearCase.Application')
    or die "Could not create Application object\n";
```

```
# Loop over the branches sprouting from a version and
# display their paths using the default property of
# ICCBranch, and other information
my $ver = $cc->Version("b:\\caroltest\\testelem.c@@\\main\\0")
     or die("Could not get version: ",
            Win32::OLE->LastError(), "\n");
my $path = $ver->Path;
my $subbranches = $ver->SubBranches;
my $enum = Win32::OLE::Enum->new($subbranches);
while (defined(my $branch = $enum->Next)) {
     print($branch->Path, " branch sprouting from ",
           $path, " has ", $branch->Versions->Count,
           " version(s); latest version is ",
           $branch->LatestVersion->VersionNumber, "\n");
}
```

Taking the Next Step

Are you finding your next few tasks a little daunting? The key to any new development effort, as with the messages embedded within each of the Schoolhouse Rock clips, is to keep things simple. How do you keep it simple? Well, we recommend you start by approaching your project with "baby steps." Take some time to understand each of your implementation options, do some reading (RDN and IBM developerWorks are great places to get started), and don't be afraid to ask questions. Like the little bill sitting on Capitol Hill, building your "perfect system" takes time and patience. And if you find yourself trying to sway your project team (or members of Congress) on certain aspects of your proposed solution, just remember: It's all about baby steps. As Elbert Hubbard said, "The reason men oppose progress is not that they hate progress, but that they love inertia."

So understand your options, take baby steps, and build some inertia. Once you've made some progress, maybe your team will accept the fact that you break out in song every so often.

15

ClearCase UCM Integration

Integrating Ideas, Tools, and Source Code

The perception of configuration management has undergone many changes over the years. Most people think the job of the CM team is to build software, but that is only part of the story. Closer to the truth is that CM is the integrator of the *whole* product, responsible for source-code management, development tools, building, testing, document packaging, and delivering the product to the customer. Keeping track of everything can therefore be a large and sometimes nerve-racking job.

There are several ways to use ClearCase to integrate and control all of the artifacts created by your development teams. ClearCase is more a framework than a standalone product because it allows you to do anything you want. However, this is a double-edged sword. You have flexibility, but with it comes complexity. Fortunately, the Supreme

Beings of ClearCase were wise, and they decided to give us mere mortals more direction and control through a common or "universal" mechanism, called Unified Change Management (UCM). With UCM, the flexibility of ClearCase is still there, but now we have a greater understanding of all the components within the system—and better control.

Basic Objects in the UCM

Where ClearCase gave us very abstract concepts such as branches, labels, hyperlinks, elements, views, and VOBs, the UCM provides the higher-level objects that we deal with every day to develop, integrate, and deliver products. These higher-level concepts are *projects*, *streams, baselines, activities*, and *components*.

Projects

A project denotes a group of people working on a single development effort. This can be a product release, a subsystem of a complete system, or a collection of products to form a suite. A project contains one integration stream and several development streams. This is where you—as the CM guru—must start planning. But before you start creating projects all over the place, you need to sit down with marketing, your software development team, QA, and your technical writers to determine how you want to work together.

Streams

A stream can be compared to a development branch. The stream groups together specific versions of elements. The key differentiator between a generic branch and a stream is the additional information stored in the stream. For example, a stream contains a baseline and a set of activities. It also contains relationships with other streams, such as a parent stream. The baseline, plus the set of activities, determines what versions of the elements the stream contains.

In Figure 15.1, two activities, Activity 1 and Activity 2, have been added to the stream. The baseline is defined by the versions of the elements represented by the bold circles in the diagram. The two activities have versions of elements that represent different patterns.

There are two basic types of streams: an integration stream and a development stream. The integration stream is where all of the development streams come together to be shared, as shown in Figure 15.2. Think of integration streams as places where everything comes together from the development streams.

Baselines

A baseline represents versions of elements that are used to start a stream or to rebase a stream. A simplistic way of looking at baselines is to compare them to labels—the difference again being that additional information and relationships are stored with baselines. Baselines are typically the starting points for many of your activities, such as creating streams, rebasing a stream, and so on.

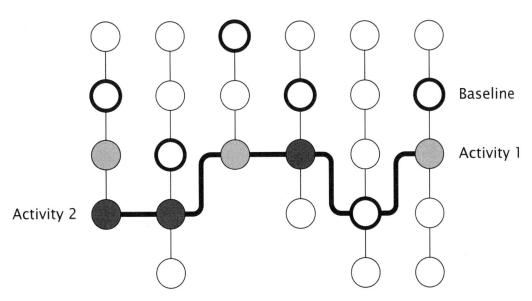

Figure 15.1   *Sample Stream Flow*

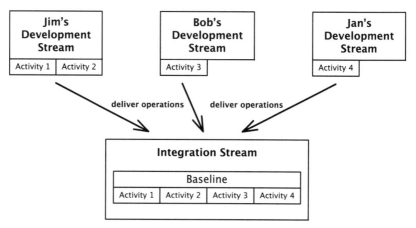

Figure 15.2   *Sample Integration Stream Flow*

Activities

An activity must be created before you can create a version of an element in a ClearCase UCM project. An activity is the basic unit of work that your team members perform. It has a headline (ID), a creator, a change set (that is, a set of elements that have changed), and a parent stream with which it corresponds. If you are using Rational's ClearQuest, an activity is usually tied directly to a defect or enhancement. All work performed in your development stream must be done in concert with an activity.

Components

A component allows you to group together a set of related directories and file elements and then tie them to a UCM project. A component is developed and integrated, and all of its parts are released together. All projects must have at least one component, and components can be shared between projects. However, a component cannot span multiple VOBs, and the largest a component can be is the size of its VOB. Other things to consider about components include:

- Elements cannot be moved from one component to another.

- An element can exist in only one component.

- Once you create a component, you cannot reorganize it into
  subcomponents.

Planning your components up front is extremely important. One
strategy is to put any elements that will be shared with other projects
into the same component, or into groups of components.

The Workflow of UCM

Now that you understand the basic concepts behind UCM, we need
to review how to use these objects to help develop and deliver on
time and with higher quality. UCM is not just for the CM team: it
requires some training on the part of the development team as well.
But let's start by reviewing the CM responsibilities as defined in the
Rational Unified Process (RUP), shown in Figure 15.3.

Planning the Project

During the planning process, the CM team will put together a configuration management plan that includes strategies for how the team
is going to work together to develop and deliver their product. This is
probably one of the most important tasks that your CM team can
perform. The Rational Unified Process has some great templates to
help you get started, and to outline each of the steps. Once you have
a plan approved, you can start creating your project.

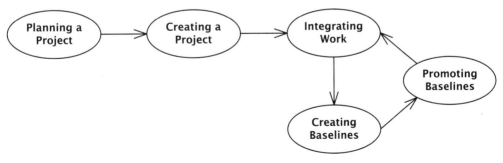

Figure 15.3   *CM Responsibilities*

Creating a Project

Although this appears as one activity in the workflow, several steps need to be performed during the creation of a project. These steps should be driven from the CM plan that was developed during planning.

Create a Process VOB for Storing Project Information

Process VOBs (PVOBs) are just like normal VOBs, but they contain additional types of ClearCase objects (streams, activities, projects, and change sets). Process VOBs are created using the `mkvob` command with the `-ucmproject` command line option:

```
cleartool mkvob -ucmproject
    -tag /vobs/kass_project /usr/vobstore/kass_project.vbs
mkdir /vobs/kass_project
```

These commands will create a UCM PVOB with the name /vobs/kass_project.

Create Components That Contain the Elements Developers Use to Start Their Work

Components are made using the `cleartool mkcomp` command. Components and VOBs usually have a one-to-one relationship, but this is not always the case:

```
cleartool mkcomp -root /vobs/kass_src
kass_comp@/vobs/kass_project
```

This creates a component named kass_comp in the /vobs/kass_project PVOB, with the complete /vobs/kass_src VOB as the component:

```
cleartool mkcomp -root /vobs/kass_src/WorkFlow
kass_WF_comp@/vobs/kass_project
```

This creates a component named kass_WF_comp in the /vobs/kass_project PVOB that contains the directory

/vobs/kass_src/WorkFlow. Please note that both commands could not be run because the second command contains directories in the first command. These are just examples.

Create Baselines for the Integration Stream, Development Streams, and Rebase Activities

Baselines are created using the command `cleartool mkbl`. The easiest way to create a baseline is from an existing label. First, place a label on the versions that should be your baseline. Use the `cleartool mklbtype` and `mklabel` commands in a view that selects the proper versions for the baseline:

```
cleartool mklbtype MY_START
cleartool mklabel -recurse -replace .
```

Now that you have a label and it has been placed on the correct versions, you can create the baseline with the following command:

```
cleartool mkbl -import MY_START@/vobs/kass_src
```

Integrating Work

Periodically, CM engineers will need to complete the delivery operations when the development team cannot. This can happen when using multi-site and UCM at the same time. The delivery operations must be finished by the project manager on a region that does not have mastership of the branch. UCM includes a useful operation called *remote deliver* that can be used to handle most cases. But essentially, it is up to you to watch out for any delivery operations that have not been completed.

Creating Baselines

Baselines are not used just for creating streams; they are used also for rebasing development streams for your developers. The key is to keep the baselines as current as possible, but not so much as to introduce instability. Having too many baselines tends to confuse your engineers.

Baselines are created when a build and test of the product are successful. This gives the engineers a stable base to work from. This type of baseline can be created with labels, as shown here.

```
cleartool mkbl -import BUILDLABEL@/vobs/kass_src BLD_2
```

Or it can be created on all of the changes since that last baseline was created.

```
cleartool mkbl BLD_2
```

Alternatively, the baseline can be created specifically for activities.

```
cleartool mkbl -activities line-lib@/vobs/kass_project
BLD_2
```

Promoting Baselines

Baselines can have state, and they pass through a number of promotion levels, typically defined as REJECTED, INITIAL, BUILT, TESTED, and RELEASED. These levels can be changed with the cleartool setplevel command; otherwise, you can change the level of a baseline using the following command:

```
cleartool chbl -level RELEASED bl2.123@/vobs/kass_project
```

In this example, the level of the baseline bl2.123 is changed to the RELEASED level.

Development Activities

It is important to understand not only what the CM's responsibilities are, but also what the developers are doing. Figure 15.4 outlines the recommended workflow from the RUP.

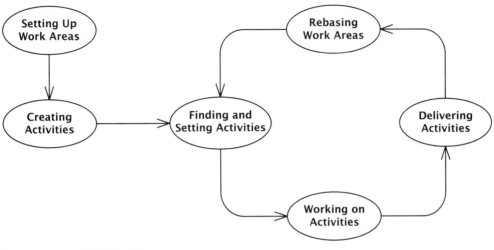

Figure 15.4   *RUP Workflow*

Setting Up Work Areas

To work on a UCM project, your developers must create at least two work areas: (1) a development area for working on activities in isolation from the changes of others and (2) an integration area for testing activities that are to be delivered. The integration area will include versions from other team members. Work areas are views that are attached to a stream.

Creating Activities

To change elements in your product, you first must create activities through which to perform the work. If you have an integration with ClearQuest, for example, this is accomplished through the ClearQuest interface (details of which we will not go through here). The commands for creating activities are shown in the following examples.

The following line will create a new activity with the name "myactivity" and a headline of "My New Activity":

```
cleartool mkactivity -nset myactivity -headline
    "My New Activity"
```

This next line will create a new activity and set it to the current view:

```
cleartool mkactivity
```

Finding and Setting Activities

ClearCase has several commands for working with activities:

- lsactivity lists activities in UCM. This can be used to find activities for the user, the view, the stream, or any combination.

- chactivity changes the activity. The activity's headline can be changed, and the version of an element can be added or removed from an activity through changing ownership of change sets.

- setactivity sets and unsets the activity to a view.

Working on Activities

Before checking files in or out, your developers need to set an activity to the current view. The activity will keep track of changes that have been made in the view. All of these changes are kept in a change set. When delivering activities, the change sets attached to the activities are delivered to the integration stream so that everyone on the team can see the changes.

Delivering Activities

- deliver changes elements from a source stream to a target stream.

  Once developers have completed working on an activity, they can deliver their changes to the default integration stream (that is, the parent stream) or any other stream that they choose. Streams can accept or reject changes depending on policies that have been established for the stream. The status of the delivery can be obtained with this command as well.

When the deliver begins, it creates a special activity to deliver the changes to the integration stream. This activity is created to help manage any possible merge conflicts and resolutions that may occur. Delivery can be accomplished in two steps or in a single step. The first step is to perform the merges of elements that have changed. The second step confirms the changes and marks the activity as completed. You can force the delivery to take only one step by using the `-complete` flag.

Rebasing Work Areas

- `rebase` changes the configuration of the stream.

Periodically, you will want to rebase your stream from the integration streams. Remember: your development streams usually hang around for a long time. Periodically, you will need to get updates from your team members' activities. In essence, the `rebase` command in ClearCase does just that. It provides the activities and therefore changes what other team members have delivered into an integration stream.

Rebasing streams is a multistep process, much like the delivering activities. You can have code merging from the integration stream to your development stream, involving moving labels and merge conflicts to be resolved. Just as with the `deliver` command, `-complete` can be used to mark the automatically created activity as completed or to force a one-step rebase.

As a CM manager, it is best that you provide recommended baselines against which developers can rebase their development streams. For example, a stable build could be put into the recommended base list, enabling developers to see that they are working from code that was functional at one time.

Policy Management

If your development team thought you were a control freak *before* discovering UCM, just wait until you figure out all of the features that UCM provides. From changing the mutability of components, to obtaining visibility of which activities and changes can be delivered and when they can be delivered, UCM offers greater flexibility and control for the software development manager.

The key to a good policy management strategy is planning. It is much harder to change policies once you have already started the development process. In an ideal world, every project would be organized, with each component in its place—but the reality is it takes work. Change will occur during the development process. Try to recognize the impact of changing policy halfway through the project before you make decisions.

There are some key areas in UCM through which policies can be enforced using triggers (see Chapter 22). These include component policies, default view types, delivery policies, and rebase policies.

- Component policies are basic, allowing you to lock a component as read-only or read/write.

- There are two types of default views: snapshot and dynamic.

- Rebase policies involve creating recommended baselines for developers to use for rebasing, and they offer the ability to determine whether rebasing is required before delivering operations can be performed.

- Delivery policies involve allowing or disallowing delivery of changes from other projects: changes made in components and not in the target stream, changes that contain nonmodifiable components, and changes in fountain baselines.

The number of different combinations of policies attached to your project can be huge, and if you want to really frustrate your development team (and increase the number of hysterical calls to your desk), implement all of them. Actually, use them in moderation. Too much control through policies can get in the way of development. The key here is to put in just enough control to steer the group in the right direction, but not so much that they get in the way of productivity.

Things to Watch For

UCM does not solve all of the problems with deploying ClearCase right out of the box, nor does it guarantee a good development strategy. You must do the planning necessary to have a good development experience. The best approach is to learn everything you can about the tools you are using, in conjunction with trying to understand what makes your team work most effectively. Then bring the two together. Time and time again, tools are thrown at development problems with no thought about how they will actually be integrated into existing processes. Avoid the slick salesman or overzealous toolsmith, pushing the perfect software development harness that just happens to solve all of the world's software development problems. That suite of tools does not yet exist, nor does UCM answer that call. But with planning, training, and execution, UCM will set you on the right path.

16

Lone Eagle Management

What in the world is a lone eagle, and what is this chapter all about? A lone eagle is someone who works outside of the office. She might work at home, in a remote office, on a sailboat somewhere in the Caribbean, or from a lodge on the ski slopes of Colorado. OK, maybe the boat and the ski slopes are pushing it, but the reality of today's technology is that an individual contributor can work from just about anywhere. Add to that reality the nature of global work teams and the need for some organizations to offer flexible schedules, and the result: more and more companies are recognizing that people no longer need to be in the same building to get their work done. This is especially true for software development. Most software developers, testers, and CM people can perform a majority of their work from home or at a remote office. Due to the availability of many multi-site tools, it is sometimes even cost-effective to have an entire team utilizing the "remote office" option.

But you can't just hire a person 1,500 miles away from headquarters and expect her to be productive. There are some things you must consider before proceeding, and these considerations will help you understand the requirements and proper setup of a remote worker.

The Success of a Lone Eagle

First, you need to consider whether or not your organization can handle a lone eagle. Some organizations just aren't designed to handle people working from their homes. For example, you would not allow your fast-food cashier (you know, the one wearing the headset, speaking the unintelligibly garbled language) to work remotely, even though—technically—it could be done. Hey, you never know—it could happen someday. The point is, you need to consider whether your organization's culture can handle this kind of change. If you tend to be a micromanager, needing to know everything going on with your team at every moment, you are probably not a good candidate for managing a lone eagle.

Second, you need to make sure that your lone eagle has the right frame of mind and work habits to be isolated from the rest of the team. You're probably thinking, "If only (insert name here) would work 1,500 miles away . . . (add your favorite complaint about the person)." Some potential lone eagles may consider your proposal for them to work remotely as a push into "voluntary exile." So be careful.

OK, back to the type of person who makes a good lone eagle. You need someone who can take vague ideas and produce something valuable. Obviously, the amount of communication this person will receive on a day-to-day basis will be less than if he were sitting in the office right next to your team, so the lone eagle needs to be able to read between the lines and decipher partially defined requirements. The person *must* be a self-starter.

It can be difficult working from a remote location: lone eagles sometimes feel isolated from the rest of the team, and out of the loop. Finally, as a manager of a lone eagle, you cannot be concerned about the number of hours worked; results should be your main focus. However, you may be surprised to learn that the typical lone eagle will put in more hours than employees back at corporate, and they are much more productive, overall.

If you are a lone eagle, there is one thing you need to remember to be successful: communication, communication, communication. It is very important that people know you still exist, so make sure the people you interface with at corporate know what you are doing as much as possible. Here are some helpful hints.

Let People Know Your Availability

There is nothing more damaging to the trust people have in you— that is, that you are indeed working—than for you to be unreachable when you are needed. Sending a friendly e-mail if you need to step out of the office is great, or placing some kind of note on your electronic calendar.

Face-to-Face Meetings

If budgets permit, go back to face-to-face meetings periodically. You can learn so much when you meet with people in person: body language, spontaneous conversations (water-cooler talk), and the frequent sidebars that come with being on site are all important to building relationships.

Communication Channels

Use several different methods of communication. The number of different communication channels now available is staggering, but you need to choose the right channel for the right type of communication. Most lone eagles rely on four basic types of remote communication: phone, instant messaging, e-mail, and Web conferencing.

Phone

The phone tends to be the most personal. Always use the phone when people need to hear the emotion in your voice, or vice versa.

Nothing is worse than saying "I'm sorry, I messed up" in an e-mail or instant message. It tells your coworkers that they are not important enough to talk to directly.

Instant Messaging

Instant messaging can be annoying, but it can also promote free-flowing communication. Such messages are analogous to someone popping his head into your office to ask a quick question. This informal "instant" communication can save hours or days of miscommunication, or worse yet, "assumption development" ("I think he said the background color should be hot pink").

E-mail

Who would have ever thought that e-mail would be considered more formal or impersonal than other forms of communication? Yet people are becoming more careful about what they write in e-mails. Maybe it has something to do with the fact that many companies now store e-mail permanently, or possibly it's related to the recent spate of corporate scandals. It is difficult to shred e-mail.

Web Conferencing

Conference calls are so much more productive when everyone can see the agenda and see action items added and discussion points modified as they talk on the phone. In many cases, phone and Web conferencing should replace face-to-face meetings. They just seem more productive, and an attendance record is automatically kept.

Whatever tools you choose, just remember there are numerous options available. Make sure you pick the right tool for the right situation. Sending an instant message to your boss about the status of a critical project is probably a bad idea.

Report Your Progress

Everyone hates writing progress reports, but as a lone eagle, you must do so regularly. You need to tell your manager and your coworkers what you are doing. The report can come weekly, monthly, or as often as your manager agrees is acceptable. However, if your progress reports are too sporadic, people will forget about you and what you are doing.

Software engineers may mistakenly think that because they have fixed a huge number of bugs in a given week, their manager is aware of their productivity. After all, such accomplishments are automatically recorded, so why wouldn't everyone know what they are doing? All of the information is there. They might think, "Why should I have to do a progress report weekly? My manager must be lazy or something."

Frankly, it is not your manager's job to babysit you and ask you what you are up to. If you are a lone eagle, it is your responsibility to make sure everyone sees the work that you do and where you are on your project.

Development Tools

OK, so far we have only talked about individuals working from home. But what does this have to do with software engineering and, more specifically, CM? Well, if you have the tools and skills mentioned previously, the engineering stuff is easy. It's virtually the same as if you were back in the corporate office. OK, maybe not easy, but pretty darn close.

Local or Remote Access

One of the first things you need to consider is whether you will be working on local machines, on remote machines at corporate, or on a combination of both.

To determine this, you should first look at your network connectivity. If you can only get a dial-up connection at 56K baud, or if your tools do not work well over the WAN, you will probably be working on local machines.

The primary benefit of working with a local setup is network speed—and if the corporate network goes down, your work can continue because your tools and data are local. In such outage situations, you might not have everything you need, but you will probably have enough to get some work done.

Working from a remote server at the corporate office has benefits, as well, especially if you are working in coordination with a team. In this scenario, you see everything that the rest of your team sees. And there are usually fewer system administration problems that you'd otherwise have to deal with if you had everything local.

CM System Local Setup

If you decide to have a local setup, here are some options to use with your CM system: snapshot views and multi-sited VOBs.

Snapshot Views

First, create snapshot views of the code on your local machines from a remote corporate VOB server. The snapshot view basically contains everything according to your config spec at the time that you created the snapshot view. The downside to a snapshot view is you will not be updated automatically with changes that have been integrated into the integration branch. This can lead to massive merge conflicts when you push your changes back to the corporate VOB server.

Local Multi-sited VOBs

Second, set up your own VOB server at your location. If this scares you, good. It means you understand that you need to learn something about VOBs and multi-sites. VOB maintenance can be easy for a single user, and it typically does not take much time if set up properly. When you set up your VOB for multi-sites, make sure you sync as frequently as your network will allow. We recommend that you set up two modes of operating the multi-site sync-ups. First is a sync-up on demand. Because lone eagles work alone, they typically know when their work is done, or when they need to integrate with other people. Allowing lone eagles to sync code when they want is power-ful, and it gives them the flexibility they need.

On the other hand, allowing them to sync only when they want to may cause problems, too. Sometimes lone eagles forget to sync, and they can be out of sync for several days or weeks at a time. Another recommendation is to set up a sync schedule for when the lone eagle's home office network is normally quiet. Sometimes this is in the middle of the night; sometimes it's the middle of the day. The important thing is not to slow down the network when the lone eagle is trying to get work done. Many engineers find that on-demand syncs provide great updates during the day and that automated syncs during the night and early morning help keep them up to date with everyone else.

The downside to working locally is that you have to purchase more equipment, and then you have to become a trained-on-the-job, part-time system administrator. Another disadvantage is the lack of avail-ability of machine resources. Unless you have a large budget—and a need for extra heating in your house—you will not have access to all the equipment that is available at the corporate office.

Remote Access Setup

With a solid network connection and tools in place, remote access to machines can be almost like sitting in the office—and you probably won't see too much of a difference. The benefit of this, of course, is you don't have to worry about becoming a part-time sys admin. Not to mention the larger number of resources accessible through the corporate office.

But not everything is perfect when logging in remotely. Networks tend to go down, and if you are not set up properly, you can lose hours of work. For example, if you telnet to a remote machine and the network goes down, you will lose the telnet session. This really stinks if you were in the middle of editing a file and you haven't saved recently.

One of the most reliable methods for working remotely is through a terminal server or a virtual X display, such as Virtual Network Computing (VNC). The benefit of these tools is their persistent nature. For example, using VNC allows you to work from home, from a remote office, or even in the corporate office without losing a window or pixel from your previous work session. Avid users of this technology start work in the morning from home and then drive into the office and pick up where they left off.

Where to Work?

If you are a lone eagle, the world really is at your doorstep. You now need to make one of the toughest decisions: Where do you want to live? Whatever you do, pick a place that you really enjoy—a place that gets your creative juices flowing. It might be in the middle of the desert, up in the mountains, along the coast, or at the center of a big city, but make sure you have the biggest Internet connection you can find. And of course, have fun.

For the rest of us, this chapter has been about understanding the lifestyle—and support requirements—of the lone eagle. Now that you have a better understanding of how the lone eagles survive, and how best to support them, you're now ready to delve into the world of ClearCase multi-site and to apply this learning to your multi-site integration planning.

17

Integrating Multi-site Teams in Your Spare Time

Multi-site development is a fact of software development, and at some point in your career, you are most likely going to run into the problem of connecting two or more locations—or at least managing teams across a great divide. With multi-site development come problems of complexity, communication, and integration. How do you set up your ClearCase multi-site, and what branching policies and integration processes should be followed? As the title says, this chapter will help shed some light on the actors, phases, and distributed team activities you will need to identify and understand in your quest to connect your multi-site development team. Hopefully our examples will also help you avoid the problems and pitfalls.

Let's take a fictitious software development company, BPT Technologies (BPT), as our example. BPT has several software development sites throughout the world. This multiple-location development strategy allows BPT to develop and test software 24 hours a day, hire in multiple locations, and support customers around the world. Setting up this type of distributed organization requires planning and coordination. Software developed in multiple locations needs to be integrated into a single product that is tested and eventually shipped to the customer. We begin by discussing the key contributors and the activities involved in accomplishing such a task. Later, we describe the phases of the software development process and show how tools and the integration of tools can improve the coordination of development teams thousands of miles away from each other.

Know Your Actors

Software Development

BPT has software developers all over the globe in several different types of offices—everything from individuals working from their homes (via ISDN or DSL) to teams of people in the same office building. Software developers work around the clock on BPT software. Their primary responsibility is to develop, compile, and test their code before marking it ready to be integrated into the product. Development is currently done on three different platforms: Solaris, HP-UX, and NT.

Configuration Management

The configuration management (CM) team is primarily responsible for source-code integrity and for making sure all the remote sites have the tools they need to accomplish their tasks. This includes source-code management, defect tracking, compilers, operating systems, reporting systems, and the tools that integrate these tools. The CM team consists of individual home offices and a team of engineers in the San Jose office.

Build-and-Release Management

After the software developers have marked their code to be integrated into the product, the build-and-release management

(B&R) team takes control of the code. It is their nightly responsibility to run the builds and the automated engineering regression tests and coordinate with the software developers on any issues regarding the compilation and testing of the code after integration. The B&R team produces a weekly build that is passed to product validation and potentially to the customer. The B&R team consists of individual home offices and a team of engineers in the San Jose office.

Product Validation

The product validation (PV) team has engineers in three locations and some in individual home offices. This gives the PV team the ability to quickly validate the builds that the B&R team produces on a weekly basis and mark the build as "gold" and ready for customer consumption.

Tools

Tools play an important part in communication between the different groups and multiple locations.

ClearCase

Source-code management is one of the most important tools used in BPT for the coordination of software development teams in multiple locations and from team to team in the development process. ClearCase offers several advantages to the distributed development paradigm that BPT uses, including parallel development stream, multi-site development, labeling, and automated merging.

Scopus

Another important tool used in BPT is the Scopus defect-tracking tool. The tool becomes invaluable during the alpha, beta, and production phases of development. Not only does the tool aid in the tracking of defects, but it is also integrated with ClearCase and the build reporting system to control the defects that are allowed into a build.

Build Reporting System

Because the team is distributed throughout the world, timely communication is important for development. Several of the key contributors are gated by the status of the product build, both nightly and weekly. The build reporting system provides real-time information about the product builds.

Hey, There Are Phases (Go Figure)

Before explaining the use cases of the actors in the development process, we must first define the different development phases for a BPT product. During the development of the product, different controlling gates are enacted to increase the quality of the code and release the product to the customer in a timely manner.

Development

During the development phase, the development teams can work independently. The purpose of the development phase is to design, code, and test features that the individual team will focus on for the upcoming release. Nightly and weekly builds and regression tests are done during this phase of development, but builds typically are not sent to the PV team for validation.

Alpha

The alpha phase includes restrictions on the code that is integrated into the build. Some teams continue to work on issues with the planned features, but no new features are added. Nightly and weekly integration builds are performed. The team uses the defect-tracking tool to track problems found during testing. Product validation begins running validation tests on the weekly integration builds.

Beta

The only code allowed in the nightly and weekly integration builds is that approved by the change control board (CCB) and marked in the

Scopus tools for a specific build. Product validation continues to validate all weekly integration builds from B&R. All problems are tracked in Scopus, and defects are scheduled for specific builds or postponed until the next version of the product.

Production and Supplemental

The only code allowed in the weekly integration builds is code that has been approved by the CCB. These are typically critical release-blocking defects that affect the quality of the product. PV validates the product, and the requestor of the defect or the customer advocate verifies the defect as being fixed for that build. After all the defects are verified as being resolved, the build goes gold and is made available on CDs for customer release.

Some Other Stuff

Because we have teams scattered all over the world, we need effective communication channels between teams. We must share not only source code between the teams, but also build status, defect information, and feature integration. One of the strategies BPT uses is the componentization of the product into distinct pieces (or directory hierarchies).

Except for a few unique cases, each component is owned by a specific team at a distinct location, as illustrated in Figure 17.1. This enables each team to work on its component independent of the other teams. Each component is self-contained. There are dependencies between components, but we try to keep them to a minimum, to decrease the amount of interteam communication required.

Self-Containment

Because components have dependencies, it is sometimes necessary for software developers to have the binaries and header files from another component. This might be a run-time dependency for testing or a build-time dependency for compilation. In the past, the software engineers built the necessary components before they could do their work.

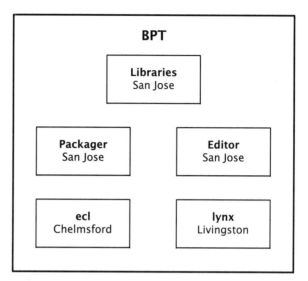

Figure 17.1 *Componentization of Product to Multiple Locations*

To decrease the time required and give a reliable source for "qualified" binaries, each component has a list of files that other R&D teams require for their development. The list is used to create a gzipped tar file that is checked into ClearCase with each weekly build that the B&R team performs. This gives the engineering teams access to the latest "good" binaries for a particular component.

Branching Strategy

To isolate changes from one component to another, a branching strategy was developed so that each component has its own branch with the same name of the stream and the component of the product. For example, if the stream is named "powder" and the component is named "sim," then the branch name would be "powder-sim." Each team works on its own component development branch independent of other teams. When code is ready to be integrated with other components, it is labeled with a "READY" label specific for the component, such as "POWDER_SIM_READY." The CM team has written scripts that automatically merge code from the component development branch with the specified label to the stream integration branch. See Figure 17.2.

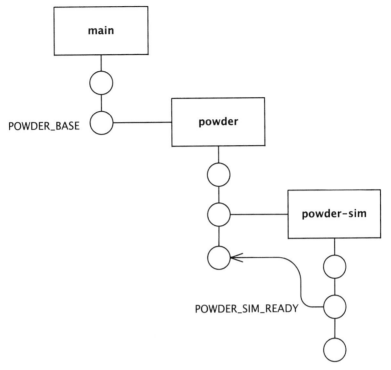

Figure 17.2 *Stream and Component Branches*

Because a specific team at a defined location owns the component, the branch ownership does not need to change. Only in some unique circumstances must the branch ownership be changed. For example, if the component development team spans more than one location, an additional branch with the name of the location can be created.

VOB Layout

ClearCase has the concept of a versioned object base (VOB), which is basically a database and versions of files and directories. We try to keep each component in its own VOB. This allows for growth of the VOB and easy maintenance of the component. There are exceptions to this for very small components, but it is best to have a consistent paradigm throughout the environment.

Although it increases the number of VOBs, ClearCase has a mechanism for administrative VOBs, which aids in the use of branches and labels. The administrative VOB contains links to the other VOBs so that every component can be accessed through a centralized directory hierarchy.

Because we deal with distributed teams, the network bandwidth or the disk space capacity of the remote sites is not always sufficient. We send the components and their VOBs to the sites only where they are needed. This decreases the sync-up time and improves the turnaround time for code at remote sites.

Multi-site Sync-ups

Multi-site sync-up is a ClearCase mechanism that keeps remote locations updated with the changes from all the other systems. There are several different ways to set up multi-site sync-ups. BPT uses a centralized star configuration for sync-ups, as shown in Figure 17.3.

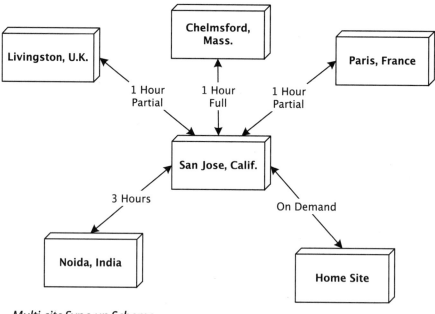

Figure 17.3   *Multi-site Sync-up Scheme*

Because we have different characteristic network connections and disk space availability at each site, we configure the promotion and retrieval of information accordingly. This includes the VOBs that are multi-sited to customers and the frequency of the updates. For example, we have a less than reliable link to our India team, so we update three hours after the last update.

Development Through Production

As we've said, multi-site development is a fact of life. And alongside multi-site development are problems of complexity, communication, and integration. For example: How should you set up your ClearCase installation across multiple sites? What branching policies and integration processes should be followed? Time is erratic and unreliable. So much of the development we do and the tools we build are focused on saving time, or using what time we do have more efficiently. So if multi-site development is such a critical factor in today's software development organization, what can we do to help our teams work more effectively and resourcefully?

Everything about managing multi-site development revolves around time. How do you coordinate activities so that each team can work efficiently? How do you manage build schedules to optimize both system and team output? Which branch is the right version to push through QA for your next customer release?

Now that we've looked at the actors, phases, and distributed team activities you will need to identify and understand in your quest to connect your multi-site development team, let's examine more closely the activities of BPT Technologies, the fictitious software company located in San Jose, California. This "case study" is a conglomeration of issues and process steps experienced with our own customers—and hopefully it will shed some light on some best practices regarding planning for and operating under a multi-site system.

In this case study, BPT has several software development sites throughout the world, and it recently went through a major effort to integrate all of its development efforts. This multiple-location development strategy gives BPT the ability to develop and test software 24 hours a day, hire the best engineers from multiple locations, and support its customers around the world. But setting up this type of distributed organization requires planning and coordination.

Software developed in multiple locations needs to be integrated into a single product that is tested and eventually shipped to the customer. Having discussed the key contributors and the activities involved in accomplishing this task, we now present the next steps: development, release, and production. We examine how BPT employed ClearCase and its related tools to overcome problems inherent in multi-site development. As part of this activity, we look at each phase of development, examine the tools used, and provide insight into how best to branch and build your products.

Preparing for Development

Now that the BPT team has things componentized and their ClearCase strategy in hand, there are several steps they need to follow to prepare for development. Developing in multiple locations will require more than just setting up ClearCase or advertising this new capability to their project teams. Communication channels need to be established, and process must be clarified.

Tools

ClearCase

Source-code control is important for the development of the product. Users work isolated from each other through private branches. Component development teams work isolated from changes in other components through component branches.

Build Reporting System

Reporting of build and regression test status is important during the development phase. Because the builds represent an integration of all the components, engineers use a homegrown, Web-based build reporting system to view the results of code changes for their component and overall system integrity. This system pulls data directly from ClearCase and provides a quick snapshot of the status of builds whenever needed.

Scopus
The defect-tracking system is used mostly for reporting problems that arise during the development phase.

Branching

During the development phase, BPT's software development team works on their own component branches. Periodically, there is a special case where a new branch is needed for additional isolation. It is the responsibility of the owner of that branch to make sure the code gets to a component branch before it is integrated into the stream branch.

The stream branch is locked down so that no one but the B&R team can merge code into the build. When a build is not running, an automated merge process runs every three hours and merges code from the component branches to the integration stream branch. So the component team can determine what code is ready for integration, they label the code with a "READY" label ("POWDER_SIM_READY," as shown in Figure 17.4). This keeps the stream branch as clean as possible. Software developers can merge from the stream branch up to their component branches to make sure that there are no nontrivial merges to the stream branch.

The component branching mechanism also handles the distributed engineering problems. To create versions on a branch, each BPT location must have ownership of the branch. Components typically do not span physical locations, and each component has its own branch. In this scheme, there is rarely the need to change ownership of a branch.

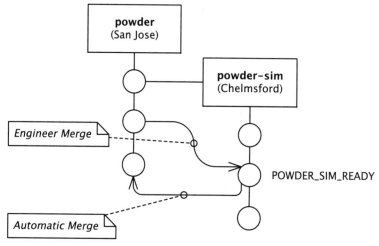

Figure 17.4   *Development Phase Merging*

Builds

During the development phase, builds and full research and development regression tests are run on a nightly basis for all platforms.
Both release and debug builds are run for each platform. ClearCase
views are not reused because the team receives a full build every
night.

Weekly builds and regression tests are run on all platforms. If the
build is successful and at least 90 percent of the regression tests pass,
then gzipped tar files are created for each component and checked
into ClearCase. These tar files are used by development for the next
week's development. BPT periodically removes old versions of components that are not used, to help decrease the amount of disk space
these tar files consume.

Alpha

With the features of the product coded, BPT's research and development team announces "Code Complete," and the project officially
enters into the alpha phase of development. At this stage, BPT begins
using the Scopus tool to track defects and enhancements to the code.

Tools

ClearCase

ClearCase continues to be used during the alpha phase of development. During this time, most of the work will be performed on component branches, and it will migrate to project change request (PCR) branches toward the end of alpha. Private branches should be avoided.

Build Reporting System

BPT's build reporting system is the primary location for engineering regression test reporting. The goal to exit alpha is to pass 100 percent of the engineering regression tests. Within this tool, additional information about the build is gathered, including change metrics, PCRs fixed for a specific build, and status on baseline and supported platforms.

Scopus

During the alpha phase of development, all defects should be entered into the Scopus database. Engineers should be working on decreasing the number of defects and should stop working on new features to the product. Periodic change control boards will be held toward that end of the alpha phase of development.

Branching

Because there should be no new code introduced during this time, the component branches are no longer used for development. All changes are made on PCR branches. The name of each branch is "pcr#####", where "#####" is the number of the PCR in Scopus. This allows for the automated build process to automatically merge the specific code for a defect into the stream branch.

Because there is typically a transition period during alpha, component branches may be left "on." That is, the development team continues to work on them and merge them into the development stream. This is generally a decision that the engineering management team has approved.

It is at this stage that BPT introduces another branch for test changes: the stream-test branch. The name of the branch is specific to the stream of development (such as powder-test). This allows engineers to update any regression tests without going through a formal defect process.

Builds

As in the development phase, builds are done on a nightly and weekly basis. One of the differences during this time is that installations of the weekly builds are performed and sent to the product validation team for validation. Another difference is that supported platforms are also tested, and engineering regression tests are run.

Installations with tarkits from a release server are also performed at this time as part of the weekly build process. The installations are taken from the B&R team and tested by the PV team.

Beta

During the beta phase of development, the change control board scrutinizes the change requests more critically, and the number of changes to the product naturally decreases. The purpose of the beta phase is to fix problems that are found by the beta customers, and to fix problems that are left over from the alpha phase of development.

Tools

ClearCase

As in the previous phases of development, ClearCase continues to be used for source-code management. In addition to source code, tarkits from other groups inside and outside of BPT are checked into a VOB for tarkits. Because of the size of the tarkit VOB, it is not usually multi-sited. All installations are performed at the BPT San Jose location.

Build Reporting System

Just as in the alpha phase of development, the baseline and supported platform builds are reported in the build reporting system. A list of PCRs that have been fixed, and the number of files that were changed to fix the PCRs, are also kept in the BRS. This gives the development team one location to see what is going on with the build.

Scopus

In addition to defects and enhancements, change requests are entered into the system before a defect can get into a build. Integration between the Scopus database, the BRS, and the automated build process requires a change request marked "APPROVED" and a defect marked "RESOLVED" for a specific build of the product. Only the CCB can approve a change request during the beta phase of development.

Change Control Board

The change control board meets three times a week to discuss change requests that are entered into Scopus by the assigned engineer or manager of a defect or enhancement. The CCB consists of the engineering managers, configuration management, product validation, program management, marketing, and IT operations. All change requests are reviewed by the CCB, and if critical enough—as determined by the CCB—and/or it can be done to meet time constraints, then the change request is approved. The defect or enhancement that has been approved by the corresponding change request will be merged into the development stream when the defect is marked resolved and the "Fixed Build" field is marked for the specific build. All changes to fix a PCR must be made on a branch with the name "pcr####", where "####" is the PCR number. The BRS will list all of the PCRs that are expected to be merged into the development stream and provide the corresponding status.

Branching

The same branches that were set up during the alpha phase continue to be used. There should be no component branches integrated into the development stream branch at this time.

The test branch is still used during the beta phase of development, but it is limited to making updates to regression tests.

Builds

The build-and-release team continues to perform nightly and weekly builds on all platforms. During the beta phase, the release builds take a higher priority over the debug builds. All builds include an automated installation of the product from tarkits that have been checked into ClearCase. The goal is to get the product into the hands of the PV team as quickly as possible.

After the PV team has validated the build, it announces it as "GREEN" and flags it as ready to be posted on the release server. All of the tarkits for the product and third-party tarkits that are checked into ClearCase are promoted to the release server when a build goes green. Green builds are used to verify that changes to the code made it into the build, and that the corresponding problem was fixed.

Production and Supplemental

When the number of defects has come as close to zero as the change control board deems acceptable, and when all of the product validation and engineering regression tests have passed 100 percent and are clean, a build can move into the production phase. There are actually more requirements for a build to move to production, but they are not important for this discussion.

Ideally, the last beta build and the first production build will be identical. This cannot always be the case, but it is something to strive for. During the production phase of development, there may be more than one production build performed, but only one moves through the process to manufacturing.

Tools

ClearCase

ClearCase is still used for source-code control as well as tarkit and installation archiving. All builds that are sent to the product validation team are labeled with the build ID.

Build Reporting System

The build reporting system continues to be used as the primary source of information about the build for the distributed team.

Scopus

Scopus data, in conjunction with the change control board, drives all decisions that are made about the product, and when the build will move to production. Queries in Scopus help the CCB monitor the defects—and the severity of the defects—every time this group meets.

Change Control Board

The change control board has absolute power during this phase of development. By looking at trends in the defect arrival and resolution, the CCB determines when a build will be moved through the process from the B&R team through PV and into manufacturing. Determining the criteria for the number of defects and their severity is left up to the CCB, which usually determines them according to market conditions, customer feedback, and business strategy.

Branching

Ideally, there should be no changes to the code from the last beta build to the first production build, but if there is a need for any code changes, the PCR branch mechanism should be used. The test branch that was introduced during the alpha phase is now disabled, and it is not used for merging to the development stream branch.

Builds

During the production and supplemental phases of development, only weekly builds of the product are done. When the build contains all the defects that have been scheduled for the build through Scopus and all of the regression tests pass, the build is sent to the PV team for validation. The PV team promotes the build to "GOLD" when all its regression tests pass and when all the defects have been verified. Then the build is sent to manufacturing to be released to the customer.

Lessons Learned

Multi-site-Enabled Tools

All of the tools should be enabled for multi-site development, but in fact, ClearCase is the only tool that is truly multi-site enabled. This means that distributed locations can work without a constant connection to the main location—in this case, BPT's San Jose facility. This is not true for the build reporting system, which is basically a Web site and the Scopus program. Because the BRS is a Web site, typically it does not have large network bandwidth requirements.

Scopus, on the other hand, works rather slowly on poor network connections. Since the client is running at the remote sites and the server is running in San Jose, the tool can, at times, be unusable from remote facilities. Since Scopus uses a Sybase database on the back end, it is possible to replicate the database to remote sites.

Change control boards need to include, at the very least, one engineering manager from each location in the decision-making process. The difficulty is finding a regular meeting time that is acceptable to all of the different locations. This can be hard at times, since most companies interested in this type of solution have organizations that cover most of the globe. Every meeting should include both a conference call and some kind of Internet meeting for presentations and to review the tools. When members of the CCB do not show up or cannot fully connect, it is difficult to maintain an open communication and to make the necessary decisions about the company's products.

Multiple Stream Development

Because each group in the development team is utilized more effectively at different times in development, work typically begins on the next stream of development during the late alpha and beta phases of the previous release. This poses problems for the tools if the tools cannot handle multiple streams at the same time. One issue that pops up is when defects are found in the current stream during the beta phase, and how that change will be promoted forward to the next stream, which is already in the development phase.

BPT created two mechanisms for promoting defect fixes from previous streams that are still alive. During the development phase, a "rebase" mechanism is used to rebase the stream on the latest build of a previous stream, as shown in Figure 17.5. Essentially, this means that the stream's branch point is moved down to the new build release of the previous stream.

Another mechanism to use in this situation, when the current phase moves into alpha and defects are needed from a previous stream, is to create a duplicate defect in the Scopus database and use the CCB process that all other defects normally follow.

Multi-site Sync-up Status

ClearCase multi-site does not have a good mechanism for reporting the status of multi-site sync-ups between sites. As a result, remote locations can become out of sync for long periods of time if not properly monitored. This can present problems in that remote locations are not getting the updates from other components in a timely manner, and vice versa.

To remedy this situation, BPT created a multi-site reporting system that reports on the status of the sync-ups between the different locations. This gives the management team a quick view of what is going on.

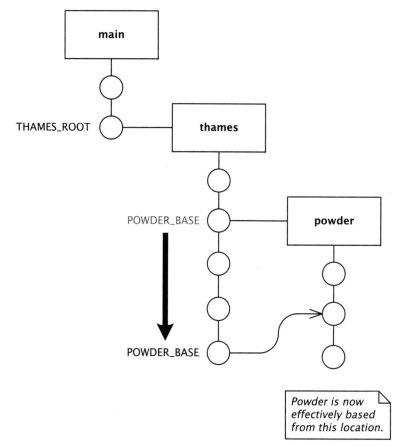

Figure 17.5   *Rebasing a Stream in ClearCase*

Many lessons were learned in the development of this configuration management system, and those lessons can be applied to your own distributed development efforts. As we've tried to illustrate through this case study, the key to staying on track is to prioritize requests for process improvement and to adhere to the original architecture. A great way to approach development and deployment of this kind of system is to treat your CM system just like any other product. Your releases will be more frequent, of course, and your customer feedback loop will be very tight (unlike your external customers, your internal customers know where you sit and may occasionally "drop by"). Try to avoid solving all of the problems that the engineering team throws your way. Try to keep the requests prioritized and focus—or else you will quickly find yourself in a quagmire of silly requests, and you'll find it difficult to make any real progress.

Whatever the feature request, whatever the prioritization, keep your overall architecture in mind and you should be just fine. As with any other product your company sells, when building a CM solution, it's always good to work from a solid product definition. This time around, the "product" just happens to be your CM solution. As you iterate on your system, focus on the purpose of the CM tool and stay true to that product definition. If you adhere to that simple rule (in this or any other product development activity), you'll improve the quality of the product you are delivering and, in this case, improve your team's productivity. And that's time well spent.

18

Hot Rods and Hardware

Growing up in California, we learned to love cars. Cruising "Main Street" was a rite of passage for most teenagers. Through some activities that will go unnamed, it was somehow determined who had the "hottest" car on the street each weekend. Some really hot-looking cars were great on the outside but nothing special on the inside. However, when push came to shove, it was the cars with the fastest and most powerful engines that earned respect and always prevailed.

The same is true for your ClearCase installation. You can have the coolest front-end scripts, triggers, and process controls, but if you don't have the correct hardware on the inside, all you will hear are complaints from your development team that the system is slow and unusable.

Understand How ClearCase Works

To understand what kind of hardware your system requires, you need to understand first how ClearCase works. Once you grasp the different aspects of the system and how they interact, you can tailor your hardware to those needs. First, remember that ClearCase uses databases. Second, it uses disks to store large amounts of data. And third, it is usually tied to several machines on a network. Figure 18.1 shows how things are generally connected.

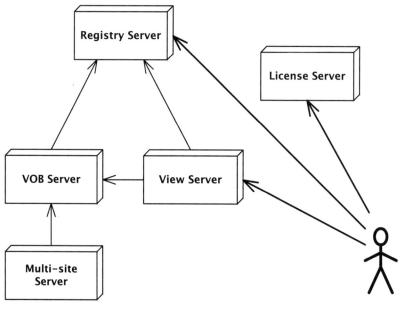

Figure 18.1   *General Connectivity for a ClearCase Server*

The Versioned Object Base Server

A versioned object base contains all of the versions of all of the elements in your project, and all associated metadata. A VOB server works with the database to store and retrieve all of the data that a user needs through a view. VOB servers work best when the complete VOB database can fit into memory. This cannot always be the case, however: VOB servers are memory hogs. The server typically runs a number of processes for each VOB (such as db_server, vob_server, vobrpc_server, and so on).

The View Server and the Multi-version File System

View servers provide elements that are set in the views configuration specification. A view uses a database and a set of storage pools and caches to access and temporarily store data. They include a process called the *view server*. The view server "serves up" a multi-version file system (MVFS) that contains all of the versions of the elements for the view. As an element is accessed in the view, the MVFS communicates with the VOB server to get the proper version of the element to be shown to the user.

The Registry Server

The registry server controls the VOB, view, and region objects for your ClearCase installation. The registry has one object per VOB and view. It also contains a tag for each object. The tag is the way the users can access the views and VOBs. The good news here is that the registry server does not take very much memory. The bad news, unfortunately, is that everyone relies on it—and expects it to be up *all* of the time. Without the registry server, no one can access the VOBs and views. Network connectivity is important. For more information, see the IBM Rational ClearCase Administrators Guide.

The License Server

The license server is very similar to the registry server in that it does not require very much CPU time, memory space, or disk space, and it needs to be accessible all of the time. Of course, the license server contains the licenses to run ClearCase. All ClearCase operations require a license to run, so network connectivity is important. Again, for more information, see the IBM Rational ClearCase Administrators Guide.

The Multi-site Server

If you have multi-site teams in your equation, then there are additional servers you need to consider. When running multi-site, you need to worry about importing and exporting sync packets. These processes typically take a large amount of memory, CPU time, disk space, and network bandwidth. So as you can see, there are several factors that can affect how powerful a machine you will need.

Sizing Your Team

Now that you have a general idea about how things are connected and their hardware needs, don't go off and buy a bunch of hardware just yet. You are still missing a key variable in the equation of success: you need to know how many people are on your current team and how big it will become. So grab your crystal ball and make an estimate of team growth. Don't consider just your developers; also include technical writers, testers, and potentially customer support staff. All of these people could participate in the larger development process and create artifacts in the system. Another thing you need to size is the amount of code, documentation, and tests you currently have or will have in the future.

These two aspects of sizing will help determine how many machines you'll require, the type of network to deploy, and the amount of disk space to invest in. For example, if your team is never going to be larger than ten people, then you probably don't need to spend hundreds of thousands of dollars on a set of VOB servers. However, some words of advice: It is much harder to grow your hardware later than you might think, so plan appropriately for growth. It is better to go bigger than you need in the beginning. This way you can grow into your hardware without experiencing substantial downtime.

Aspects of Hardware

With an understanding of the processes, the size of the project, and your team's current and future needs, you can now start looking at hardware.

Memory

You can never have enough memory for your VOB server—period. If the VOB can fit into memory, it will perform much faster than if it is swapping all of the time. So you can either have smaller machines with fewer VOBs per machine or get a bigger machine with several VOBs. We recommend more machines and splitting the VOBs across the machines. Between five and ten VOBs per machine is a good ratio, as long as your total memory can handle the complete VOB database set in memory. Accessing disk space is about a million times slower than accessing memory, so make sure you have sufficient memory to handle the workload.

Horsepower (Number of CPUs)

As mentioned earlier, multi-site and view processes take CPU cycles. Some people have put their VOB and view servers on four-way-processor machines. This is not necessarily the most cost-effective way of getting the performance that you need. Look at what is needed for each CPU-bound process.

Multi-site processes take CPU time for decompressing operation logs and performing the operations in the logs. It is beneficial to have the multi-site processes running on the same machine as the VOBs with which it is syncing.

View processes, on the other hand, do not take up more CPU processing than a VOB server, but there are typically many more views than VOBs. If you have a centralized view server machine strategy, then you will need more CPUs to handle the load. One option is to use local views dispersed across ClearCase client machines.

Disk Space

A couple of aspects of disk storage need to be considered. First, and probably most important, is speed to access disk storage. Several storage devices are now available that make storage cheaper and faster than what was available in the past.

In studies comparing performance between hardware and software RAID 5 or RAID 0+1 configurations, RAID 0+1 has been shown to be 1.2 to 2 times faster than RAID 5. Local disk storage is even slower, so take that into consideration for view and VOB storage.

Consult with the IBM Rational ClearCase release notes on supported storage devices before purchasing hardware.

Network Connectivity

If you are still using 10 Base-T connections on your network, join the rest of the world and move to at least a 100 MB network. In some larger organizations, 1 GB networks are standard between servers. Remember that ClearCase is a very distributed application, and because of that it is highly network bound. Do not make the mistake of having an insufficiently architected network to handle the load. The key server processes that need to have reliable and sufficient network connections are the VOB server, registry server, and license server.

In small configurations, you might see all three of these servers collocated on the same machine. In larger configurations, doing so can actually swamp a machine with network traffic; so it is wise to put the registry server and license servers on the same machine, but not with the VOB servers. This is especially true if there is more than one VOB server in your configuration.

In large configurations that use several VOB servers and view servers, we recommend installing GB network connections between these large machines with additional network cards to handle 100 MB connections for client machines. And multiple network cards can help isolate network traffic on separate subnets, if needed.

Configurations (Remote Storage Strategies)

VOBs and Views on the Same Machine

Many would say that this configuration is the best way to do things, because the network is now taken out of the equation. This approach works fine for small configurations, but it begins to break down quickly with mid-size to large configurations. The problem is that the view and VOB server processes begin to thrash with context switches. So this configuration is not very useful.

Local View and VOB Storage

This configuration is typical for most ClearCase installations for small to mid-size organizations. Views are created on local machines using local disk space that is exported, allowing them to be seen on all of the machines in the region. The VOBs are on a VOB server machine, usually handling the multi-site and VOBs. The registry and license servers may be on the same machine as well, but they should be put on a smaller machine separate from that of the VOB server. The VOBs use local disk space that is exported via NFS to all of the machines in the region.

This configuration is easy to manage and fairly inexpensive. If additional VOBs or views are needed, adding another machine can help with the load fairly easily. The size of the VOBs can determine how many VOBs can fit on the machine. But remember, the databases should fit into memory. More than anything, VOBs are memory bound.

Remote VOB Storage

Large organizations normally need large VOBs—and *several* of them. This situation requires a more reliable and robust storage device. Network storage can be used to handle this requirement.

Network storage devices are much faster than local storage, and they have built-in reliability. As your team expands, and therefore as the cost of downtime grows, you cannot afford to have your VOBs offline for any period of time. This is a good solution for your organization. Again, please check the IBM Rational ClearCase release notes for the storage devices supported by ClearCase. To create remote storage pools for your VOBs, see the `cleartool mkvob` command for more information.

Remote View Storage

Remote view storage pools can be found in mid-size to large organizations. These configurations are good if you are using any kind of multi-platform development, server farm, or NT/UNIX development. Any time you need to access a view from more than one machine, a view server with remote view storage is a good option. As mentioned previously, the speed and reliability of network storage devices are huge benefits.

To create these types of views, see the `cleartool mkview` command for instructions on how to create remote storage pools. Look at the `-ln` option.

And don't go buying hardware without first consulting the IBM Rational ClearCase release notes for supported hardware configurations.

What Can You Afford? (Price/Performance)

Most projects are underfunded, so you need to look closely at the price/performance of your VOB server hosts and your view server hosts. Remember: you can probably get away with a lesser machine if you add more memory for a VOB server. Additionally, if you use views on your local machines, you may not need a separate machine for serving views. Of course, there are trade-offs for all of these decisions. In a CM organization, you must have a reliable and *fast* network, or everyone will suffer and there will be rioting in the streets.

Think about the hot rod analogy: If you are smart, you spend money on the best engine and suspension you can get, and then you spend much of your own time fixing up the rest of the car. You don't want to buy something like a 1979 Ford Pinto and spend tons of money dressing it up. That is the same as spending next to nothing on hardware, and instead writing scripts and triggers to manage the process. The result can be disastrous. And no matter how perfect the paint job, you're still driving a Ford Pinto.

19

The Magical World of VOB Sizing

One thing about rolling out ClearCase to a geographically dispersed team is true: if you fail to plan, you plan to fail. And that's the underlying premise of this book. It's easy enough to find books and articles that walk through the minutiae of installation and configuration, but far too few address the activities that lead up to those steps: the requirements of your software development team and the limitations on your environment.

In Chapter 7, "Planning Your ClearCase Deployment," we presented a framework of questions geared toward jump-starting your planning activities and to get you thinking about the prerequisites (that is, the things that need to happen before deployment) and the dependencies (everything that ClearCase will touch once it's on your system) of deployment. These questions included:

- How big do you think the project will be?

- How many people will be involved in the product development?

- At how many locations will the product be developed, tested, and deployed?

- What third-party tools will you be using?

- Do you have the hardware you need?

- Do you have the infrastructure ready to support your plans?

In Chapter 8, "Modeling Your Configuration Management System," we started down the requirements path by identifying each of the artifacts within the system, including the actors, use cases, activities, and components. This time around, we'll discuss the process of VOB sizing, as well as some of the hardware considerations involved in a large ClearCase deployment.

So now that you have an understanding of the different business and technical drivers for your system, you need to move to the next step: understanding the internal requirements of managing a multi-site CM solution. First off, you need to realize that this system will grow, change, and quickly become unmanageable if you don't plan accordingly. There's a lot of risk management involved in the deployment of this kind of application. And to understand how to plan properly for this huge task, it helps first to grasp the inner workings of the tool.

Setting Up ClearCase

ClearCase is a distributed application with a client/server architecture. The execution of a single ClearCase command usually involves several processes running on several hosts. The vast majority of ClearCase commands access information that is stored in a VOB database. But what is a VOB database? Well, a VOB, which as you know by now stands for versioned object base, is a mountable file system. ClearCase stores its files and directories in a VOB. For each file or directory, ClearCase keeps track of each version anyone creates. VOBs can be physically located throughout the local area network, and they can be mounted on various workstations and server machines. In fact, the data storage for an individual VOB can be distributed across the network, even to hosts that are not running ClearCase software.

This information is accessed either directly (by communicating with a process that interacts with the database) or indirectly (by referring to data stored in a cache either at the MVFS or the view). You usually keep source files in Rational ClearCase. In fact, ClearCase is sometimes called a source-control system. However, the types of files you store in the document VOB depend on the tools you are using. Actually, ClearCase can be used to manage a wide variety of artifacts. Some examples are shown in Table 19.1.

The purpose of the ClearCase client/server architecture is to optimize usage of network resources. Typically, VOBs containing shared data (and associated server processes) are located on high-speed network server hosts, while developers and their views are located on individual workstations. As additional developers and workstations are added to a project, more computing and storage resources become available for ClearCase usage. In addition, busy VOBs should

Table 19.1 *Files to Keep Under Source Control*[1]

Tool	Files to Keep Under Source Control
Adobe FrameMaker	• .fm (Frame files) • .book (book files) • graphics and other files included by reference into your book
Microsoft Word	• .doc (the basic Word file)
ForeFront ForeHelp	• .fhb
eHelp RoboHelp	• .rtf (the Rich Text Format file that you edit) • .hpj (the WinHelp project file) • graphics files that you use with your help project

1. Reprinted by permission based on material from "How Technical Writers Use Rational ClearCase" by Liz Augustine, © 2001 IBM Corporation. All rights reserved.

be kept smaller to allow for growth. Having more, smaller VOBs, rather than fewer, larger ones will also benefit NFS, and thus ClearCase, performance.

And for those history buffs out there, here's another interesting tidbit: ClearCase for UNIX preceded ClearCase for Windows NT. As a result, ClearCase was designed to work in an environment where all of the users and machines that want to use ClearCase together (that is, sharing a set of views and VOBs) belong to a single domain. (Within a UNIX environment, it would not be possible for these users and machines to work together to any meaningful degree if the systems did not use the same YP password map.) Therefore, significant development would be required to make ClearCase fully domain-aware, especially with the restriction that this modified ClearCase would still be able to interoperate with ClearCase on UNIX.

Despite this, ClearCase for Windows NT can be used in multidomain environments. In addition, changes were made to ClearCase to improve its operation in some common multidomain environments.

Understanding the Server Types

There are some basic rules of thumb for ClearCase deployment and hardware:

1. The various ClearCase servers should be as powerful and have as much memory as possible.

2. Ensure that nobody can log onto the server. Removing the Network Information Service (NIS) password table prevents this temptation. NIS allows administrators to maintain a single copy of various administrative databases and have this copy replicated as NIS "maps" from the server machine to client systems. One of these maps is the password database, which defines all the accounts allowed to use the system.

3. Confine the ClearCase license to one of these machines. Most ClearCase sites have only a single ClearCase machine, but some larger sites do have multiple VOB servers and view servers. It makes sense that the license server should be confined to these fast and secure machines.

4. The ClearCase administrator, and nobody else, should own and have root access to these machines.

Now, before you run out and start estimating your server needs, let's review some of the various server types involved in a large ClearCase deployment. As mentioned earlier, ClearCase is a client/server application. VOBs are stored on VOB servers, and the user's client system requests information—which is sent to the user's machine. The ClearCase administrator's manual mentions several different ClearCase server types, which we'll describe here. Most of these servers can be the same system as the VOB server, with no segregation of service. With the help of the "Not-So-Official ClearCase Page" (http://www.weintraubworld.net/clearcase/), here are the different server types you need to be aware of.

View Server

Although there is no reference to a view server in the ClearCase administrator's manual, many sites simply allow users to set up views under the user's $HOME directory, versus storing views on another server—which could slow performance. As mentioned in previous chapters, we're not the biggest fans of view servers. Compilation on the view server is generally faster than accessing the view over the network, but when you have a parallel build and a farm of fast machines, you need to have a centralized view server. Plus, keeping all of the views together makes backups and rebuilds easier. It is also easier to rebuild the view registry if all the views are in a single known location. In sites with a single ClearCase server, views may simply be stored on the same system as VOBs. The network connection to this machine should be fast, or there should be multiple network cards. The faster card is a better solution, so we recommend a gigabit network card in the view server, as well.

License Server

This is a server with low CPU usage, usually placed on the same machine as the VOB server. If your site has a dedicated machine that serves licenses for a variety of software, then that system could serve as the license server. The ClearCase administrator's manual recommends splitting your licenses between systems and having multiple ClearCase license servers, so if one goes down, others will still be available. However, if you keep your licenses on the same system as your VOB server, this is unnecessary. If the system crashes, your VOBs will be down anyway, so it won't matter if the licenses are unavailable.

Registry Server

> The registry can be thought of as the "Table of Contents" to ClearCase's VOBs and views. The ClearCase VOB registry links the VOB tags (the mount points of the VOBs on the ClearCase user's machine) to the directories where the VOBs are actually stored. The ClearCase view registry links the view tags (the name of the view) to the directories where the view is actually stored. It is recommended that a single registry be used, and the registry server be placed on one of the standard ClearCase server systems (usually the VOB server).
>
> —*David Weintraub, "The Not-So-Official ClearCase Page,"*
>   *http://www.weintraubworld.net/clearcase/*

There are some scenarios in which it is necessary to have more than one registry server; check your ClearCase manuals for more information.

Release Server

The release server is simply the machine onto which you loaded the ClearCase CD. Except for the installation of upgrades, the release server rarely sees activity. However, if you are planning to do link or standard installations, (versus full or mounted installations), this server could host a lot of activity. To maintain top performance, if you plan to provide link and standard installations, we recommend you install ClearCase to some kind of high-speed application server, not directly to your ClearCase servers.

VOB Server

Not surprisingly, this is the machine that contains the VOB storage area. Depending on the speed of the system, the number of users, and your budget, there may be more than one VOB server. One concept that you need to understand is that the VOBs are stored in one area, and the *VOB tag* is the mount point on the client machine. As far as the ClearCase user is concerned, the files he accesses are located right on his own machine.

> **Note: ClearCase version 4.x has experienced some changes. The lock manager no longer limits VOB servers. The old configurations of more (smaller) VOB servers have given way to smaller numbers of large machines. With the number of VOBs and users increased, you need to consider the network connections to the VOB server in your planning.**

Factors to Determine VOB Boundaries

Now that you have a grasp of all of the different servers involved in a ClearCase deployment, we'd like to focus on what is, by far, the most complicated aspect of your system deployment: the scope and sizing of your VOB server(s). Figure 19.1 provides the high-level VOBs that can be used in a typical product development.

You may say, "Why not just put everything in one big VOB?" Well, while the new database schema in ClearCase 4.x makes it possible to maintain very large VOBs, we don't recommend it. Here are some reasons why you may prefer to have several smaller VOBs versus one large VOB:

- As the size of your VOB increases, your performance will decrease.

- As the number of developers increases (large VOBs tend to have more users), the VOB server quickly becomes swamped, and performance decreases.

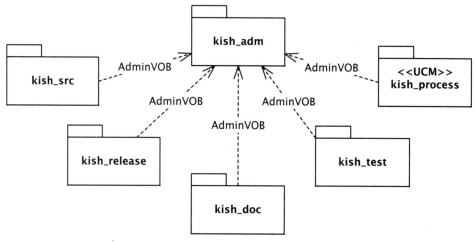

Figure 19.1   *High-Level VOB Structure*

- As development costs increase in your area, you may need to look at remote development. Going multi-site with really large VOBs can be problematic, and performance will really take a hit.

Logical Software Components—Software Architecture

Source VOBs can be segmented along software component boundaries. First, look along component subsystem lines and divide VOBs along those boundaries. This can be determined from the logical view or the component view of the software architecture. As a CM manager or architect, make sure you are a part of the overall software architecture process. Consider yourself the "CM Police" and your job will be much easier in the long run.

If you already have a VOB structure, start looking at the top-level directories for component boundaries. You can group components and directories together and put them into a single VOB. Make sure that you decrease the dependencies between these VOBs as much as possible. This will make your job easier when you are working on your build and release scripts. The lower the number of dependencies, the better you can "parallelize" your development to multiple locations and "parallelize" your automated build system.

It is best to plan for these VOB divisions before you get started. If you don't do this up front, you'll likely have to split your VOB later. Splitting a VOB can be likened, at best, to removing your own abscessed tooth without the Novocaine. It's fun stuff.

Test Architecture

Another area that can be segmented is the test architecture. Typically, test harnesses are organized very well and have very few dependencies. This is beneficial to segmenting the VOBs along operational groups. If you have teams that are geographically dispersed, you should be able to divide easily the test suites into VOBs that can be multi-sited geographically. This limits the amount of information that needs to be sent over the Internet.

Operational Segmentation

You may be asking, "Why not just have a VOB for every test suite or software component?" Our advice is: Don't go overboard! Separate VOBs according to your organizational needs. Take a few things into account.

Size of the Organization

If you have a small organization, you may not need to segment your VOBs at all. But don't think that your team will never grow. Remember those guys who developed code in the late 1960s who thought their code would be rewritten before Y2K? Guess what: in some cases, that code sat there for 40 years. Our advice is not to think too small. Just make sure your plans are reasonable and somewhat forward thinking.

If you have a large organization, try to look at the different teams as owning a VOB or set of VOBs. If this is not the case, assert yourself and help your team develop smarter. Segment the code and the teams along component boundaries and apply the preceding ideas for VOB segmentation.

Types of Artifacts

It is important to understand the types of artifacts you are going to store in your VOBs. Normal file types that contain ASCII text are stored in the VOBs as deltas, while binary-type data is stored as whole copies. If you have several versions of binary files stored in the VOB, this can increase the VOB size dramatically. Sometimes keeping binary files in their own VOBs is a good idea.

Builds and Derived Objects

If your organization is using clearmake and build avoidance, then ClearCase keeps metadata called configuration records in the VOB database. In addition to these records, the VOBs keep track of derived objects as well. So if you are building very often, and your builds produce large files, then you will need to take this into consideration.

Location

Increased economic pressure has forced several development teams to look at remote development and testing options. There is a cost involved that most managers do not understand: data synchronization. Getting source code synced up between all of your locations can be a full-time job unto itself. Decreasing the amount of information that actually gets synced can make this job much faster and more manageable. This can be done through VOB segmentation and by sending only those VOBs that the location needs to work with.

Deployment diagrams and the timing between locations is a great way to show management and your engineering teams exactly what is happening within your system. See Figure 19.2.

Don't Over-Segment

And remember: as the number of VOBs increases, management of the VOBs also increases. Scripts need to be smarter to handle uni-

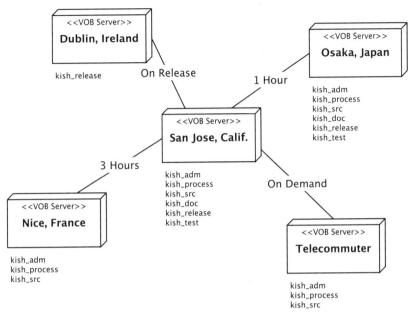

Figure 19.2 *VOB Deployment Diagram*

form labeling, backup coordination, and any other global actions that need to be managed across all of the VOBs. You need to find a balance that best fits your organization.

Other Hardware Considerations

Before we wrap up this important step in the ClearCase deployment process, we think it is important to touch on two additional areas of concern when looking at hardware: compute machines and network configuration. Our recommendation? For large deployments, consider building a server farm. From Chapter 18, "Hot Rods and Hardware," here are our suggestions on what to buy and how to construct your system.

Get a Big Network Switch

Your network switch becomes more important as your server farm grows; get one, and make it big. Server farms that perform builds are typically very network-intensive. A switch with a big back plane will help the information flow uninhibited. All of the machines should be connected directly to the switch, including the VOB, view, and compute machines.

Set Up a File System Server

As far as data access goes, you need to have a central location to store your data so all of the compute machines in your server farm can access one repository. The central file server should be able to serve data to jobs that run on any one of the compute machines. The data on this central file server can be view storage data, scripting tools, raw input data, or anything that your jobs need to run.

Choose More Powerful Computation Machines

The purpose of the compute machine is to compile or test your product. You are hunting for pure speed and memory. These machines are typically multiple-processor machines with as much memory as you can put into them. The network connection on these machines can be a 100 Base-T network card, which is standard for most servers. Putting faster cards in the compute machines is not a good idea, however, as the VOB server and view servers will most likely become the slowest part of your network connection.

Several hardware vendors have compute or server farm solutions. Sun, Hewlett-Packard, IBM, Linux, and Windows platforms are supported by a myriad of vendors. The key to compute machines is having common platform definitions. Depending on your budget and infrastructure plans, you can purchase an out-of-the-box solution. When considering the purchase of a compute machine, your primary concerns should be CPU and RAM. Unlike the VOB servers, disk I/O is not as important if you are going to use your compute machine as some sort of centralized file server. Most file server solutions can actually have disk I/O comparable to the internal disks on a compute machine.

Increase Network Bandwidth

One way of limiting the amount of traffic on the VOB and file servers is to limit the bandwidth to the compute machines. All of the VOB servers and view servers should have 1-Gigabit connections to the switch (if VOB network performance is still an issue, just remember that additional network cards can be added). All compute machines should have 100 Base-T connections directly to a large switch. This will somewhat control the amount of data requests to the VOB and view servers. Because more than one VOB server and more than one view server—in addition to the compute servers—may need access to the file server, it should have multiple 1-Gigabit network cards.

Optimize Performance

To optimize the performance of your server farm, you will need to set up methods to monitor what is going on with your hardware. Several different tools are available for monitoring and analyzing hardware and network configurations, including TeamQuest, HP OpenView, and LSF Analyzer, just to name a few. The key thing to remember when purchasing any kind of monitoring tool is to gather enough information to make a smart decision. Gathering data on your system processes for one week is not nearly enough if your cycle time itself is one week. As any good marketing person will tell you, you need to gather enough data so you can begin seeing trends and can identify problem areas. The primary statistics that you will need to monitor are CPU utilization, one-minute run queue, swap, memory, disk I/O, network I/O, and paging. Some of the tools out on the market will present this information in easy-to-use graphs and models, and some will even run prediction models—depending on the amount of money you want to spend.

20

Constructing Your CM System

Tree House Construction Theory

Did you ever build a tree house when you were a kid? When we were growing up in California, summer days were long and warm, and parents usually pushed their kids out the door as early in the day as possible. With all of the growth we experienced out here (and are still experiencing), scrap wood was easy enough to find. Most neighborhoods adjoined one or more new developments, providing a bounty of material for building that dream mansion in the treetops.

But the tree house never really turned out the way we wanted. We drew up (what we considered to be) complex architectural diagrams, with our best estimates of the materials it would take to construct our vision and the time we would need to dedicate to building the dream. And then reality set in. After a couple hours of dragging wood to the secure, often remote location, we were ready to be done with the whole effort. But we hadn't even begun building. So we cut corners. Not that we knew how to properly build a structure, or even a platform that could support the weight of all of us—much less even use a hammer without someone getting hurt.

And then came the arguments about which branches to build from, which wood scraps to use, who would go get more wood, more tools, some lunch. A group of kids on a hot summer day out in the middle of a field—a power struggle was inevitable. We just couldn't agree on what we wanted. Finally, someone suggested splitting up roles: two people hold the boards while a third nails them in place. But as the day wore on, and things weren't working out with the design, everyone just kind of . . . gave up.

In short, we started off with the best intentions but quickly realized that we had not properly planned, had not properly estimated the workload, and had not brought into the project the people with the know-how to successfully build our tree house.

Months later, a pile of weathered wood scraps and a few rusted tools could still be found at the bottom of that oak tree, with several boards still clinging to the high branches.

What in the world does this have to do with your software development process? Plenty! Whether you realize it or not, you need tools and a common strategy when developing your software product. Tools come in several different flavors (compilers, test harnesses, libraries) and several different sizes (different operating systems and platforms). And you need to make these tools available to your development, build-and-release, and QA teams in a consistent manner. And then there is your strategy—your building plans. Putting everything on a central file server is not enough. Before you go off to develop a solution, there are many other factors you need to consider. Your goals should be consistency and speed. Nothing frustrates a development team or kills a product development effort faster than variability of the system. If your development team uses different tools than your B&R team, your build will never complete. If QA is not testing with the same set of tools coded to by development, what are they really testing?

Look Before You Jump

Now relate the tree house analogy to your current project. Do you see any parallels? So many projects start off with the best intentions, but have you properly planned for the effort? Do you have a sound design? Do you have all of the right tools? Is your team the right fit? Human nature is fairly constant: we all typically want to get right into solving the problem. After all, that is what we get paid for—solving problems. But before you embark on your next project, first make sure you understand the problem.

First, Know Your Customers

Your customers are the friends gathered around the bottom of the tree, waiting for you to lead the effort to build that tree house. Your customers are the development team. Customers don't customarily sit idle and watch the construction, but as you know, they play an important role in the development process.

With all of their different personalities, needs, and wants, you need to better understand what makes your "developers" tick. Do they need (or want) root access on their UNIX boxes? Do they like to be in control of their tools? Are they part of the Free Software Foundation? Do they write packages on Linux on the weekend for fun? If this describes your software developers, then join the club. The problem with these developers is they need to feel as if they are in control.

As a configuration manager, you have to be in control, or anarchy in your development process will destroy your product and company. You need to take control of the tools that your developers use, or at least guide them down the right path. If you work in a large organization, try to coordinate with other CM people to share a common tool area. There is safety in numbers, and the workload is much lighter when more people are involved. That is, as long as you all can agree on some basic architecture for your tools area. We'll get to that later.

On the other hand, if you're the sorry sap who controls the company's tool area all by yourself, you have a mighty task ahead. You will need to be the grunt, the evangelist, the psychiatrist, and of course, the consummate salesperson. In any case, you will need help. Find a couple of the self-appointed tool gurus to help you out. Those guys generally love to port tools to different platforms, and they can do some of the grunt work for you.

Don't forget to enlist help from quality assurance and your build-and-release team. They use tools as well. But as we all know, they are one of the easiest groups to work with (ha-ha).

Second, Know Your Tools

Now that you know your customers, find out what tools they are using. It's simple: start a spreadsheet of every tool *and its version number* that your engineers are using in their development work. Compare that list with what the B&R and QA teams are using. If they are the same, then the battle is half over. If they are different, then you have ammunition to take to management. During the next meeting, when management asks why things have slipped so much, you can whip out your Excel spreadsheet that shows five different versions of GCC or Tk are being used by the same development team. Or that two product groups are attempting to integrate their products.

Table 20.1 is an example of what this spreadsheet might look like. Notice in this example that the Gadget product team is just a little bit out of touch, and there does not appear to be any consistency in the group. At your next meeting when management announces their desire to integrate two products, don't forget to bring your spread-sheet with you. It will save the company from spinning a few cycles while trying to figure out why the tools are not matching up well, and it'll make you seem like a hero. Yes—some good old ego massaging!

Table 20.1 *Sample Tools Spreadsheet*

	GCC			
Group	**2.7.23**	**2.8.5**	**2.8.23**	
Gadget—Dev	X	X		
Gadget—Build			X	
Gadget—Test			X	
Midget—Dev	X			
Midget—Build	X			
Midget—Test	X			

But before your head gets too big, you need to be prepared for the next step: platforms.

Third, Develop Multiplatform Development Strategies

Some of you are thinking that you don't develop on multiple platforms. "We are a Linux house, and we only have one platform!" Are you sure? When was the last time you checked all of the machines that your development, build-and-release, and testing teams are using? Each operating system company has its own way of versioning things. Don't be fooled by the OS version number by itself. Patch levels, patch sets, and kernel levels versus OS levels can really throw a kink into your system. Here are some of the things to watch out for.

Solaris

Thanks, Sun, for allowing us to download individual patches into the operating system. This allows us to pick and choose the particular patches that we want to apply to our machines. At first glance, this appears to be a good thing. But when everyone has root access (remember, there are developers who want to feel like God), patches are downloaded onto their machines *willy-nilly* (a highly technical term—look it up). The result? Broken builds, late-night pages to the network operating center, and quality problems for the end product.

You need to get control of the patches that are applied and form patch sets of your own. Write a tool that runs periodically on all of the machines to check each configuration. This will, at least, give you a heads up about what is going on.

Linux

Nothing like free software. They version the kernel and the operating system. A recent vendor mentioned that they ran on the 2.4x Linux kernel, and that is all he would say. No OS version was mentioned. He said it didn't matter. Being curious, we investigated his tool. Not surprisingly, it did not work with three of the four versions of Linux (Red Hat and SUSE) that we were evaluating at the time. Don't forget to control things based on both version numbers. The good thing is that Linux changes the version every time they touch the kernel.

Windows

Microsoft is famous for its service packs. Some people insist that you should not upgrade on Windows until they've hit Service Pack 2.x, unless you have a strong stomach. There are different service packs for different tools. This needs to be coordinated as well.

Fourth, Define Your Multiple Development Sites

Do you have multiple sites that work on your development? Most companies do. Do you need to coordinate the tools across different sites? In most cases, the answer is going to be yes. If you say no, we suggest you look again at how your sites interact, and how your development, build-and-release, and testing teams work together. It may be that each site does not need all of the tools of another site, but it is a safe assumption that they share some tools. It might be a good idea to add another column to your tools spreadsheet. When filling it out, your first thought might be just to force all of the sites to use the exact same tools. This sounds great and should be your goal, but make sure that the hardware—and especially disk space—can handle all of the tools at each site.

Roll Up Your Sleeves

Now that you have a spreadsheet with all of your tools, groups, and locations, you are ready to start doing some real work. In terms of our tree house analogy, you have selected your tree, collected as much scrap wood as you think you'll need, and have raided your father's tool chest for hammers, saws, and nails. At this point, you have not made any decisions—and now it's time to get started. Your first design decision: How will you access your tree house? By ladder? Rope? Stairs?

Probably the biggest decision you will make in the rollout of your common tool strategy solution is somewhat similar: How will your team access the tools? There are several options, all of which have been tried and tested. In fact, if you have tried something that worked better than these suggestions, please let us know.

Each mechanism has its pros and cons.

To ClearCase or Not to ClearCase?

The first thing you need to do is look at each group, at each location, and find out if they are all using ClearCase. If the answer is no, then you already know that your tool server will not be accessed via ClearCase. Don't even try to convert all of the groups to ClearCase at the same time as rolling out a ClearCase-centric tools server solution. There are far too many barriers to entry when you attempt something this size. Tackle one problem at a time.

So how does a ClearCase tool server solution work?

There are different options, of course. The simplest is to create tool VOBs for each of your platform definitions. Then store the installations in the VOB. The following paths are UNIX centric:

```
/vobs/linux7.3/
/vobs/sol27/
/vobs/sol28/
```

Most freeware and shareware tools that are compiled require the code to be compiled in the location that it will reside. This requires that you be in a view when building, testing, and running the tool. You can use ClearCase to label tools together into tool sets, allowing you to label all of the tools that you built with the same label. For example:

TOOLS_09_2002—**Tool set for September 2002**

Now that the tool set is labeled, you can access the tool set by the label in your config spec:

```
element * CHECKEDOUT
element * TOOLS_09_2002
element * /main/LATEST
```

This way, it's guaranteed that you are using the same tools for all of your groups (development, build, and test). This also spans product teams and can help unify teams that have to start talking to each other.

Another thing to look at is how the tools are placed in each VOB. Do I store each tool by name and version, or just by name? We recommend storing the tools by name and version in the same directory. This allows you to have a tool set with multiple versions of the same tool. This may sound bad, but sometimes it is a necessary evil when groups begin merging. The following example shows how tools are stored in the sol27 VOB:

```
/vobs/sol27/gcc-2.95.2
/vobs/sol27/gcc-3.1
/vobs/sol27/tcltk-8.3.3
/vobs/sol27/python-2.2.1
```

Now that the tools are accessible in the VOB, the user needs to add each tool to her path, and then she should be up and running with the tool. Another thing that may be beneficial is to create a bin directory that has symbolic links to the tool binaries. Make sure to pick one version of the tool and create a link to it. For example:

```
/vobs/sol27/bin/gcc -> /vobs/sol27/gcc-3.1/bin/gcc
/vobs/sol27/bin/tclsh -> /vobs/sol27/tcltk-8.3.3/bin/tclsh
```

Now the user needs only to put the `/vobs/sol27/bin` directory in his path when he runs on a Solaris platform.

Controlling Your Tool Suites

Don't forget to version-control your tools. You may want to create a VOB to handle the versioning of your tools from the source-code perspective. You have to build most of the tools that you can get out there right now, so you might as well put them under a formal CM process. This will help you control the quality of your tools, as well. Not only should you check in the source code for the tools, but you should also come up with a set of suites to test the tools that are in your tool suite. This VOB should be separate from the tool VOBs mentioned before. Those are tool *release* VOBS. Remember, everyone should be able to see those tools. Before you push things into those VOBs, you should run tests on them. So you might have a VOB structure like this:

```
/vobs/tools_src/gcc-3.1
/vobs/tools_test/gcc
/vobs/tools_adm # An admin VOB for these VOBs and all of
                # the tool release VOBs.
```

Any time you get a new update to a tool, you should run the tests in the test VOB against the update. When the tests pass, you can then check the binaries into the release tool VOBs and then label them accordingly. Make sure you follow the same CM processes that you would expect your development teams to follow. It is important to eat your own dog food.

Multi-site to Locations

One of the huge benefits of using ClearCase to access the tools is that multi-site is handled for you. You don't need to come up with a tool to replicate your data to all of your locations. Make sure that you set up your multi-site in a star configuration, if this is the solution you select. Only one location should have the responsibility to release tools. The other replicas are really read-only replicas. The multi-site sync-up looks something like Figure 20.1.

All of the syncs should be on demand. Syncing periodically might cause sites to be partially updated with the latest releases of your tool sets. You can also control which sites get what platforms of your tool sets. So if in Paris they are working only on Linux boxes, then you need only the Linux VOB replicas created there.

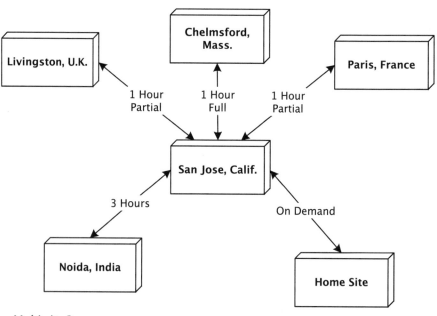

Figure 20.1   *Multi-site Sync*

ClearCase and Speed

When you propose this solution, you will get several people telling you that it will not work, because running tools in a VOB is slow. Guess what: they are right. It is slower running tools from a VOB. A snapshot view solution has the same problem with speed. You are going to have to make trade-offs for consistency and slowness. But how slow is it really? In our experience, we have seen only a 10 to 20 percent slowdown in using ClearCase VOBs to run tools. This could be significant if your build already takes ten hours. Adding an additional one to two hours could get your developers complaining. There are other options, of course, and we'll get into those later.

Non-ClearCase Release Area

If you have groups that are not using ClearCase and need to access centralized tools, then this is probably a good option for you. Many of the same rules apply as in the ClearCase option; the only difference is that the release area is outside of ClearCase. In fact, it may be beneficial to use both the ClearCase and non-ClearCase options. This may require building the software twice if the installation path is hard-coded in the binary. Most of the freeware stuff has this limitation. The release area is set up a little differently.

Select a Common Directory

When you pick a name, make sure it is not used at any location that you need for the common tools area.

Pick a Physical Location That Is Accessible from the Entire Machine at Your Site

If you have a centralized file server, create a directory for each platform that follows the naming convention in automount maps. On a machine named Fileserver, for example, the directories that are created should be:

```
/export/tools_installs/Linux/2.4.2-2
/export/tools_installs/SunOS/5.7
/export/tools/ # This contains a directory for each tool set
```

Modify Automount Maps Appropriately

The automount maps could be as follows:

```
/tools_install   Fileserver:/export/tools_installs/$OSNAME/$OSREL
/tools           Fileserver:/export/tools
```

Just as in the ClearCase example, you create a `bin` directory that has symbolic links to the versions of the tools for each tool set. The only difference is that the `/tools` directory has the tool version in the path name. So

```
/tools/TOOLS_09_2002/bin
```

will contain links to the versions of the tools in the tool set, as shown here:

```
/tools/TOOLS_09_2002/bin/gcc -> /tools_install/gcc-3.1/bin/gcc
/tools/TOOLS_09_2002/bin/tclsh -> /tools_install/
                                      tcltk-8.3.3/bin/tclsh
```

Push Maps to All Machines per Site

Remember, the name of the machine will be different for each site, so the automount maps will need to change. Try to keep the directory names the same. Just the machine name should be different. This will make it easier for replication of automount maps and directories.

Replicate Directories

There are several options for replicating these directories. Make sure that the tool you use fits your needs.

If you have no budget and your tools don't change often try `rdist` or `rsync`. These are free and pretty easy to install and configure. They do push everything over the network, and if your network is slow, that can take some time. If you need real-time data replication and have a budget, try:

- IBM data replication with the hardware and ESS data storage software

- Various other hardware and software solutions from your vendor of choice

- Veritas data replication—software solution

All of these solutions cost money, but your data will be replicated reliably. If you wait a couple more years, more solutions will be available.

The Developer's Environment

Good news. The developer in this solution accesses all of the tools the same way: `/tools/TOOLS_09_2002/bin`—independent of platform. The automounter handles all of this for you. This means you don't need to put information about platforms into your test or build scripts to set up paths that depend on the platform. This simplifies things dramatically and increases the quality of your build or test system.

Pick an Option

The ClearCase option allows you to use the power of ClearCase to handle all of your versioning and distribution. This is very powerful, but you suffer with speed and accessibility. If all of your developers are not on ClearCase, this can be a problem. We suggest using ClearCase, no matter what, for storing the tools' source code. You just need to weigh whether or not to use ClearCase for distribution of your tool sets. And then you're back to where we started: you need to know your group.

Just about every article you'll read on the subject mentions something about understanding the model before you begin building. Well, understanding your developers is the first step—and key step—to successfully building your tool strategy. Or your tree house. But once you have an understanding and can agree on a path forward, you'll be headed in the right direction.

21

Training and Scripting to Control Process

Fishing Lessons

Give a man a fish and you feed him for a day.
Teach him how to fish and you feed him for a lifetime.

Everyone knows that old fishing allegory. Well, let's expand that bit of wisdom into the world of technology. Instead of just teaching a man to fish, what if you, in your efforts to help this man (or woman), were to set about decreasing the amount of mistakes he made while fishing, increasing his ability to be successful? Sounds like a good idea, right?

First, you might give him a boat. No longer restricted to the shore of the lake or river, he would surely find more fish available to him, and his potential for catching larger fish in greater quantities would be increased exponentially. Next, maybe you would suggest improvements to the fishing pole itself. Maybe even propose adding multiple fishing poles to the boat, allowing him to catch more than one fish at a time. Better than multiple poles, of course, would be a net. The bigger net, the better. So he wouldn't have to waste his time casting his net into an empty part of the lake, you might give him radar, so he could more readily identify entire schools of fish hiding in the deep recesses of the lake, and cast his net appropriately.

Your next suggestion might be to connect some kind of GPS guidance system and a relational database to his boat, to capture and store historical information gathered from his radar tracking system. With these new tools, the fisherman could more accurately predict where the fish will be—and possibly the volume of fish he could expect from each day's labor.

Because he would be catching so many fish with his new tools and tracking system, the fisherman would quickly outgrow the cart and baskets he used to sell his fish. You would then need to help him to set up the proper distribution channels to sell his product, which would include hiring and training additional people on how to maintain the tools and processes that have been created to support this emerging business.

Things might appear to be running great, and you might start feeling that your time and money have been well spent. The man seems happy, and the business is growing at a steady 10 percent each year.

Until one day, the radar system breaks, and the boat engine needs repair—and it will be weeks before the mechanic can get it all working again. Because the fisherman is not generating revenue, he needs to cut costs. He decides to lay off 50 percent of his staff, which only prolongs the pain, because there won't be fish enough to support operations for weeks, and competition moves in fast. You quickly realize that you have not taught the man to fish at all, but you have taught him to become dependent on things that don't have anything to do with fishing. The art of fishing, and the goal of simply applying a trade to support the man and his family, has been lost in the technology surrounding the business. The man finds that he does not know how to fish at all, and he is even more dependent on you than before.

In configuration management, we tend to use technology instead of training to help software developers do their work. We look to scripting languages to solve all of our problems. In many situations, we write scripts to eliminate redundant steps, to force process on team members, or to do any number of other things that we CM-ers can dream up. Scripts are great, and they enrich our development environments, but if they are not managed properly, scaling and maintaining scripts can become a full-blown project in itself.

Maybe it has to do with the personal history of most configuration managers, or at least those of us who have been doing this for some time. Most CM people first start as software developers and then find that they have a knack for makefile systems and system administration. When the organization grows and more people are added, configuration management becomes more important to the company, and those who are at the helm of the source-code management solution suddenly find themselves in the official role of configuration manager. Although it often takes some software development creativity to find yourself in this position, many CM-ers realize quickly that there are very few creative outlets in their new role. As a result, many start writing scripts to get that technology fix.

Before you know it, you wake up groggy and confused after a night of vendor sales pitches and general post-RUC debauchery somewhere outside of Orlando, and you suddenly realize that your small "helpful" script has exceeded 10,000 lines, and it requires its own CM processes and a small staff to keep it running. These are dark times, indeed.

Just like the fisherman in our story, software developers can become so dependent on technology that things come to a screeching halt if that automated script suddenly breaks. Even simple scripts that automate common, redundant steps can become stumbling blocks when they don't work. Any knowledge of the original steps can be lost, and the development process comes to a standstill. The result? Product schedules are missed, people are laid off, and everyone gets mad at the configuration manager.

When to Write Scripts

Don't get us wrong: we believe automation is the way to go. Automation improves quality because it fosters repeatable and predictable process. However, automation that replaces knowledge and training can be problematic. There are some specific areas in which scripts become important and should be used in conjunction with training: integration of tools, automation of redundant steps, and enforcement of process adherence.

Integration of Tools

As we have discussed in some of our previous chapters, the integration of tools can increase quality, communication, and productivity. These integration scripts can easily become very complex projects in themselves. Make sure you map out the integrations between the tools before you get started. Many software development tools allow you to define how that tool can be used. If you first define and document how you want the tool to be used independently, followed by how it will be integrated with other tools, managing feature creep will be much easier later on. This documentation should also be used to train your developers.

Automation

Automation scripts typically come about from observing developers working or, more than likely, developers complaining about the steps that they have to follow. These scripts are usually written by engineers themselves and sent to CM managers to add to the scripting arsenal. Make sure these scripts are kept simple and don't "solve" more than they are designed to solve. One good habit is to make sure that a description of the manual steps being automated is also documented in the script. This will give engineers a clear picture of what the script is attempting to resolve and point them in the right direction when the script is not behaving properly.

Process Adherence

Most of the time, you may find yourself considering building a script to help enforce process. As discussed in Chapter 22, "Trigger-Happy," scripts and ClearCase triggers can be used effectively to enforce quality and process. Some examples of this are reviewing code before integration for builds, adding comments for each check-in, or even running code analyzers or memory checkers before code is put into main development streams. Even though scripts will automate these steps, your developers need to know what to expect when the scripts or triggers are run. Once again, documentation is important to your overall success.

Types of Training

Let's all admit it to ourselves: sometimes we focus on the technology instead of the principles suggested by that technology in the first place. Proper training on how to build your product, maintain your system, or solve a problem is many times more important than the technology that you use. There is much more to training than just your typical "man" pages that tell how the tool can be used, but this is—most of the time—all your developer will get. Just like the fisherman in the opening story, training should teach software developers the art of software development, not just the mechanics of using tools. This includes building a foundation of knowledge of the tools being used, indoctrinating developers in the philosophy of development, and teaching them the process to follow when developing.

Build a Foundation of Knowledge

"Just use the script we wrote. You don't need to know ClearCase. We've wrapped it so that it's easy to use." How many times have we heard this and even said it ourselves? This is great for the job security of the configuration manager; however, the reality around heavily scripted CM solutions is that your CM guy is likely overwhelmed with questions about the system, creating more work for him, and possibly requiring more people just to field these questions. In the end, you may be creating as much—or more—work as you had before your automated solution.

Another option is to teach the developers how the tools work. Some CM people think this is the wrong thing to do because "engineers can now find ways around their scripts, and maybe they won't follow the process." This is a legitimate concern, but the next section helps the developer understand why things are done a specific way. We think what you will find is that developers who are empowered with knowledge of how the tools work will be able to understand and much more easily adhere to your established processes.

A good example of this is a basic ClearCase training class. Rational offers some good courses on basic ClearCase philosophy and usage. That's a great place to start. Even though you might not use all of the tools that the course teaches, it is a foundation of knowledge on top of which you can build. Although you don't typically send developers to the ClearCase administration class, you might want to have at least one developer attend so that you have someone who understands how the solution works.

Philosophy of Development

It is not good enough to train people on the individual tools they will be using; you also need to train them how to use the tools according to your philosophy of development. Many development tools today allow users to customize and configure them every which way. ClearCase is another great example of this kind of configuration flexibility. It is a very powerful tool that supports many different methodologies of developing software.

So maybe your engineers have already attended the ClearCase fundamentals course. This does not mean they have the ability to just sit down and start using the tool. There are several questions that still need to be answered and much process to be learned. What is your branching strategy? What rules do you have for code reviews? The list goes on and on.

Software development can be very much like religion: everyone has the same central focus, but there are many different approaches to the same goal. The important thing to maintain within your own company is that everyone follows the same software development doctrine. You must become an evangelist for whatever philosophy that you want everyone to follow. It is not good enough to simply post your standards online and expect compliance. You need to get your engineers to understand why you use the tool the way you do.

Figure 21.1 is an example. You can publish this branching strategy diagram, providing text on what each piece means.

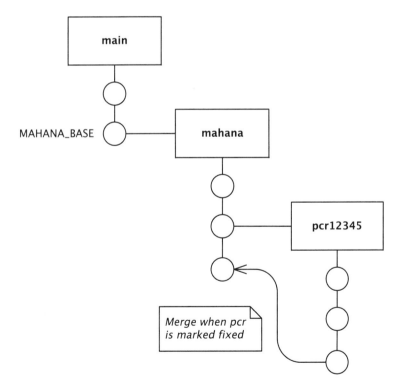

Figure 21.1   *Branching Strategy*

All development is done on PCR branches, with the name of the branch being "pcr####". When a PCR is marked "FIXED" and its code has been reviewed, it is merged to a development stream ("mahana") to be integrated into the product.

The previous paragraph is a simple example, but it's a common one that we give our engineers about branching strategy. What is missing is the why? A better description of the process would be this:

> The main stream of development should be as clean as possible to prevent an error from being propagated to others' work areas. Additionally, individual files that have been changed to resolve PCRs should be grouped together. Integration from the main development branch should occur anytime another PCR(s) change is merged to the development branch. This will decrease the divergent nature of multiple people working on the code at the same time.

If the developers understand why the branching strategy is the way it is, they will more likely adhere to the process—rather than following it blindly, and looking for opportunities to subvert the process.

Process Training

Now that your engineers understand the tools and appreciate how and why you are going to use them, it is time to document and train them on the process that helps them adhere to your company's philosophy of development. This training should include, where possible, simple workflows that clearly illustrate the steps to be taken, responsibility for each step, and any artifacts that are used or generated. The Rational Unified Process does a good job of describing these workflows. Whatever process you develop and roll out to your team, make sure that you provide multiple vehicles of information distribution: teach it, promote it, and then make it available in server forms, on the Web, and in paper format. If people understand the process steps and the philosophy behind what is going on, you'll find that they can even work without those additional scripts that you wrote to automate the process. This decreases the potential downtime that you may experience due to errors in your tools and scripts.

Good Fishing Techniques

In our experience, when rolling out development environments, try to limit the number of tools that the engineers need to learn. Focus instead on training them on the critical tools for the job, and constantly touch on your philosophy of development. This gives the engineers more flexibility in how they get their work done by keeping things simple and by allowing them—with their understanding of the company's development philosophies—some flexibility in how they solve a problem.

Not everything can be solved by a script, and not every script can handle all of the different permutations that may occur in normal software development. Make sure that your process is not so limiting that it slows down development. The end goal is to make the developer more productive, not to establish your own bureaucratic red tape. The last thing you want is to just slow things down.

Don't get sucked into the belief that job security is about building tools and processes that cannot be run without you. This destructive cycle must be broken. It is better to teach someone the art of fishing—or in this case, how to develop software within your organization—than to set up a lot of tools and processes. A fisherman who encounters a storm simply takes up his pole and waits out the storm. But a developer who relies too heavily on automated solutions will find himself stuck when that storm hits.

22

Trigger-Happy

As you probably know, *entropy* is defined as "the tendency for all matter and energy in the universe to evolve toward a state of inert uniformity." You can see examples of this in nature: from something as simple as water running downhill, to interplanetary matter collapsing and transforming into some kind of physical mass. Arguably, entropy may also explain the "love handles" and other physical attributes usually seen on the engineering elite and other seat-warming technologists. (We're not singling out anyone here—we're all victims.)

Over the years, entropy has become rather prevalent in the world of software development. It can be attributed to budget constraints, time-to-market pressures, and big engineering egos. So how do you control this? As a configuration manager or business system owner, you're probably tired of the finger pointing whenever there are questions about the quality of builds and the product—but what can you do? Look at nature. There are some interesting principles we can learn from nature and its ongoing fight against disorder and chaos. The key is to acquire the relevant knowledge using a rational thought process in order to take advantage of it.

To optimize the effectiveness of our actions, it is helpful to understand the implications of entropy. Look at one of the most universal powers in the universe: gravity. It is one of the main forces, which causes matter and energy to come together. It keeps the universe from completely dispersing and becoming a whole lot of nothing. So how does gravity help your software engineers develop better code? First, it keeps your engineers from floating out to space (physically, not mentally). That's always a plus. But we should look at why gravity is so successful at what it does. It is consistent. It is constant. And it is invisible. The goal is to develop something similar to gravity to help your software development team keep their feet on the ground and focused on the product—not on the little things that don't matter.

Consistent

Gravity does not play favorites. It works the same on everyone. Some would argue that there are those who are affected more by gravity than others—the effects of which are typically seen around age 30 or so. But in general, the law is the same across the board. Whatever system you develop for your development team needs to be consistent. Exceptions to the rules should be just that: exceptions. Don't make exceptions all of the time. Doing so will increase the variability and decrease the overall quality of your product. More important, make sure that you as a CM engineer follow the rules as well. Don't exclude yourself (as if you were a member of Congress).

Constant

Gravity is always there. It does not turn off when we fall. Maybe there's that one guy on "Ripley's Believe It Or Not!" who can somehow defy gravity—but for the rest of us, it's a fact of life. In fact, gravity can be really painful at times—but we've come to expect that it's there. And it will always be there. You can count on it. Understanding this, it can even be used to our advantage. The same should be true of your development system. It needs to be on all of the time. Even under pressure, you need to hold your ground and make sure the process is always running. We've all seen process go out the window when time—or customer demand—becomes an issue. But turning things off just postpones or prolongs the issue.

Invisible

We cannot see gravity. Ghosts, maybe, but not gravity. If we could see it, we might try to avoid it or find some way around it. If your system hampers or otherwise obstructs the process of your engineers—and they are aware that it is your system causing these problems—not surprisingly, they will circumvent it at all costs. The best technology is invisible.

Types of Triggers

Most configuration management tools have some kind of mechanism that allows for automation of software development processes. In ClearCase, these mechanisms are called triggers. Software developers can be guided to follow process through triggers, which are scripts that are called before (pre-triggers) and after (post-triggers) a specific ClearCase operation (check-in, check-out, make element). For any operation that requires some kind of control, you first need to determine whether it is a pre-trigger or a post-trigger.

For those of you who are new to ClearCase, this chapter provides a fairly comprehensive overview of triggers. Once you're more comfortable with the application, you can use this material as a reference. Here's a quick rundown of the reasons for triggers and other ClearCase mechanisms, such as locks.

Preventive Triggers and Locks

These triggers don't allow users to perform specific actions with source code or artifacts. ClearCase allows you to do anything you want to your artifacts. Well, almost anything. It also allows you to prevent things from happening to your artifacts. By using triggers and locks, you can prevent artifacts from being modified, checked in, checked out, or anything else you can imagine. This restriction can be limited to branches, elements, and even versions of elements in the VOB. Most of the time, locks are sufficient to handle everything that you need.

One problem with the lock mechanism, typically, is that it is static. You can use triggers on most of the operations in ClearCase to prevent things from happening. To enable this, you need to use a pre-trigger. If the trigger exists with a nonzero value, for example, it will prevent the operation from running. Preventive triggers are closely related to integration triggers.

Integration Triggers

ClearCase integrates well with other software development tools. Most of the time, triggers are used to track the work that users perform in ClearCase and "record" them into other tools. One of the most popular integrations is combining a defect-tracking system with build-and-release tools and ClearCase. In this case, keeping the other tools updated with changes in ClearCase is the primary reason for triggers.

Triggers for `mkelem`, `co`, and `ci` are typical operations that are written. These triggers are normally post-execution commands (pre- and post-execution commands can be any arbitrary command lines to be run before a job is started or after a job finishes). Not only do you want to run these operations in post-exec triggers, but you probably also want to run them in the background. Running post-exec commands in the background provides results from the post-exec part of the trigger much more quickly. Remember, you want your triggers to be invisible, if possible. Perceived speed can be just as good as real speed to your users.

Interactive Triggers

The problem with interactive triggers is that they can consume mass quantities of your developer's time. That is, generally speaking, bad. When you need to ask the user for information, make it possible for the trigger to read environment variables as input, as well. This allows your engineering teams to run operations in batch mode. A great example of this is the "mass check-in." If your trigger requires that the user supply a comment, you can allow the user to set an environment variable with the comment and read that in a pre-trigger.

Most interactive triggers are pre-triggers.

Pre-triggers

A pre-event trigger monitors the usage of a specified ClearCase operation or class of operations. For example, a pre-event trigger can require that some check be applied before the check-in command is allowed to run. It can allow the command to proceed, or it can cancel the command.

Pre-triggers are typically used to enforce process or to disallow the operation from occurring if certain conditions are not met.

Again, try to avoid triggers that prompt the user. Such prompts can become annoying when engineers perform those mass check-ins, because they force the engineers to hit the Return key for each check-in. If you require user input, make sure you can get the information from an environment variable or file. The prompt should be seen as a backup input mechanism, not as your leading solution. Another option would be to prompt once, using the input information for the rest of the triggers that are called.

Post-triggers

A post-event trigger runs after a specified operation completes. Typically, this type of trigger notifies one or more users that a command was executed, or it attaches an attribute to an object. For example, a post-event trigger might send an e-mail notification to the QA department when a modified file is checked in, along with any user-supplied information or comments from check-in.

Running post-triggers in the background will decrease the operation completion time. This is not a big deal for checking in one or two files, but checking in hundreds of files at a time can waste a developer's time.

The other negative effect is speed. Nothing is more frustrating for an engineer than a slow file check-in. In fact, the result of a slow check-in process usually (and quickly) leads to developers ignoring the process, developing the bad habit of not checking in their files. Inevitably, this will lead to engineers forgetting to check in a file for a build later down the road. When this happens, of course, builds fail, and timelines are affected.

On the other hand, post-triggers are great for tool integration. If you have any integration with other tools, this should probably be done in the post-triggers of operations.

Controlling Triggers

Where you put your triggers completely determines how they can be accessed. You need to ensure that they can be accessed at all of your sites, and by all of your VOBs. And you need to make sure that they are accessed the same way—through the same methods and processes—in each location. This will make things consistent and constant across your organization.

Recommendations

As outlined in Chapter 3, "Standards Enforcement Using Configuration Management Tools," most software development standards have some kind of process requirements in place that must be followed and thoroughly documented. This is where event-driven triggers can help you manage your project. In Chapter 3, we also gave an example of working with the program Lint, used for checking in your source code for certain standards. If your requirement is for all of your source code to adhere to a specific coding standard, you can register a trigger to run Lint before it allows users to check in their code. Triggers can also help solve problems with event notifications or error handling. For example, triggers can send out e-mail notifications to a group of reviewers when code has been checked in, so that the team can review the modified code before approving it for a certain build. On the flip side, triggers can notify the team in the event that files are not checked back in before a scheduled build, or when an upload fails.

Some basic rules of thumb come into play when creating triggers: Performance is king. Understand the scope of what you deploy. Simple is better. Here is our advice on each.

Speed Is Good

One of the great unwritten rules about working with software developers is, whenever possible, stay out of their way. And one of the ways to impede their progress is to develop slow and cumbersome triggers. If you do this, your software developers will complain, and as is their nature, most of them will do everything they can to subvert your process. It is important to streamline your processes, creating triggers that improve, not impede. Ensure that your process improvement efforts focus on what is most important to the developers, and make performance your top priority.

Have You Thought It Through?

Maybe you've identified a problem area in your process—but how do you go about making your triggers faster? One surefire design method is first to analyze the scope and purpose of the trigger. Far too many engineers jump into a problem without first understanding the full scope. If you understand the drivers behind the problem, you're more apt to find a long-term solution. If the trigger is used to disallow an operation from occurring, for example, it should be in the pre-trigger category (to be run before the operation is executed). In general, these triggers need to be fast. If you're looking for unabashed rebellion, make your developers wait to check in or check out code from a version control system. Not a wise move.

Another technique we recommend is to run all other triggers in the post-operation mode. Anything that can be run in the background will allow your engineering team to optimize their productivity. Without having to monitor the system, they can get back to work again much more quickly—and they won't have to sit there and wait for all of the triggers to finish. They'll thank you for that.

Try to Solve One Problem at a Time

Finally, we recommend that you bite off only what you can chew. Don't get "trigger-happy." One of the biggest mistakes with trigger development is the interactive trigger. If you need to get information from an engineer, try to work directly with the source-code management system and allow for environment variables or other mechanisms that can be used to apply the same information to all files for a given operation. If you thought slowing down the check-in, check-out process frustrated your development team, you'll triple that pain by forcing your developers to answer the same question again and again for the hundred or so files that they just checked in to the source-code management system. Simplify your designs and, as the section header states, try to solve just one problem at a time.

As we alluded to in our introduction, entropy "is the ultimate Natural Law because it determines the flow of what we call 'time'. Thus, entropy deals with the very existence of the universe. The term entropy describes phenomena that have the most profound effect on all events in human existence, including our ability to achieve happiness by aligning ourselves with Objective Reality" (Walter E. Requadt, http://www.rationality.net).

So tell your spouse that they're not "love handles"—they're just part of your "objective reality."

More About Triggers, in General

Now that we have walked through the different types of triggers (preventive, integration, interactive, pre-, and post-) and provided some insight into how to control and manage them, we thought we'd share some useful information and links to help you research some of the functionality possible in ClearCase.

As we're sure most of you know, triggers are not unique to ClearCase. In the wide world of database management, triggers are very common. They are special, user-defined actions—usually in the form of stored procedures—that are automatically invoked by the server based on data-related events. Triggers can perform complex actions and can use the full power of procedural language. A rule is a special type of trigger that is used to perform simple checks on data. Both triggers and rules are attached to specific operations on specific tables. In other words, an event tells you something happened to the database; a trigger or rule is an event handler you write to take proper action in response to that event.

Triggers and rules are typically used to perform tasks related to changes in tables, such as auditing, looking for value thresholds, or setting column defaults. Enabled triggers or rules are executed whenever a table is updated by a SQL Delete, Insert, or Update command. A separate trigger or rule can be defined for each of these commands, or a single trigger may be defined for any updates to a table.

In general, triggers can call other triggers or stored procedures. So what makes a trigger different from a stored procedure? Triggers are called implicitly by database-generated events, while stored procedures are called explicitly by client applications. Server implementations of triggers are extremely nonstandard and vendor-specific.

Triggers are written in proprietary SQL procedural extensions. Different implementations limit what triggers can do. Several tools provide "hooks" or "triggers": these are built-in "slots" in the tool to make room for you to insert your own custom actions that take place before and/or after a given tool operation. ClearCase provides a rich set of triggers and allows users to add hooks/triggers to almost anything.

More About Triggers, in ClearCase

Online user groups are an excellent resource for learning about new technologies from other engineers working in the trenches. We came across an excellent overview on CMcrossroads.com (an online community for configuration management) of working with triggers in ClearCase, provided by Paul M. Sander and summarized here: Triggers can be installed for almost any event that modifies a ClearCase repository, as either a pre-op (a test before action, with early abort) or a post-op (a follow-up action without abort). They can be applied to manipulations of data types as well as specific file system artifacts.

Triggers can be applied to the following:

- Creating, modifying, removing, or renaming metadata types (that is, source file type descriptions, label types, branch types, hyperlink types, and attribute types)

- Locking and unlocking versions, branches, and labels

- Changing the contents of history events

- Checking out a source file; also undoing a check-out and changing the reserved status of a checked-out file

- Checking in a source file

- Changing a source file's data type

- Creating a hard or symbolic link

- Creating or removing a branch on a file

- Creating a new source file or deleting a source file in the repository

- Removing a directory entry

- Removing a version

- Setting or removing an attribute on a source file

- Creating or deleting a hyperlink

- Creating or removing a label on a source file

- Creating or removing a trigger

All in all, the trigger mechanism in ClearCase is fairly comprehensive, though there are some warts:

- Merges are recorded as special instances of hyperlinks. Triggers created to act on merges have been reported to not be working.

- Triggers act on each specific file or other database metadata artifact. There is no way to create a single instance of a trigger that operates on multiple files; for example, the CVS notion of a per-directory commit message that can be mailed is difficult to implement in ClearCase reliably.

- There are no command-level triggers (that is, triggers that fire once per command invocation). As a workaround, the user is directed to write wrappers around the ClearCase command-line interface.

- Post-op triggers do not abort a transaction; changes are committed to the database regardless of whether or not the trigger exited successfully. (Pre-op triggers can prevent commission of erroneous data.)

- State information is passed from ClearCase to the triggers by way of environment variables. There are a few conditions that are not passed into the trigger properly, thus making it necessary occasionally to parse the command line. One example of this is when a user checks out a file: a profile file states whether files are checked out reserved or unreserved by default, and ClearCase has options to override the default.

- The trigger environment shows only the command-line overrides, and it does not account for the user's profile.

Configuration Management of Your Triggers

Because you are good configuration managers and you practice what you preach, we assume you make sure all of your triggers are under some source-code management system. Right? OK, none of us follows all of the steps all of the time. To be honest, sometimes we feel we are above the rules as far as configuration management goes, because we write the rules for our organizations. But what we turn into is something like the textbook bad parent (or government official), constantly telling our children, "Do as I say, not as I do." Just like children (sorry for the condescending tone), our software engineers will call our bluff if we don't follow our own rules.

So where do you put your trigger code? We've seen a number of different options—some are good, and some, well . . . keep us scratching our heads in disbelief. The most consistent solution is to create a configuration management VOB, either for your entire site or for the individual project you are working on. For example:

```
/vobs/cmtools
```

This is a good place to put trigger code, support code for build-and-release processes, and any other CM stuff lying around the shop floor. You should run your CM coding project the same way that your software engineering teams work. In short: live by your own rules.

Installing Triggers

Now that you have your triggers under version control, you need to figure out how the triggers can be accessed. Triggers are called by the client side of ClearCase. This means that the triggers are called on the same machine on which the cleartool command is called. This is true for both the pre- and the post-trigger types. So what does that mean to you? Consider the following:

Triggers must be accessible by all of the machines on which you have ClearCase installed. The different options here are:

- Running the triggers out of the VOB. This may seem like a good idea, but you cannot assume that all of your triggers are running in a view. As a result, it requires that you have a view that is always accessible on all of your machines.

- Place the triggers in a directory that has guaranteed accessibility on all platforms. One option is the VOB storage directory area for your configuration management VOB.

- Any commands or scripts called by your trigger need to be accessible on all machines. Make sure you don't call platform-specific tools like grep, awk, or sed if you are working with Windows and UNIX.

- Don't assume the user's environment contains environment variables. You may need to make sure any environment variables such as PATH are set in the trigger script.

- Remember the different platforms in your ClearCase configuration, and use a platform-independent language. Perl is the best bet. But make sure you have the same version of Perl on all of your machines.

- Again, you have different platforms and versions in your system, so don't think that csh, ksh, or sh are the same on all UNIX boxes. You will find some minor but disastrous differences on different versions of UNIX.

Windows and UNIX triggers can be registered in ClearCase independently or on the same command line. The following example shows the registration happening independently:

```
cleartool mktrtype . . . -execunix "Command"
cleartool mktrtype . . . -execwin "Command"
```

So now that you have selected a location to house your triggers and supporting code, you need to come up with an installation procedure. *Do not* simply copy stuff out to your installation area whenever you feel like it. We recommend you automate this process with a make system or scripts. This process should include at least two steps:

1. Copy the files to your installation area.

2. Register your triggers with ClearCase.

```
cleartool mktrtype . . .
```

Multi-site and Triggers

Triggers are not automatically multi-sited with the replicas that are multi-sited—unless, of course, they are in a ClearCase VOB that has been multi-sited. But even then, the triggers need to be installed. So, some of your sites in a multi-site configuration may not have the same set of triggers installed at another site. Of course, this can lead to confusion and possible holes in your trigger strategy. You must make sure that when you create a replica, or add a new trigger to a replica, that you duplicate the installation in each replica.

Additional Trigger Pitfalls

Here are some additional pearls of knowledge about triggers, gathered from the Web:

- They're designed to work on all ClearCase platforms, UNIX and Windows.

- They work in dynamic and snapshot views.

- They do everything possible to stay in process, meaning that they use OS interfaces to manipulate files directly rather than calling out to system utilities. This is important for performance, for portability, and for reliability.

- They're written as a family, meaning that they share common coding conventions and prefix logic.

- They attempt to anticipate uncommon scenarios, such as the user not having cleartool in his or her PATH (which can happen in cron jobs or when the root user needs to run ClearCase operations).

- A trigger is always attached to a cleartool operation.

- Any trigger script that does something more than "`exit 1`" very likely invokes additional cleartool operations.

- As with any database transaction, write operations are much slower than reads.

- Triggers can be attached only to write operations. In fact, the categories of opkinds have names such as `MODIFY_ELEM`, `MODIFY_TYPE`, `MODIFY_DATA`, and `MODIFY_MD`.

- Thus, any trigger script that falls into the "performance-sensitive" category likely involves at least two cleartool ops, with at least one being a slow write.

Tapping into the Web

Speaking of the Web, there is a wide variety of resources available online for database management generally and ClearCase specifically. We've compiled a short list of trigger-related resources, which may or may not help your project but will at least provide you with some insight into the options available out there.

http://www.cleartool.com/triggers/

This site contains a collection of trigger scripts that have been published, donated, and otherwise found for the online ClearCase community. The Webmaster has published this list in an attempt to pull together those tools, which seek to "aspire to a standard."

http://www.cmcrossroads.com/bradapp/acme/clearcase/

As the introduction reads, this page "attempts to catalog common practices with the ClearCase software configuration management tool. At present, no attempt is made to distinguish which practices are 'good' and which ones aren't. At a later date, I hope to be able to sort the common usage patterns listed here into best practices and traps and pitfalls."

This site lists numerous triggers and their functions, and it is a good online resource for ClearCase trigger hints and tips.

http://www.weintraubworld.net/clearcase/cc.env.html

A Web site dedicated to setting up the proper ClearCase environment. As stated by the author, "It is important that all of your ClearCase users have the same environment. Otherwise, it may be hard to tell if an error is due to environment problems or software problems."

http://www-136.ibm.com/developerworks/rational/

Well, we'd be remiss if we did not include the Rational Developer Network—now part of the IBM developerWorks site—in our list of online resources, as the site is a veritable cornucopia of ClearCase administration and power-user hints and tips, with information on ClearCase hooks and triggers.

http://www.highley-recommended.com/sw_process/triggers.html

An overview of trigger installation, removal, debugging, and branching/labeling policies recommended by Highley Recommended, Inc.

http://www.abs-consulting.com/abs_consulting_products.html

A Better Solution (ABS) Inc. are ClearCase consultants and a Rational Unified Partner. Their product, ClearTrigger, provides a framework to manage triggers across multiple projects and VOBs. It has a large number of triggers for both Windows and UNIX. It also has a trigger-control language that allows users to set bits that turn triggers on and off. They have developed a highly integrated solution with ClearCase, which includes several GUI dialogs for triggers and managing the triggers.

ABS's product is a nice framework and a good starting point for developing your own triggers or policies, but it is not freeware. They require a license per site, costing about $500, or two licenses if you are running Windows and UNIX machines. If you are getting started for the first time, this is an inexpensive way to begin your setup.

The Benefits of Triggers

A number of benefits can be realized in the ClearCase environment by using triggers. For example, triggers can enable faster application development. Because triggers are stored in the application, the actions performed by triggers do not have to be coded into each stream. They also allow for global enforcement of business rules. In fact, a trigger can be defined once and then reused for any application using the database.

From a cost and performance perspective, for example, triggers can provide valuable savings in ongoing maintenance. If a business policy changes, it is necessary to change only the trigger program linked to a database file instead of every application program that touches it. Triggers can also improve performance in client/server environments where one I/O from the client can in fact trigger multiple actions at the server level, thus freeing the wire between the client and the server for other transactions.

But most important, triggers can automate enforcement of complex business rules (that's right—they can provide actual business value!). Triggers can stand alone, or they can be used in conjunction with other system controls your company may have developed. With these tools, one could potentially make business rules practically self-enforcing—regardless of the application that touches the data. For example, you could use triggers to guarantee that when a specific operation is performed, related actions are performed. You could also use triggers only for centralized, global operations that should be fired for the triggering statement, regardless of which user or application issues the statement.

Triggers can be installed for almost any event that modifies a ClearCase repository, as either a pre-op or post-op. They can be applied to manipulations of data types as well as specific file system artifacts.

Triggers à la Carte

Now that you have a better sense of what can be done with triggers, you are ready to explore how triggers are constructed and implemented.

Example: Don't Let the User Check In a File Without a Comment

First, write a script that checks for the comment and rejects or accepts the check-in. To do this, you will need to determine on what platforms the trigger will run. Of course, in 99 percent of the cases, you really only need to worry about NT or UNIX. Both are handled differently if you write the script correctly. In the following example, we chose Perl as the language because it is highly portable:

```
#!/usr/local/bin/perl

# Check if the comment is greater than 5 characters
if(length($ENV{CLEARCASE_COMMENT}) > 5)
{
# This will allow the check-in to finish.
exit 0;
}

# This will fail the check-in.
exit -1;
```

You may have noticed that we used an environment variable to see what the comment was set to on the command line,

CLEARCASE_COMMENT. A list of environment variables that can be used in triggers appears at the end of this section.

You will need to save this file in a location that can be accessed by any of the machines from which the cleartool command is called. If you ask several people, you'll get several answers on where to put your triggers. Some have stored them in the VOB storage directory. Whatever your strategy, just remember that the script must be accessible from all of the machines, plain and simple.

Next, you'll need to register the trigger for the check-in operation. You can place a trigger on almost any command from the command line. There are even some internal commands onto which you can attach triggers (there are too many options to cover here), but our focus here is on when the trigger will be called.

There are two options: pre-execution operation and post-execution operation. Pre-exec triggers are great for preventing the command from happening. Post-exec triggers are great for compute-intensive or back-end processing.

In our example, we want to prevent the check-in, so we are going to use a pre-exec trigger:

```
mktrtype -element -all -preop check-in-nc -execunix
      '/usr/local/trigger/comment.pl' comment_tr
```

Please note that the –execunix switch installs this trigger for UNIX platforms only. Use the –execwin switch to handle triggers on Windows platforms. When you install a Windows trigger, make sure you put the trigger in a globally accessible location. Here is an example:

```
mktrtype -element -all -preop check-in-nc -execwin
      '\\wert\triggers\comment.pl' comment_tr
```

You'll need to make sure you have registered the .pl extension to be handled with Perl. If you haven't, your trigger will fail. Also, if you call a command built into the Windows shell (for example, cd, del, dir, or copy), you must invoke the shell with "cmd /c".

For those interested in how triggers are developed within ClearCase, we also recommend you take a look at "ClearCase: The Ten Best Triggers," by Daniel Diebolt (http://www-106.ibm.com/developerworks/rational/library/content/RationalEdge/oct03/rdn.pdf), for a ground-level view of the trigger types outlined in this chapter, which includes the scripts and installation procedures for each example.

Here now is the list of environment variables that can be used in triggers. For the latest ClearCase environment variables, see the ClearCase user's guide, as this list may change as new versions are released.

- CLEARCASE_ACTIVITY—The name of the activity called—only for post-exec triggers.

- CLEARCASE_ATTACH—Set to 1 if an element trigger type; 0 if it is on a directory element's inheritance list.

- CLEARCASE_ATTYPE—Attribute type involved in operation that caused the trigger to fire. In a rename operation, the old name of the renamed attribute type object.

- CLEARCASE_BASELINES—A space-separated list of all UCM baselines that the destination stream is rebased.

- CLEARCASE_BRTYPE—Branch type involved in the call. In a branch rename, it will be the old name of the branch type.

- CLEARCASE_CI_FPN—Pathname of the element that is checked in.

- CLEARCASE_CMDLINE—This contains the command and arguments run from cleartool.

- CLEARCASE_COMMENT—Comment string for the command.

- CLEARCASE_COMPONENT—The UCM component.

- CLEARCASE_DLVR_ACTS—A space-separated list of all UCM activities merged during the deliver operation.

- CLEARCASE_ELTYPE—Element type of the element.

- CLEARCASE_FOLDER—The folder that contains the project.

- CLEARCASE_FREPLICA—The old master replica, or from-replica.

- CLEARCASE_FTEXT—Text associated with hyperlink from-object.

- CLEARCASE_FTYPE—The type of element from which the hyperlink being applied or removed is pointed.

- CLEARCASE_FVOB_PN—Pathname of VOB containing hyperlink from-object.

- CLEARCASE_FXPN—VOB-extended pathname of hyperlink from-object.

- CLEARCASE_HLTYPE—Hyperlink type.

- CLEARCASE_ID_STR—Version-ID of a version, or branch path name of branch.

- CLEARCASE_IS_FROM—Set to 1 if CLEARCASE_PN contains name of hyperlink from-object; set to 0 if CLEARCASE_PN contains name of hyperlink to-object.

- CLEARCASE_LBTYPE—Label type.

- CLEARCASE_MODTYPE—Object selector of the type for which the attribute or hyperlink is being applied or removed.

- CLEARCASE_MTYPE—Kind (element type, branch type, directory version, and so on).

- CLEARCASE_NEW_TYPE—New name of the renamed type object.

- CLEARCASE_OP_KIND—Operation that caused the trigger to fire.

- CLEARCASE_OUT_PN—Path name in checkout -out.

- CLEARCASE_PN—Name of element specified in the command.

- CLEARCASE_POP_KIND—Parent operation kind.

- CLEARCASE_PPID—Parent process ID.

- CLEARCASE_PROJECT—The UCM project.

- CLEARCASE_REPLACE—Set to 1 if the user specified -replace on the command line.

- CLEARCASE_RESERVED—Set to 1 if the -reserved checkedout command is specified.

- CLEARCASE_SLNKTXT—Text of the new VOB symbolic link.

- CLEARCASE_SNAPSHOT_PN—The path to the root of the snap-shot view directory.

- CLEARCASE_STREAM—The UCM stream.

- CLEARCASE_TO_ACTIVITY—The activity that will contain the versions of elements.

- CLEARCASE_TO_FOLDER—The folder that will contain the project or folder.

- CLEARCASE_TREPLICA—The new master replica, or to-replica.

- CLEARCASE_TRTYPE—Trigger type.

- CLEARCASE_TRTYPE_KIND—Kind of trigger type.

- CLEARCASE_TTEXT—Text associated with hyperlink to-object.

- CLEARCASE_TVOB_PN—Path name of the VOB containing hyperlink to-object.

- CLEARCASE_TXPN—VOB-extended path name of hyperlink to-object.

- CLEARCASE_TYPE—The type of element to which the hyperlink being applied or removed is pointed.

- CLEARCASE_USER—The user who issued the command.

- CLEARCASE_VIEW_KIND—The kind of view.

- CLEARCASE_VIEW_TAG—View-tag of the view.

- CLEARCASE_VOB_PN—VOB-tag of the VOB or UCM project VOB.

- CLEARCASE_XN_SFX—Extended naming symbol (such as @@) for host.

- CLEARCASE_XPN—Same as CLEARCASE_ID_STR, but prepended with CLEARCASE_PN and CLEARCASE_XN_SFX values.

Conclusion

The trigger mechanism within ClearCase is fairly comprehensive, but like every application, there is always room for improvement. Here are some areas we've identified that could use some improvement:

- Merges are recorded as special instances of hyperlinks. Triggers created to act on merges have been reported to not be working.

- Triggers act on each specific file or other database meta-data artifact. There is no way to create a single instance of a trigger that operates on multiple files; for example, the CVS notion of a per-directory commit message that can be mailed is difficult to implement in ClearCase reliably.

- There are no command-level triggers (that is, triggers that fire once per command invocation). As a workaround, the user is directed to write wrappers around the ClearCase command-line interface.

- Post-op triggers do not abort a transaction; changes are committed to the database regardless of whether or not the trigger exited successfully. (Pre-op triggers can prevent commission of erroneous data.)

State information is passed from ClearCase to the triggers by way of environment variables. There are a few conditions that are not passed into the trigger properly, thus making parsing the command line occasionally necessary. One example of this is when a user checks out a file: A profile states whether files are checked out reserved or unreserved by default, and ClearCase has options to override the default. The trigger environment shows only the command line overrides, and does not account for the user's profile.

A word of advice: Just because you can put triggers into your ClearCase system, that does not mean you should, or that you would even benefit from implementing them. The first thing you need to do is find out more about your use model and know what CM system your company has deployed. Then you can hunt for the triggers you need.

Another word of advice: Be careful about adding too many triggers. Doing so will slow down your developers. Developers hate it when you deploy things that slow them down, and they may subvert your process just to avoid whatever it is that you added the trigger for in the first place. You do not want the tools to get in the way of the developers' coding, affecting their productivity. You do want to increase their productivity.

Finally, be flexible with your triggers. Improvement in process only comes through change. If your triggers are too restrictive, then your process will become stagnant and you will not improve the system. Remember the acronym "K.I.S.S."—Keep It Simple, Stupid.

23

Efficiencies in Your CM System

Automation + Optimization = Project Optimism

As we discussed (ad nauseam) in our previous chapters, the ultimate reward for software process improvement is increased quality and decreased development cycle time. However, the question we've posed in each chapter remains the same: How do we get there? The running theme across these chapters can be summarized by the following three methods—which can be applied just as readily to the management of build-and-release activities surrounding large multi-site development efforts as to your seemingly small, one-time, internal software projects:

- Decrease build cycle times, to get results back to the software developers. (Decrease development cycle.)

- Decrease test cycle times while maintaining code coverage and use case coverage. (Increase product quality.)

- Accurately report results of build and test cycles. (Increase schedule estimation accuracy.)

This chapter will walk through the prominent methods and tools for multi-site development collaboration and, more important, automating your build-reporting system. We've put a lot of thought and effort into our recommendations—in fact, the two of us worked together to deploy a system very similar to what we'll discuss here—and hopefully you will find this information helpful as you seek to improve your own environment.

The Evolution of a Build-and-Release System

You've probably recognized that the bulk of this book is geared toward the configuration management crowd. While we're going to delve into a broader theme of collaboration technologies, we'll try our best to bring it all back around to answer one very important question: How do you accurately report the real-time results of your build and test cycles? Although the world of collaboration technologies may not apply entirely to the CM world, there are definitely tools and techniques for automation of the build-and-release cycles that you can apply, bringing your humble project into the modern world of collaboration and automation.

It Begins with an Embryo

When they first look at a new product to be developed, most engineers start with a basic makefile that will compile and link their program. The software engineer will focus on getting his or her code compiled and working before checking in the code. Some nominal self-testing occurs, everything seems to work great, and the code and makefile are checked in. In this first phase of our automation evolution, our makefile system needs to report information to one or two people, and most of the reporting is done in an interactive mode.

As the team grows and the numbers of subsystems and directories grow, additional makefiles and scripts are created to handle the dependencies between the compilation and linking of these subsystems. Slowly but surely, the meandering path toward an automated CM build-and-release system begins to form.

Typically, an engineer with some system administration experience will be given the duties of CM "build-meister" (please excuse the technical lingo) and will spend his evenings babysitting builds. You know the type: it needs to run overnight, but while it only took an hour to run before, it's now taking as long as five hours. Eventually, the engineer gets tired of watching builds while simultaneously coding, and he opts to become a configuration manager. Or maybe he decides he likes development more (we can't imagine why), and the team is forced to hire a configuration manager.

It's a good thing the CM manager was hired at this time, because someone has to manage the team of developers who are pushing to get their code out the door. Build reporting is becoming a daily process. As the product release schedules begin to tighten, daily build-and-release meetings are held so the CM manager can report back to the engineering managers that the build failed again last night because of disk space problems or someone forgetting to check in a header file.

"Why can't CM get a build turned over in one night?" is the constant theme of these sessions. The CM manager, out of frustration, begins reporting the status of the build on a quickly deployed Web site. The meetings are still held daily, but now the CM manager refers people to his Web site. The engineering managers like the pretty colors and information on the Web page. They are satisfied with the great work the CM manager is doing, even though the build is still failing periodically. But you throw something up on the Web, and people associate the activity with progress, even though nothing actually gets improved.

Things are quiet for the CM manager for a while. And then, suddenly, out of nowhere, unforeseen by current metrics, and so on, and so on . . . the 9-week development cycle everyone was focusing on slides into week 15. The build, which originally went from an hour to five hours, is now approaching ten hours because of reruns, caused by a wide variety of problems: hanging compilers, lack of disk space, machines going down, engineers forgetting to check in the directory to which they just added files, or—our personal favorite—an IT person tripping over the network cord to the build and test machine. (That was a classic.)

In addition to the increase in the amount of code that needs to be compiled, the marketing team has told customers that the Linux and Windows versions of the product will be available in the next release. The CM problem is now three times more complicated, and things are getting out of control.

Did we mention that thanks to the infinite wisdom of the management team, your product development is now spread to India and France? That's right, you are also now a 24-hour development shop. Development teams all over the world are now waiting for the build report to come out at the end of the builds on the now *five* different platforms that require your support. Oh yes, and the icing on the cake is that *all* groups point to CM as the bottleneck in the organization. You can just feel the love.

Back to Our Hero: The CM Manager

After hiring a couple of CM engineers to handle the increased amount of work, the CM manager gets his first vacation in two years and has time to reflect on what has happened. He reads an article in a business magazine somewhere that talks about information distribution, automation, and collaboration. The article describes how important it is to get the correct information to the correct people as soon as possible, increasing overall productivity across the organization.

Could this resolve the problems within his organization? Or were the daily meetings simply not frequent enough? What is the problem?

This scenario, although exaggerated (only slightly), is pretty typical of what happens as a configuration management solution evolves over time. The reporting is usually ad hoc and post mortem. Reactive, not proactive. Our advice? When looking at reporting, you need to take a system-level approach.

The Proliferation of Collaboration Technologies

OK, for those of you who are only partially engaged in reading this chapter, this is the section where we're going to talk about collaboration technologies (the section heading should have been an indication). Anyway . . .

In these unprecedented times, we are seeing people travel less and rely more on technology to work together. Less face time between members of the global development community requires a greater level of systems integration and automation. Expectations for online, real-time tools are growing, and not just inside the engineering world. Arguably, software developers were the early adopters of the network and Internet technologies that make possible most of the software and Web-based applications we use today. If we remember correctly, a long, long, long time ago (in the late 1980s), the majority of Bulletin Board Service users consisted of engineers and other homegrown technical geeks. But the people who brought us to where we are today were not necessarily the software engineers.

We are not going to dive into the chronological order or nuances of each of the technologies that created and shaped this space, but it's probably safe to say that a pocket-protector crowd of a different sort were at the forefront of the collaborative product movement.

While competitive forces kept software developers embroiled in battles over communications standards and ownership of key intellectual property, managers of massive documentation libraries were searching for any way to manage their ever-growing repositories. About this time, someone, somewhere had an epiphany, and the term "one version of the truth" was coined. The proliferation of *groupware* in the late 80s and into the early 90s was the result.

For those of you unfamiliar with the collaborative tool marketplace, here's a quick primer. Automated reporting and documentation processes (routing, workflow, dynamic reporting, and so on) and the larger collaboration space are, for the most part, flourishing—even in this tender economic environment. This class of technology is more than just groupware, which is a class of software that helps groups of colleagues (such as teams, workgroups, and business units) attached to a local area network to organize their activities. The larger collaboration tool space is considered to include the following tools and operations.

E-mail

The way this technology has expanded over the last decade is amazing. It has become a major part of our lives. E-mail is the fundamental building block of groupware.

Even though we like to think that our configuration management engineers love to stay up at night and watch the build, let us assure you that this is not the case. As long as we're talking about e-mail, one of the things that we found to increase productivity was to notify interested parties through e-mail alerts whenever an error was found in a build. The key is not to wait until the build has completed. For best results, find out who made the last change to the file that failed compilation and send that engineer and his team an e-mail. This may not be the best way to do things; you may want to refer to a static list of people who need to be notified when a specific directory build fails. But this approach typically gets a very quick response, and the build can be stopped if needed and started again—usually from the point of failure.

But we digress.

Shared Calendars and Resources

Once team members have access to each other through a shared network, it makes sense to start sharing calendars and tapping into the organization's resource pool.

Shared Storage and File Distribution

Document repositories, knowledge management systems, and other shared project activities enable teams to keep in contact across geographical and time zone barriers. Developments in this area have rapidly accelerated acceptance of the common repository model in the modern company. Technical writers were one group that quickly adopted anything that helped manage the constantly changing collateral of their teams.

Take a look at how ClearCase has been used to manage documentation:

> Technical writers, like software developers, use Rational ClearCase to track changes to their work and to ensure that they can reliably repeat the development processes that their group follows. When you work with Rational ClearCase, you don't have to worry about these issues. ClearCase tracks each version for you so that you always know which one is the latest. And if someone else is working on a file, ClearCase tells you, letting you decide—before you make changes—whether you want to proceed.
>
> —Liz Augustine, *"How Technical Writers Use Rational ClearCase," The Rational Edge*

While cruising through the Rational Developer Network, we came across another great testimonial to the repository model:

> A requirements repository gives managers a powerful tool for tracking and reporting project status. Critical milestones are more easily identified. Schedule risks are better quantified. Priorities and ownership are kept visible. Querying the repository can quickly uncover facts that provide answers to important questions, such as:
>
> "How many requirements do we have on this project? How many are high priority?"
>
> "What percentage of the requirements are incorporated in the baseline? When will they be implemented?"

"Which requirements changed since the last customer review? Who is responsible for the changes?"

"What's the estimated cost impact of the proposed changes?" High-level reports aid management reviews of product features. Requirements can be prioritized by customer need, difficulty and cost to implement, or by user safety considerations. These specialized reports help managers better allocate scarce resources by focusing attention on key project issues. The net result is that managers make better decisions and thereby improve the outcomes of their company's application development efforts.

—*Reprinted with permission based on material from "Using Requirements Management to Speed Delivery of Higher-Quality Applications," by Alan M. Davis and Dean A. Leffingwell, © Copyright 1995–1996 IBM Corporation. All rights reserved.*

Workgroup Productivity Software (Groupware)

While this can generally take on a number of different forms and definitions, it's basically a category of software that enables colleagues, especially geographically dispersed colleagues, to collaborate on projects. Typically, team groupware uses the Internet and the World Wide Web to facilitate communication among the team. Products in this category include Lotus Notes and e-mail services such as Microsoft's Exchange, which can incorporate e-mail features with shared file systems over the workplace LAN.

Workflow

Workflow can be defined as a specified series of tasks within an organization performed to produce a final outcome. Sophisticated workgroup computing applications, which are usually integrated into a larger application or solution, such as product data management tools, allow you to define different workflows for different types of jobs. So for example, in a publishing setting, a document might be automatically routed from writer to editor to proofreader to production. At each stage in the workflow, one individual or group is responsible for a specific task. Once the task is complete, the workflow software ensures that the individuals responsible for the next task are notified and receive the data they need to execute their stage of the process. Although some of these tools can be very expensive (both for licensing and for integration), more and more solutions include some workflow capability. However, over the next few years, the market will likely become saturated with a variety of workflow tools—good for the users, not so good for the workflow tool vendors.

So who is using this technology? How does it apply to software development and configuration management? Well, companies with large product development organizations such as 3M are quickly realizing the benefits of the collaborative model. Even in sluggish economic times, 3M is sinking resources into new groupware projects such as collaborative engineering tools. 3M has developed a data warehouse, for example, "that gives them access to information, such as where to find a list of accounts receivable to generate a report, that they used to have to call an IT person to dig up" ("Hard Times Are the Best Times," *CIO*, August 2001).

We've shown one example of how ClearCase is being used as a document management data warehouse. These kinds of simple solutions have actually cut costs by making collaboration easier.

Let's face it: in the current environment, we must justify every dollar we spend, and every technology we implement. So why automate your reporting and document management systems? Well, ask yourself how important it is to provide accuracy in your projects? By adopting the real-time data paradigm, document and information relevance will become more evident.

There is a general lack of automation in most companies, and yet if you look at the bulk of technology firms entering the market, you'll see products and services that focus on integration of key applications and data sources. Real-time data transfer is moving beyond the Electronic Data Interchange (EDI) standard or the transfer of data between different companies using networks, such as the Internet. Though let's not push EDI out of the picture: as more and more companies get connected to the Internet, EDI is becoming increasingly important as an easy mechanism for companies to buy, sell, and trade information. And the Universal Description, Discovery, and Integration (UDDI) standard is also becoming more prominent.

UDDI is a Web-based, distributed directory that enables businesses to list themselves on the Internet and discover each other, similar to a traditional phone book's yellow and white pages.

But these standards operate under very controlled environments, where the systems and data shared between them are clearly defined. What most teams need, however, is something more dynamic, something malleable. Something that directly addresses the automation and collaboration issues facing software teams today.

So what can your software development team do to collaborate better with each other? One solution is an automated build-reporting system that is linked directly into your code management infrastructure. Here's what we did at one customer site.

The CM Manager's Solution

Moving from the Monolithic

Break monolithic scripts into small chunks that can be reported on. It is much harder for people to look at a process that takes five hours to finish. Reporting on the progress of a script can be done by breaking the script into small chunks that get reported as subscripts or activities. The benefit comes from reporting work completion through percentages, instead of only reporting an entire build.

Subactivities

Use hierarchal aggregation to report status, allowing users to drill down into different views of the process. Most of the time, your process will have errors that need to be reported. Instead of reporting that the whole build is bad, you can report that subactivities of your build are bad or have failed. This allows engineers to drill down to the real cause of the build failure much more quickly than through the manual process.

Let's look at a simple example. Consider the hierarchy of activities in Figure 23.1.

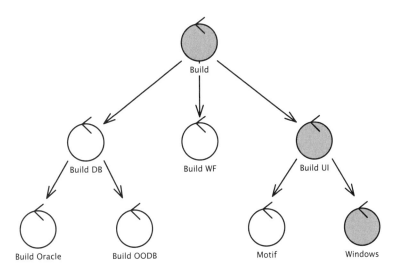

Figure 23.1   *Hierarchy of Activities*

In this example, we have broken the build script into three subscripts. Each subscript builds different subsystems (DB, WF, and UI). We have then broken both DB and UI into subactivities to identify small pieces of the build. The benefit of this is that you can quickly see what is going on at different sections of your build.

The status of an activity depends on the status of its subactivities. In this case, the Windows build failed (in dark gray), therefore the Build UI, its parent, is dark gray. And of course, the build itself is dark gray. The same propagation is true with the Build OODB (light gray means warning), but notice when it gets to Build that the most severe state wins. Therefore, the Build is still dark gray. You can use any algorithm you wish to propagate the status to the top.

An engineer can see that the build failed and then quickly look at the subactivities and see that Build UI and then Windows failed. The engineer will then try to figure out what happened to cause the error.

Stdout and Stderr Logs

The output and error logs for the individual activities should be accessible at the same level as the activity. This is easily accomplished with a Web page that has a hyperlink to the stdout and stderr of the command that was run to perform the activity.

Let's take a look at the example again. Figure 23.2 shows a single, monolithic script with one log. Figure 23.3 shows an activity aggregation and multiple logs. Notice that not all activities have logs. This is true if the activity does not really do anything. It may just be a placeholder for a number of sub-jobs.

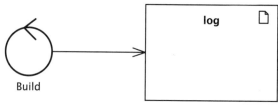

Figure 23.2   *One Log File*

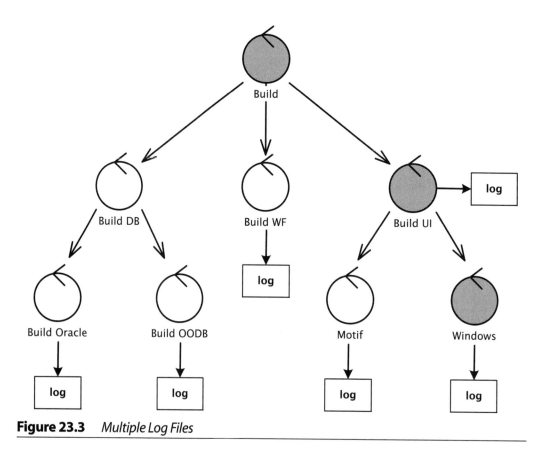

Figure 23.3   *Multiple Log Files*

Believe it or not, we have had people complain at first about the increased number of logs and how to check all the logs for errors. It turned out that most of the engineers had written scripts to move them to the line where the error resided. It took some training, and some people had to give up their cool emacs and vi macros, but—overall—people liked the Web layout better.

The other benefit is that the logs are faster to download to remote sites. Using the Web, engineers have to download only the log that is specific to the activity they are watching, not the entire five-meg log.

Real-Time Active Status and Logs

Another important aspect to build and test reporting is to make the status and logs as real-time or active as possible. There is nothing worse than pushing the logs up to the Web site after a 12-hour build cycle, only to find out that the very first activity failed—5 minutes into the build, no less—and thereby caused a cascade of link errors in the remaining build. If the information is live, progress can be watched, errors caught early, and problems potentially fixed—and the build can then be quickly restarted.

Another benefit of the real-time status is that you can show the percentage complete for an entire process (aggregated builds).

If we drill down to the unfinished activity, which is the Build DB, we find that this subactivity is 50% complete. This technique is also very useful if you are trying to find out if a current build has hung.

Opportunities for Collaboration

There are numerous opportunities for expansion of collaboration of the automated build-reporting system outlined here. Depending on your organization, you might be interested in building mechanisms to track and store threaded messages, attaching these as artifacts to builds at the subactivity level. Or maybe an instant-messaging utility for real-time conversations between your CM engineering team and your users, who are spread across the globe.

Looking back at the list of collaboration options in this chapter, we see that a few of these can be successfully integrated into a BRS solution to offer more robust, automated functionality. One possibility is e-mail alerts. Or a pager alert when a build fails. And if you, for example, link the system to your Exchange server, you can drag and drop alerts into your calendar and set up meetings to discuss any issues you uncover. And in combination with ClearCase, you have a powerful code and document storage facility at your hands, with numerous ways of meeting the needs of your development teams.

Oh, and about our friend, the distressed CM manager who escaped to his vacation. Well, as he makes his way back to work in bumper-to-bumper traffic on a Monday morning after his vacation, he realizes the changes he has uncovered will help break down the communication problems that his team has been experiencing. The question now is which engineering manager will take credit for the increased productivity that he has just enabled. As long as the problem is solved and he can get back to a normal sleeping schedule, he decides that this is one problem he can deal with.

24

Reducing Build Cycle Times

Eating an Elephant, One Bite at a Time

The African elephant is the world's largest land animal. According to the Pittsburgh Zoo and PPG Aquarium, males grow to 10–12 feet tall at the shoulder and weigh 10,000–12,000 pounds when fully matured. The elephant's skin, which withstands blistering sun and torrential rains, is between 0.25 and 1.5 inches thick. An elephant will spend the majority of each day foraging for 300-plus pounds of vegetation in the form of grasses, tree limbs, tubers, fruits, vines, and shrubs just to meet its daily nutritional needs. An elephant's digestive system is geared toward quantity: while it consumes large amounts of food, only 45 percent of what it takes in is actually digested and used. Interestingly, the partially digested feces of the African elephant are an ecologically important method of seed dispersal, opening up dense areas of trees and shrubs, allowing the generation of plants and grasses on the forest floor. One species of plant, in fact, germinates by passing through an elephant's system.[1]

Sizing Your Elephant

For argument's sake, let's assume you are the build-and-release manager of a large product that is developed at six locations across the globe (very similar in sheer size to our African elephant friend). The current build-and-release cycle takes two days to integrate, with an additional 24 hours to construct the integrated code. Testing takes another 48 hours, which needs to occur before the product validation team checks the soundness of the installation and pushes the final product out to the customer. In a best-case scenario, the complete cycle takes more than five days. The count begins when an engineer has checked in code to fix a bug, and it completes when the defect has been verified. This effort can be massive and cumbersome. No wonder product schedules slip. No wonder the overhead costs for distributed computing are not realized until the product is ready to ship out the door. Distributed computing has benefits, but if not managed and controlled, the integration and distribution of code and executables can be overwhelming.

As we mentioned, elephant skin can be as thick as 1.5 inches—and like the elephant, your product can also wear a "thick skin." So how can you decrease product development cycle times while maintaining product quality?

Well, you can decrease the integration costs of distributed teams—or even nondistributed teams. How? You need to integrate early and often. But with build cycles over five days long, how do you integrate often? Five days come and go quickly, and it means the build-and-release teams will be spending all of their time building, testing, and

---

1. http://zoo.pgh.pa.us

releasing the product, with no time to look at process improvement and optimization. It is a cyclical—and deadly—problem. It's the goose and the golden egg problem: You need the golden eggs right now, and so you kill the goose—only to destroy your one and only source of golden eggs. The same is true with B&R teams. If they spend all of their time pushing buttons, they won't find the improvements that you need to decrease build cycle times, and to increase productivity. Elephants will spend up to 16 hours a day foraging for more than 300 pounds of vegetation. That's a lot of vegetation. Do you have that kind of time for your product?

The rewards of process improvement are increased quality and decreased development cycle time. But how do you get there? Well, as mentioned in Chapter 23, we can think of three methods to manage the build and release of large multi-site development efforts:

- Decrease build cycle times, to get results back to the software developers. (Decrease development cycle.)

- Decrease test cycle times while maintaining code coverage and use case coverage. (Increase product quality.)

- Accurately report results of build and test cycles. (Increase schedule estimation accuracy.)

Build Cycle Reduction Solutions

In this chapter, we're going to focus on build cycle reductions. Why only build cycle reductions? Well, like the elephant, whose digestive system processes massive quantities of bulk—of which only 45 percent is actually digested and used—we thought it would be helpful to attack these concepts one chapter at a time. In upcoming chapters, we will discuss test cycle reduction solutions and automated build-and-test systems. We plan to walk through the typical build-and-test cycles, and if that huge government grant comes through, we may even venture into the product build-and-release cycle.

The first place that most CM managers look for efficiencies is always in build cycle reduction. "How can I get the code to compile and link faster?" Well, there are several different approaches to the problem, such as revamping the make system, buying more hardware to make it go faster, and automating as many manual steps as possible.

Reconstruct the Make System

When looking at revamping a make system, you need to be involved with the software engineering architect. Many times the software engineering architect was the one who originally designed the product, and he will have a good idea of the dependencies and methods used to build the product. If the product has some history, you will quickly find out that the code is just short of a sentient life form—doing whatever it likes, despite the architects' original designs.

OK, enough about religion. The code seems to evolve over time and the dependencies and compilation rules can easily become inconsistent and hard to manage. Here are some ideas on how to approach a problem such as this: look for multiple compilations of the same code, componentize your code, remove circular dependencies, and then decrease dependencies between components.

Eliminate Multiple Paths to Compile the Same Code

Although everyone knows better, this problem typically pops up when an engineer needs a library in another directory and cannot wait for the next clean build to get the library to test his stuff. Makefiles are changed and inadvertently checked into ClearCase, which then make it into the build. If you are lucky, the build will break and the problem will be noticed and fixed. Worse—and most often the mistake: it is not caught and your build becomes that much longer because of the additional time to build that library. You may think that this outcome is fine, since `clearmake` and `make` are smart enough to avoid building the target again. Don't be tempted to think that all is well in your make system because of this process. Different environments, targets, and so on can allow the library to be built more than once. And when looking at parallelizing the code, this problem can literally paralyze your build. How do you find the problem? It's a hard one to find, but `clearmake` can help; looking at configuration records is a good place to find how a library or binary has been built. The other approach would be to start looking at `makefile` and making sure that the system only builds files in the directory where they reside. Most code has some good notion of source-code directory hierarchies.

Componentize Your Product

While you are going through all of your makefiles and directories, you should start to look at the componentization of your code. A component will typically match the directory hierarchy in some fashion. If you have determined that a component spans two or more directories, look at putting them together under another directory with the name of the component. It is also okay to have a hierarchy of components and subcomponents. This will make it much easier when you start parallelizing the build.

Remove Circular Dependencies

If the product you are building has been around for some time, you will see circular dependencies between the components that you have just defined. They typically present themselves as rebuilding the same library twice with different dependencies. Circular dependencies are like driving 25 miles per hour on a freeway when all the other cars are going 70. It is a stupid thing to do, and it takes forever for you to get to your destination—not to mention aggravating every other person driving on the freeway. The easiest way to remove the circular dependency is to create another component upon which the original two components depend. All of the shared code should be made available in the new component. Another approach is to place all of the common code in one of the components. This last approach can be problematic for future growth of the product, so be careful.

Decrease Dependencies

Using a tool such as Rational Rose or SNiFF+, you can see the dependencies between your components. If your dependency graph looks like a map of San Jose or Los Angeles, you should probably consider simplifying it. This can be done by shifting code from component to component, creating new common components with global dependencies, and creating a hierarchy of components and subcomponents. The fewer dependencies you have between components, the more parallelism you will obtain and the faster your build will be.

A recent project went through the exercise of reworking a make system that had de-evolved into a mess of circular dependencies. Over a span of two weeks, we took a build that averaged 24 hours to less than eight hours—just by cleaning up the component structure of the product. The product was still being built sequentially, and we got a 3× improvement in speed. When we parallelized the build, we achieved another 3× improvement.

Throw Hardware at It

In the last three years, the big UNIX machine shops have started pushing their "server farm" solutions. Every engineer's and configuration manager's dream has come true: 48 CPUs, 96 gigabytes of RAM, and 2.8 terabytes of hard-disk space, all in a single rack. Even with more hardware, you can continue having speed problems if you don't address the build system directly. You also need to plan out your hardware configuration—if not, you will have all that horsepower, but you will still be driving in the slow lane. There are several things to consider for speed improvements: VOB server layout, compute machines, centralized tools, and network configuration.

VOB Servers

With some changes to ClearCase in version 4.x, the VOB servers are no longer limited by the lock manager. The old configuration of more (smaller) VOB servers has given way to smaller numbers of large machines. We have used machines such as the Sun E420R (4 CPUs, 8 gigabytes of RAM) as a VOB server, serving 60 VOBs and over 100 users. The E420 is connected to a fiber-channel RAID array of 375 gigabytes mirrored. With the number of VOBs and users increased, you must look at the network connections to the VOB server, as well.

Most of these big servers can handle multiple network cards, or the larger network cards, such as a 1-gigabit card. Remember, your VOB server will be hammered by several different machines in your server farm.

View Servers

In most cases, we have not been thrilled with view servers. Compilation on the machine on which a view resides is generally faster than accessing the view over the net. But when you have a parallel build and a farm of fast machines, you need to have a centralized view server. The network connection to this machine should be fast—or there should be multiple network cards. The faster card is a better solution, so we recommend a 1-gigabit network card in the view server, as well.

Compute Machines

The purpose of the compute machine is to compile or test your product. You are hunting for pure speed and memory. These machines are typically multiple-processor machines with as much memory as you can put into them. The network connection on these machines can be a 100 Base-T network card, which is standard for most servers. Putting faster cards in the compute machines is not a good idea, however, as the VOB server and view servers will most likely become the slowest part of your network connection.

Network Configuration

Get a switch and make it big. Server farms that perform builds are typically very network-intensive. A switch with a big back plane will help the information flow freely. All of the machines should be connected directly to the switch, including the VOB, view, and compute machines.

File Servers

If you have a server farm that has several users and products, you may want to consider one of the large file servers. Most of them come with multiple large gigabit network cards and fast disks. This can increase your performance and decrease your maintenance.

Conclusion

Partially digested feces are an ecologically important method of seed dispersal, and one species of plant actually must be passed through an elephant's gut in order to germinate and grow . . .

OK, maybe this is not the best way to close out a chapter, but our point is simple: Large, multi-site software projects are like an elephant. They're big, bulky, and natively inefficient. But there are ways that you can make them more efficient—train them, if you will. And amid all those systems and all of that bulk, there is that seed that germinates and grows. That is your project—your software. But you should probably wash your hands after handling it.

## 25

The Drag Coefficient of Test-Cycle Reduction

The drag coefficient is a number that aerodynamicists use to model all of the complex dependencies of shape, inclination, and flow conditions on aircraft drag. This equation is simply a rearrangement of the drag equation where we solve for the drag coefficient in terms of the other variables. The drag coefficient **Cd** is equal to the drag **D** divided by the quantity: density **r** times half the velocity **V** squared times the reference area **A**. . . .

This equation gives us a way to determine a value for the drag coefficient. In a controlled environment . . . we can set the velocity, density, and area and measure the drag produced. Through division we arrive at a value for the drag coefficient. . . . [T]he choice of reference area (wing area, frontal area, surface area, . . .) will affect the actual numerical value of the drag coefficient that is calculated. When reporting drag coefficient values, it is important to specify the reference area that is used to determine the coefficient. We can predict the drag that will be produced under a different set of velocity, density (altitude), and area conditions using the drag equation.

—*From the NASA Glenn Learning Technologies Project Web site,*
http://www.grc.nasa.gov/WWW/K-12/airplane/dragco.html

How do you reduce the "drag coefficient" in software development? Well, the best place to start is to determine what is slowing you down. Much like an Olympic runner training for a marathon, software teams need to find ways of reducing the amount of friction pushing against their momentum—what is affecting overall cycle time—by optimizing their performance through test-cycle reduction. Professional runners are constantly tracking performance metrics, identifying food and exercise variables that may affect their strength and endurance. They may occasionally resort to shaving their head as a way of minimizing their own drag coefficient. It takes dedication to get through the barriers that come with running marathons.

> The marathon is the most psychologically demanding of all running events because it requires that the mind withstand enormous stress, fatigue, tension and pain. And no one is excused from its clutches. . . . At the first signs of increased fatigue, your worst fears are confirmed: You've hit the wall. You panic and become even more fearful, which again feeds your negative physical response. You become even more fatigued. Finally, when your mind says, "Stop," your body stops.
> —*Dr. Jerry Lynch, "Mind Over Marathon,"*
>   *http://www.runnersworld.com/events/boston98/training/jlpsych.htm*

To avoid hitting this wall in software development, we must continually optimize our systems and practices. In addition to his famous quote, "Optimize the system," management guru W. Edwards Deming, one of the key American leaders who helped reconstruct Japan's economy after World War II, made a very important statement about identifying and pursuing paths to system and process optimization. "The prevailing style of management must undergo transformation. A system cannot understand itself. The transformation requires a view from outside."

This is the key to testing: setting up processes for examining your software with an "outside" perspective. But testing needs to be managed. Without process and a systematic approach, testing schemas can become overly complicated and burden your development organization with yet another legacy system. This chapter will illustrate different methods of getting "a view from the outside" of your system—and managing those activities—through test-cycle optimization.

Levels of Testing

Once you have improved the speed of your code (that is, its ability to compile and link), the next phase of process improvement is decreasing test-cycle time. To accomplish this, you must have a "view from the outside," which includes testing the overall class structure. Additionally, you need to examine the interfaces, the internal relationships, and the behaviors between aggregated elements. Through this holistic approach, you must optimize each of the following:

- Class test cases

- Package test cases

- System or flow test cases

- Defect regression tests

- Responsibility for test creation

Class Test Cases

Class test cases should test the class structure and behavior. For each class that has operations, there should be a class test case. There are several different UML elements that can be examined to determine the tests that should be written.

Class Definitions (Diagrams)

When you first write a class test case, you typically write a small test case for each operation in your class. At first, this seems like a great idea, but is it really necessary? If a class is defined properly, the public operations of the class should be the only things to consider when you write a test case for the class. The class diagram in Figure 25.1 presents two classes for which test cases need to be written.

The `Work_impl` class test case should have at least four tests, one for each public operation: `new()`, `run()`, `started()`, and `completed()`. When writing the `Job_impl` class test case, consider all of the public

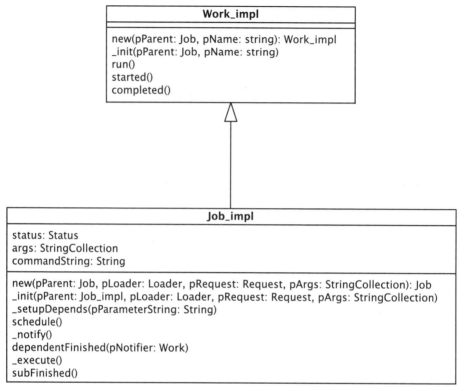

Figure 25.1   *Class Diagram*

operations of the class that include the inherited operations. So? Do
we need to write four or seven tests for the Job_impl class? If the
superclass Work_impl class test case is well written, we will need to
write only four tests for the Job_impl class test case. When the
Job_impl class test case is run, it should kick off seven different tests.
The class test cases should use the same inheritance that exists in the
class definition.

Test Objects

You may notice that some of the operations have other classes as
parameters to the class. This implies some kind of dependency on
your tests by another class. One way of getting around having tests
depend on each other is to have the class maintain a default or test
instance of the class. For example, the new() operator for Work_impl

requires parameters (pParent: Job, pName: String). We can have a static operation in the Job class named createTestObject() : Job that will create a Job, so that we can use it for our test cases. Every class in your system should use the same mechanism, so there is no confusion when writing tests.

State Diagrams

If the class has a state diagram, it can be used to create additional tests for the class test case. For an example, review the state diagram in Figure 25.2.

The state diagram shows an additional test for each unique path through the state net. In this case, there are, at most, 15 additional tests that can be written here. We need to make sure that we don't overdo our testing. We should look for ways to decrease our testing while maintaining the same coverage. One approach is to decrease the number of tests by eliminating paths for test runs.

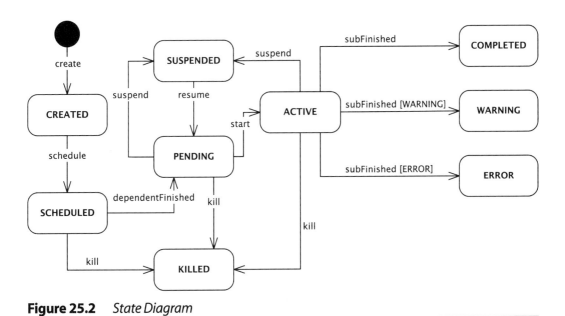

Figure 25.2   *State Diagram*

Look first for paths through the state net that have a common path leading up to a certain state. For example, the ACTIVE state appears to be the center point in the state diagram, on which four end states rely. There are three different paths to get to the ACTIVE state. You need to pick one of the paths—probably the shortest or the most commonly used. In this case, CREATED → SCHEDULED → PENDING → ACTIVE. Now, write a test for each state that follows the ACTIVE state (KILLED, ERROR, WARNING, and COMPLETED). Now, pick one of the next states to write the other two tests for the paths up to ACTIVE. For example, selecting COMPLETED would yield two additional tests with the flows CREATED → SCHEDULED → PENDING → SUSPENDED → PENDING → ACTIVE → COMPLETED and CREATED → SCHEDULED → PENDING → ACTIVE → SUSPENDED → PENDING → ACTIVE → COMPLETED.

This reduction method can decrease the number of tests from 15 tests to about eight tests. This reduction does not seem like much, but when looking at a large system of 300 or 400 classes, this can be a substantial decrease in class testing time.

Of course, scenario and active diagrams for classes can be analyzed for class test cases, but make sure these are specific to the class. If they aren't specific to the class, they belong in the package-level test cases. We will cover this point in the next section.

Package Test Cases

Package test cases test the interface of the package, as well as the internal relationships and behaviors between aggregated elements in the package. The interface of the package consists of a set of classes—usually of the stereotype interface—that are public for the package. The subelements can be classes or packages. They are virtually handled the same way.

Package Interfaces

The first place to look for tests for a package test case is at the interface of the package, as shown in Figure 25.3. In a well-designed system, these are normally the classes defined with the stereotype <<interface>>. Treat each interface definition just as we did in the class test cases.

Only the classes DependJob, Job, Work, and Task need to be used for the package test cases. If the class test cases have been written for these classes, we simply include them in the package test case. If they haven't been written for these classes, they should be written as class test cases and then included in the package test case. This will allow us to test at different granularities as needed.

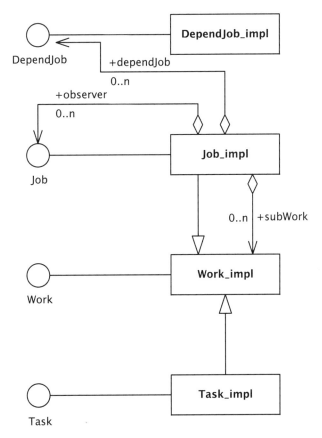

Figure 25.3   *Package Interface*

Test Objects

It is important, as described in the discussion of class test cases, that we create a static operation `createTestObject()` for each class in the system. The same concept exists for the package. We need to ensure a class is created (`TestHarness`) that handles the initialization of the package so that it can be used for testing. Most packages require some set of objects to exist before running some of the interfaces to the package. The initial step of the package test case should create a `TestHarness` object that will, in turn, initialize the package for testing. It is important to remember from the start that tests should be able to be run in parallel and on separate machines. If the package initialization takes a long time, you may be limited in the amount of parallel work you can accomplish.

Interaction and Collaboration Diagrams

Another place to look for tests is within interaction and collaboration diagrams. Most of these diagrams should show objects in the system interacting with each other. Look for those diagrams that define only the internal interactions of the package. If the diagram contains an object that is outside of the package, it might not belong in this package. Instead, it may belong to a parent or grandparent package in the system.

First, look at all of the objects in the diagram, as shown in Figure 25.4. If the objects need to be created, call `createTestObject()` for each class in the scenario. Make sure the object is not created by some message in the scenario diagram. If this is the case, you will not need to create the object ahead of time. Next, look at the messages passed between objects. Take only the first-level messages: these are the operations that you will need to call in your test case.

In this example, only `theMatrix : Manager` class needs to be created ahead of time. Only top-level messages are needed to test this scenario. So 1.1, 1.2, 1.3, 1.4, 1.5, and 1.6 are needed to define this test.

In most cases, you will have one test per scenario. However, if you show exceptions or different event flows of the scenario with the diagram, you could have more.

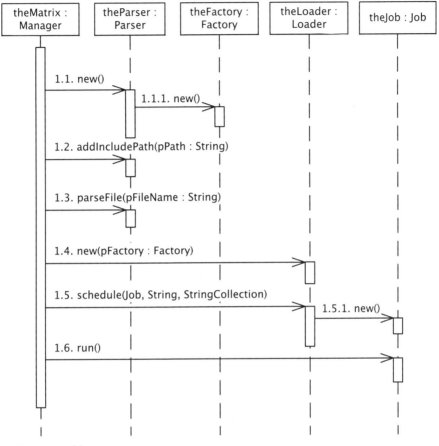

Figure 25.4   *Sequence Diagram*

Activity Diagrams and State Diagrams

Activity diagrams can yield a plethora of tests because they show different flows through the system, as well as interaction between objects in the package. Activity diagrams are very similar to state diagrams in that they show state and transitions, but they can have multiple objects involved.

System or Flow Test Cases

The system or flow test cases can be derived within use cases and scenarios. There should be at least one test for each scenario of your analysis model. It is always a good idea to group the tests in these test cases so that they map with the use case groupings. Typically, the scenarios for a use case will cover the "good" path of system execution. This is not enough testing for the system and flow test cases. Asynchronous user interfaces to programs give the user the ability to create several different scenarios that most analysts and designers have not considered.

Determining the user scenarios is important when creating the flow test cases. These flow tests can be very large and time-consuming to create and execute. Recording these scenarios using automated testing tools is one method of easily capturing these test cases for automated rerunning. One thing to watch out for is to have too many of these cases covering the same portions of scenarios—with slightly different permutations. Although it would be great to handle all scenarios that the user can do, it is not feasible, and the return on investment is not there. It is better to approach your testing with a plan, rather than just to record everything.

One approach to reducing flow testing is to evaluate the different flows and, in much the same way we did with activity and state diagrams, find the common steps of flows and combine them. This will decrease the amount of time needed to run these tests.

In many cases, product validation organizations need to verify programs against different third-party tools and operating systems. A great example of this is with Internet browsers. What looks fine on Internet Explorer does not look so great on Netscape, and vice versa. One approach to this problem is to blame the third-party tool manufacturers for the quality of their software. But as we saw with the Firestone and Ford tire fiasco, this kind of back-and-forth just leaves frustrated customers and unmet requirements. Such finger pointing, of course, does not solve problems and is unacceptable. We need to be flexible to the different third-party tools that we use. A bad habit is to run all tests on one platform configuration and then run a subset of the tests on "supported" platforms. This may not be acceptable to customers, especially if they are crashing or experiencing other problems on these "supported" platforms. Just be careful when reducing test cases in system and flow tests and ensure that these supported platforms aren't sacrificed for some minor time savings.

Flow test cases can have certain characteristics that need to be analyzed, including performance, memory usage, disk usage, and so forth. Many of these test cases can be found within the requirements and target platforms of the product. Rational has a suite of tools to help with different kinds of tests. Purify, Quantify, and Pure Coverage are great tools for quality evaluation.

Defect Regression Tests

Another place to find test cases is in your defect-tracking system. Although we like to think we don't have bugs in our code, defects are a reality of software development. Most bugs are found by running through some scenario that the user or engineer has executed within the program. Test cases that mirror these real-life scenarios are critical. Such test cases are invaluable to showing improvement from one release of your product to another.

Automating these regression tests is a great idea, as they can be run or executed by automated build-and-test scripts on a nightly or weekly basis. One drawback to this practice is the proliferation of tests as the product ages. In one organization that we worked with, they did a great job writing and running test cases for each defect that had been repaired. Over a five-year period, they collected quite an impressive set of defect regression tests—so impressive, in fact, it took weeks to run the regression for each build-and-release cycle. Avoid this problem through proper planning. You will need to phase out regression test cases over time or at least look for duplicates. Managing these regression tests is a full-time job, and it will require resources to keep it manageable.

Responsibility for Test Creation

Product validation or quality assurance organizations are typically pointed to as being responsible for detailed product testing. In reality, testing blankets several different organizations. Table 25.1 shows how testing responsibilities should flow across organizations.

Table 25.1 *Testing Responsibilities*

Class Test Cases	Software Development
Package Test Cases	Software Architects and Development
System/Flow Test Cases	Marketing, Software Architects, and Product Validation
Defect Regression Test Cases	Customer Support, Software Development, and Product Validation
Automated Test Runs	CM and Build & Release

Reducing the Drag Coefficient

> The most important lesson I learned is that there are no simple recipes for training successfully for a marathon. Part of the marathon's allure is that it's difficult—not only to race but to train for properly. Over a period of years, I developed basic guidelines about marathon training that have worked for me. I didn't have great speed, but I knew how to get ready for a marathon by following a well-conceived plan.
>
> —*Benji Durden, "The Path to Marathon Success," www.runnersworld.com*

What your development team needs is a well-conceived plan. Just as the runner is responsible for the condition of his or her body and how he or she prepares for a marathon, ultimately it is product validation or QA that will need to make sure things are managed and controlled in an effective manner—and to constantly look for ways to optimize the system through test-cycle reduction. There are several places to find test cases, but if the test cycles are not watched, your product, which takes two hours to build, might take weeks to test. And shaving your head won't help that problem.

Decreasing Testing Time

As a product ages, the number of test cases can also grow. Just like an Olympic runner who needs to be careful about what he eats and how he trains to optimize his performance, there are things you can do to manage what your project "eats" and how it "exercises." As a product ages, more care needs to be taken to manage the test suite so that it does not become overburdened with unnecessary test cases that eat up valuable cycle time. We now discuss some specific strategies for keeping your testing effectiveness up and your testing cycle time down.

Improve the Process

We've seen a vast array of software development and testing processes in business. The software world is a veritable cornucopia, if you will, of rapid development schemes and antiquated practices. But if we were asked to categorize all of them into two major groups, we'd put them in two simple categories: ad hoc (shoot-from-the-hip) processes and architected (planned, organized) processes. All right, we're generalizing things a bit—and when you generalize, you often spend an inordinate amount of time discussing exceptions. Well, please bear with us.

Automate Manual Processes

It's an unfortunate fact that most product validation organizations work in the ad hoc mode most of the time. Or at best, they begin optimistically on the architected side of the aisle and quickly move to ad hoc when schedules become tight, or a key player changes jobs, or maybe someone gets "forcibly downsized" or whatever the company calls it. In any event, the processes that typically get neglected the most are those that are manual and that exist among the common collective. When someone leaves the team or the company, these are the processes that get shuffled to the bottom of the priority basket or are lost forever. This is not good.

By automating your tests and testing processes, you can have a more stable and persistent record of what was accomplished and how it was accomplished. Training of new employees should include some kind of instruction on how to modify and augment the automated process. You need to circumvent the possibility of "historical layering" of automation—the habit of adding process without refining what is already there. This typically happens when a new employee begins in an organization and adds more automation on top of what is already automated. This can result in massive, out-of-control test harnesses that require the use of several different languages and tools.

Here's a quick rule of thumb: Come up with one way of automating process and stick with it. Make sure everyone is trained on how to use it and enforce its use. The best way to train and enforce usage is to document it and distribute it to the team. Documentation can be magic that way: it's amazing (and scary) how people will support something if it is well documented. Just make sure your process is a living and breathing thing that can be changed and adapted as your team and product grow.

Massively Parallelize Test Suites

One way to decrease cycle time is to parallelize the tests in your test cases. When designing your tests, make sure that those tests have no dependencies, or as few as possible. This can be hard to determine if you have tests that have been running sequentially for long periods of time. Some tests may have always run after another test has completed, and in some unknown way these tests depend on the state of resources after the first test has finished. This is something we've seen up close. After converting to parallel testing a set of tests that had been running sequentially for years, we found several of these so-called independent tests. Things that had once been passing through unnoticed were no longer getting through because they relied on a change to a configuration file or input data that was modified by a previously run test. When run in parallel, the tests identified several bugs in both the test scripts and the product itself.

Remove Testing Dependencies

Decrease or Remove the Amount of Shared Resources for Tests

Finding a testing dependency can be both difficult and time-consuming. One approach is to parallelize everything, but that is not the best way of finding dependencies. Because you are not guaranteed the order of execution, shared resources can cause intermittent errors. You need to find out which resources, data files, databases, configuration files, servers, and the like are being used by each test, and make sure that they don't implicitly depend on each other through shared resources.

Once you have found these shared resources, you can duplicate the resource and put it in a context that each test has exclusive control over, or you can sequence the tests such that they don't interfere with each other. Trade-offs between disk space and cycle time reduction will have to be considered when determining which approach to use.

Remove Redundant and Obsolete Tests

As a product ages, original requirements and features become obsolete. Sometimes the code is even taken out of the product. Tests should also be removed when they no longer assess the functionality of the product. If tests are well organized, it becomes very evident when it is time for them to be removed. For example, if a complete package is removed from the design, the package test cases and all of the class test cases can be removed without reservation. However, flow and system test cases are another issue. Removal of these test cases needs to be coordinated with marketing and customer support.

Another area to look at when cleaning up tests is redundant tests, which are usually harder to find. They appear in test suites that have not been managed over time, or in the defect regression tests. Many people feel it is easier just to write another test case without examining what is already available. Remember, doing so does not test the product any more than it is already being tested—it just takes more time. You never hear about the "benefits" of increasing development cycle times, because there aren't any. Time is critical because no matter what you're building, you have competitors who are trying to reduce their own development cycle times.

Run Tests As Soon As the Package Has Been Built

Because we have layered our test suite, we can run different levels of tests at different times in the build, test, and release cycle. Let's take a look at the traditional cycle in Table 25.2.

Table 25.2 *Sample Test Cycles*

Time

	Build			Test	Release
	DB	**WF**	**UI**	DB Package Test Case	
				WF Package Test Case	
				UI Package Test Case	
				DB Class Test Cases	
				WF Class Test Cases	
				UI Class Test Cases	
				System Test Cases	

(Number of Processes — vertical axis label)

In this example, the build has to be run sequentially because of package dependencies, but notice that all of the tests can be run at the same time. Running this build-and-test cycle requires seven concurrently running processes, at most. If you have limited resources, this can be problematic. There is software that will take this massively parallel portion of your process and balance it over your machine resources, such as Load Sharing Facility from Platform Computing. However, your cycle will take longer to complete as the number of resources becomes smaller.

There is another way, as shown in Table 25.3. Let's reorganize our cycle by running class and package test cases as soon as possible—right after the package is built.

Table 25.3 *Revised Test Cycles*

Time

	Build			Test	Release
	DB	**WF**	**UI**	UI Class	
		DB Class	WF Class	UI Package	
		DB Package	WF Package	System Test Cases	

(Number of Processes — vertical axis label)

This example becomes even more beneficial as the number of packages in your system increases. Testing immediately after a package is built can get information back to the software engineers faster, as well. No need to wait for the entire product to build before running new tests for the class or package. You can also stop your cycle if a critical package test case fails, therefore saving CPU cycle times for other builds and tests.

Remove Test-to-Test Dependencies

Software engineers and test engineers often design tests that depend on other tests. At first thought, it seems like a great idea. If I have one test that sets up an environment that other tests can use to validate their functionality, this should decrease the code that others have to write and, as a result, decrease the product development cycle. In most cases, such reasoning is incorrect. Test-to-test dependencies may decrease the amount of time it takes to produce code, but the ripple effect can be detrimental to product quality and cycle time.

In Figure 25.5, we justify testing the WF package after the DB package is tested because it sets up a database that we need to run the workflow tests. We do the same thing for the UI package and the WF package.

Now, these tests have to be run sequentially. If the test result for each test is identical, we have just tripled our test time. Not a good thing. There is another interesting effect of this design. Any changes to Setup DB Test or Test DB are felt in all of the tests. This actually increases the amount of maintenance time you'll need to spend to keep your tests up to date. Yet another problem with this testing

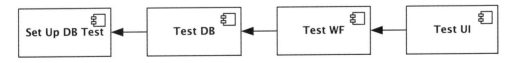

Figure 25.5   *Understanding Dependencies*

method can be demonstrated with statistical analysis. The success rates for each test are shown in stereotypes in Figure 25.6. When two tests depend on each other, the probability of successfully executing the test is the product of the two success rates, if they were independent. For example, if Test DB succeeded 98 percent of the time and Test WF succeeded 95 percent of the time if they were independent, then the Test WF that is dependent on Test DB would succeed 93 percent of the time (0.98×0.93).

As you can see, this gives erroneous results and sends the wrong message about product quality. The poor UI team gets hammered with bugs while the DB and WF teams move on to the next release of the product—all because of dependencies in the test suite.

Dependency graphs can also be used to focus on how much testing needs to be done for a particular product. As the lower-level packages in your architecture become more stable and the reliability number increases toward 1.00, the rest of the package tests will have better results as well.

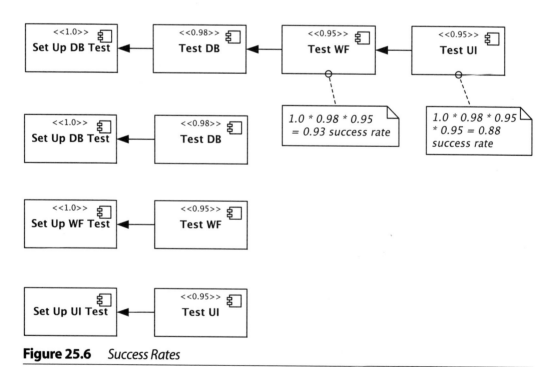

Figure 25.6   *Success Rates*

Conclusion

Testing a product can be a great tool for revealing product quality. It can also become a black hole for resources and cycle time. Edwards Deming once said, "It is a mistake to assume that if everybody does his job, it will be all right. The whole system may be in trouble." Never assume that because someone wrote a test case, it must be acceptable—or even relevant. Here are some tips to keep in mind when managing your test suite.

1. **Architect testing from the beginning.** A QA architect should be involved in the architecture of the product. The QA architect can make sure certain procedures are followed from the beginning, to make the product more reliable and easier to test.

2. **Don't neglect your test suite.** Just like a tree in your backyard, it will need to be pruned periodically, fertilized, and sometimes cut down because of disease. Testing does not occur at the end of product development.

3. **Automate everything.** Eliminating manual steps decreases the variability of the testing and ensures repeatability.

4. **Don't try to test quality into your product.** All testing does is let you know what you have already done. It does not give your product higher quality. Some companies have two organizations: quality assurance and product validation. Consider the names when you are performing duties.

26

What to Do When Things Go Wrong

Solving Problems with ClearCase

Your project has been moving along at a quick pace, largely without incident. Not a single build has broken, and the customer's review of the beta was a huge success. Not only have the customer and your development team been working together to resolve design issues, but everyone seems to be following your processes without the usual complaining and attempts to cut corners and go around established standards and procedures.

And then you wake up.

Ah, the pain of reality. An unchecked .dll that brings down a very important build in the middle of the night. A poorly configured source-control system, designed and built by someone who no longer works for your company. A recently expanded multi-site setup that constantly sets off your pager in the middle of the night. It's silly to think that you can plan around every possible problem and every user scenario; but there are steps you can take to diminish the possibility of your system breaking, which, as Murphy's Law states, always happens at the worst possible time.

The following are some of our recommendations for minimizing problems with ClearCase.

Playing It Safe

Protecting your VOBs

When trying to avoid problems with ClearCase, the best place to start is with your data. Are you backing up your VOBs? How do you know for certain you are correctly backing up your VOBs? Don't make any assumptions about what is happening with your data. There are far too many unfortunate situations where people believe their IT departments are automatically backing up their VOBs. In one (very personal) situation, for example, we ran into problems with one of our VOBs and found that our request for backup was assigned to someone who happened to have left the company—and had not passed along the request. Remember that *you* are ultimately responsible for your VOBs. And it does not hurt to make more than one backup copy of your VOBs. Remember: VOBs contain your company's intellectual property, and they need the proper safeguards and attention.

What is your data backup strategy? How often do you back up your VOBs? That all depends! Some organizations back up using multi-site more than once a day. Other firms back up in the middle of the night every 24 hours. It all depends on the activity level of your development group. One important note: **The VOBs should be locked when you do a backup**. Make sure you follow the manual when you do your backups, and everything should go smoothly. The ClearCase manuals have plenty of information about backup strategies, so find what works for your organization and formalize the process.

Making View Backups?

You might be asking yourself, What about my views? Should I be worried about backing those up as well? Our answer is no. We have had several battles with management and engineers about this one. But views are temporary things, and they don't require a regular backup process.

Many engineers are afraid to check in their code because they worry that it will be put into the build or that other people will see it. So they want their views backed up. A better strategy is to have your engineers work on a branch. Have them check in often, more than once a day. Remind them that when they check something into their branch that it is safe, and no one else will see it—not until they are ready for other people to see it.

This strategy has several benefits. First, backups of the VOB will back up the user's changes. Second, if you are using multi-site, you now have a disaster recovery scheme (if there's an earthquake in California, people are able to keep working in Boston). Third, this molds the engineers into true ClearCase users—instead of having them just sit around and complain about it all the time.

Avoiding Problems

Education is the primary key to avoiding real problems with ClearCase. Many of the day-to-day problems you'll experience are, strangely enough (heavy sarcasm intended), caused by users or administrators not knowing what they are doing. If you are an administrator, get educated. Rational has some great courses on ClearCase administration, so if you've been asked to manage your company's solution or if you have inherited a system, get some formal training.

VOBs need care and maintenance. To our earlier point, if you are now in control of your company's intellectual property, you had better know what you are doing. Rational has some standard administrative tools that run periodically. Some basic training on these utilities will give you an understanding of what you can do to help keep your VOBs from getting sick.

vob_scrubber

This command frees up records that are no longer needed from the VOB database. This includes events and oplogs from the database. The vob_scrubber program does not decrease the size of the database, but it creates open records for new information. Aggressive use of vob_scrubber and frequent multi-site sync-ups can help keep your VOB database from growing wildly out of control. By default, vob_scrubber is run only periodically. See the ClearCase Scheduler for more information on how to run this program more frequently.

view_scrubber

We don't recommend using this program at all, but if you keep views around for long periods of time, they can become large and contain several derived objects. To free up record space, this command can be run indirectly through the `view_scrubber.sh` command supplied with ClearCase. But there are plenty of caveats to running this. From the ClearCase man pages:

> WARNING: This command modifies the way in which view-resident objects are combined with VOB-resident objects to produce a virtual workspace. To avoid errors, make sure that no application or development tool is using the view's files when this command is executed.

A better way to go is to use views, because they were created for temporary transient work—and *not* for long workspaces to be used for years. (All right, we'll get off the soapbox now.)

scrubber

This program removes derived objects from the VOB database and deletes data containers from the VOB storage pools. What does this mean? It means that your VOB can shrink after using this command. This is especially true if you perform several builds. As the number of derived objects increases, the VOB will increase in the database and in the storage pools. We recommend that you clean up with scrubber before you perform any large task on a VOB, such as reformatting, backing up, or upgrading. This decreases the amount of useless data on the database that needs to be interpreted.

Remember that you are dealing with a very complex piece of software, and one of your company's most critical databases. These things need maintenance time. If at all possible, schedule quarterly downtime, usually over a weekend, to upgrade ClearCase versions, fix problems, or just to clean things up. Put the downtime in the project plan for development. Let people know at the beginning of the year when you are going to take their ClearCase down, and stand by your plans. This time is important, and it will greatly reduce the amount of unscheduled downtime over the course of the year.

Finding the Logs

Because ClearCase involves many different machines, problems you encounter may encompass machines, networks, and storage devices. When you are looking for a problem, you need to know where to look. One really nice ClearCase feature is the ClearCase Administration UI. This provides you with access to all of the logs on all of the machines. But using the Administration UI may not always be an option. The following is a complete list of the logs, and the different types of information you can find in them. On UNIX, look in /var/adm/atria/logs. On NT, look in c:\Program Files\Rational\ClearCase\var\logs.

- **abe_log**—Used by the audited build executor during parallel clearmake builds (`clearmake -J ...`).

- **albd_log**—Used by the albd_server. Typically contains information about scheduled activities and their status.

- **ccfs_log**—This has information about the ClearCase file system, which is used for snapshot views.

- **credmap_log**—This shows information about user credentials across platforms. Specifically NT and UNIX interop.

- **db_server_log**—Used by the db_server. This is where you will find problems with the VOB database.

- **epoch_logs**—Directory that contains information for multi-site epoch. The epoch_watchdog uses these logs to compare current state with logged state.

- **error_log**—A general-purpose error log. Used by user programs such as cleartool.

- **export_mvfs_log**—Used by the export_mvfs program. This is used to export to NFS file systems. Great for platforms that are not supported by ClearCase.

- **lockmgr_log**—Used by the lockmgr program. This is where you will find problems with the locking mechanism in accessing the VOBs on a single host.

- **mntrpc_server_log**—Used by the mntrpc_server program. This is where you can find information about mounting the VOBs on a machine (`cleartool mount`).

- **msadm_log**—Used by the MultiSite administrative server, which handles requests for mastership (`cleartool chmaster`).

- **mvfs_log**—This log shows errors that typically occur when accessing files or directories in a view.

- **promote_log**—Used by the promote_server. This has to do with derived objects and their locations. The commands `cleartool`, `winkin`, and `omake` use the promote_server. Any errors with promoting derived objects to views will be found in here.

- **scrubber_log**—Used by the scrubber program. Contains information about the removal of data objects and data storage pools in VOBs.

- **shipping_server_log**—This contains information about what has been shipped to or received from a remote location for multi-site.

- **snap_log, snapshot_log**—Records information about the vob_snapshot command. This is used for taking copies of local VOBs.

- **sync_logs**—Contains information about the syncing of VOBs between replicas for multi-site.

- **view_log**—Used by the view_server. This shows if there are any problems with the view database.

- **vob_log**—Used by the vob_server. This typically reports problems with pools in the VOB. Database errors can be found in the db_server_log.

- **vob_scrubber_log**—Used by the vob_scrubber program. This shows what old event records and MultiSite oplogs have been deleted.

- **vobrpc_server_log**—Used by the vobrpc_server. Any problems with RPC calls between the VOB and views can be found here.

- **ws_helper_log**—Attached views and ClearCase VOBs log information.

Administration Problems

Interop Problems (UNIX and NT)

Most of problems with interop have to do with permissions, authentication, and setup. If you are accessing UNIX VOBs or views from a Windows box, you will need to be careful of a couple of things:

1. **Make sure the user has accounts on both systems.** The person's user name should be the same on both systems. If possible, the user should be part of the same group on both systems. Make sure that the group names are the same, not the group IDs. Follow this same rule for the user names and IDs.

2. **If your Windows OS does not support NFS clients, you will need to set up an SMB server on your UNIX box.** Make sure that the SMB server authenticates the user properly. You will typically find problems in the mvfs_log if this is not set up properly. Additionally, the credmap_log can be investigated for authentication problems. To check for this, try running the `credmap` command.

Multi-site Problems

Several logs are involved in common multi-site problems. Sometimes it can be hard to know where to start. Most of the problems we've seen have to do with epoch tables being out of sync between locations. This can be found in the sync_logs directory. Look for the newest log and you will find the problem.

If you are having problems with your replicas becoming out of sync, then the following example should help. Let's assume you have two sites, sanjose and nome. The sanjose location is pushing information to the nome location. If you get failures, you should first look at the epoch tables.

On a machine in the sanjose location:

```
multitool lsepoch Nome
For VOB replica "/vobs/kish":
Oplog IDs for row "nome" (@ ccvob-nome):
oid:4885755d.62a811d6.a390.00:01:83:02:9a:2e=1640  (nome)
oid:78b20e7d.a91311d4.bb60.00:01:80:b6:5b:a9=1951917  (sanjose)
```

Now you need to find out what nome thinks it has.

```
multitool lsepoch -actual nome
For VOB replica "/vobs/kish":
Oplog IDs for row "nome" (@ ccvob-nome):
oid:4885755d.62a811d6.a390.00:01:83:02:9a:2e=1534  (nome)
oid:78b20e7d.a91311d4.bb60.00:01:80:b6:5b:a9=1951917  (sanjose)
```

To fix the problem, first make sure that there is no sync running. Then you can run the following command to get things back in sync:

```
multitool chepoch -actual vobs/kish@/vobs/kish
```

This should fix the problem. Afterward, start a sync for the VOB. Remember: if one VOB is out of sync, chances are all of the VOBs between sites are out of sync. Check all of the VOBs between the sites.

Additionally, the shipping logs can be looked at for information on connectivity between sites.

Deployment Problems

We would be remiss if we did not mention some of the key avoidance measures in the deployment of ClearCase. Hands down, the biggest deployment pitfalls surround the training of engineers and your support team. If you fail in this area, your new system may never be widely accepted nor your processes followed. The majority of training issues have to do with maintaining two repositories of all of your file versions, which is necessary for continuity between old and new systems. Whether you are moving from a homegrown tool or from CVS, when you are moving to ClearCase, ensure your team has been trained on the new processes surrounding these key areas:

- Directory versioning

- Configuration specifications

- View creations and destructions

- Permission problems

These are some specifics, but don't forget about the "fuzzier" training issues. In Chapter 4, "Selling ClearCase into the Rest of Your Organization," we described some of the issues you will need to address when promoting a new ClearCase install to your team. Many of these points apply to this chapter, as well. For example, one of the biggest problems when moving to any new software solution is getting your team to adjust to the new processes, methodologies, and *quirks* of the new system. Ask yourself: How does the new system interact with the old repositories that need to be maintained? Does your new methodology take into account *how* your developers work, and on what *systems* they work? One of the most common failures of ClearCase administrators is not taking these kinds of issues into account, thinking that whatever changes they are adopting will "magically" roll out to the team without issues, and will not cause problems in the product environment.

It's never that easy. Take the time to think through all of your training needs, and be prepared to fix some mistakes—because you *will* make some.

Contacting the Experts

IBM Rational Software has great self-serve support. This service includes patch downloads, a knowledge center, and if you own a license to one of their products, access to the fabulous Rational Developer Network at http://www.rational.net. When you have a problem, however, we recommend that you start looking on http://www.ibm.com/software/rational/support. There are links from here to everything you will need on both IBM.com and Rational.net. If you cannot find a solution to your problem here, give IBM Rational a call.

But before you call IBM Rational with your problem, there are a few things you can do to decrease the amount of time you have to spend on the phone—and these steps may even prevent additional problems from occurring:

1. **If you think it is a VOB problem, lock your VOB and back it up.** On UNIX, tar works fine for this.

2. **Find out the operating system version and patch levels.** This varies from platform to platform, so look at your OS manual to get the correct information. On most UNIX systems, `uname -a` will give you most of what you will need.

3. **Find out what versions of ClearCase and the database you are using.** For ClearCase, `cleartool version` will give you this information.

4. **Tar up the log files from the log directory.** Again, on UNIX:

```
cd /var/adm/atria/log;
tar cvf ../logs.tar .
```

5. **Get your customer ID or contact information ready.** This just saves time when you are on the phone.

Here is the contact information for Rational support:

Web site: http://www.ibm.com/software/rational/support

E-mail: Customers should use the IBM ESR tool located at http://www-306.ibm.com/software/support/probsub.html.
E-mail submission is no longer being accepted.

Phone: 1-800-IBM-SERV

27

Bringing It All Together

The single common thread that runs throughout this book is that CM managers need to communicate—and communicate well. When people first think of communication, they usually think of talking, writing, and disseminating information electronically. The most important aspect of communication is often missing from these definitions: listening. If CM managers can really learn to listen and *then* communicate with their team, they will find success.

Changing the way your product is developed can be much more difficult than making other types of change. This is primarily due to the nature of development teams. Battles over CM systems, editors, or coding styles can flare into full-blown religious wars. Software developers are part scientist, part artist. They are difficult to convince to upgrade their software, much less change the entire mechanics of how they develop their code. And their way is *always* the best way, even if it involves a fax machine and some obscure terminology. The key is to pick your battles appropriately.

One of the areas that seems to be a good place for change is the configuration management system. Most software developers know that configuration management needs to be done, but they don't want anything to do with it. Surprisingly enough, CM systems are typically the glue that binds together development, testing, manufacturing, and the customer. As a result, this is where process can best be enforced.

Integration of the CM system with different development, test, change management, and project management tools is a natural fit, but it just does not happen on its own. A formal analysis, design, and implementation cycle needs to be executed to identify and validate the benefits of a CM system. Too often, CM systems are grown organically over time. This approach tends to generate fragile, rigid systems that are in constant need of repair. These systems create job security for some and management nightmares for others. The key is to plan it out, execute against that plan, and train the users to follow the new system.

Building and releasing software is not as easy as most people think. It involves integrating development activities with testing, manufacturing, and the customer. Just typing "make" against a makefile is not sufficient most of the time, unless of course the development team is a team of one. Typical build-and-release cycles include:

- Gathering code by merging code from development to integration branches and possibly several different locations.

- Compiling code from several different platforms, languages, and parameters (debug and purify, for example).

- Creating binaries by linking compile code together to form executables for the customer to use the product.

- Labeling or tagging the code and binaries with a unique identifier.

- Packaging deliverables. This includes binaries, documentation, demos, examples, and so forth.

Build-and-release systems are not as trivial as they first look. The key is to analyze the team's needs, work habits, and integration points and then to come up with a plan to implement the required changes.

Testing would not be needed if our software engineers could produce bug-free code, right? Wrong. Utopia does not exist in the software industry. And because of the complexity of systems, it does not look like it will get better anytime soon. There are both good ways and bad ways to test code. Having a test strategy is the first step to creating a successful testing system. Even with the best of plans, tests are constantly being added, and constant evaluation and optimization are needed to keep things in control.

Each part of a complete CM system requires planning, analysis, design, and implementation. Sounds like a real product is being produced, doesn't it? The fact is that CM systems are probably one of the more difficult products to develop. They have to integrate several systems together to act as one. They must be highly reliable. Their deployment cannot affect the current development cycle at all. Sounds fun, doesn't it?

Configuration management experts are necessary, but so are change agents, at every level within the organization. Change can be driven by a wide range of project participants, but they need to have a solid footing in the problem space and a good understanding of the potential issues that could arise. Whether driving a change to a CM system, implementing a new CM system, or ensuring the timely delivery of a new product or patch, there will always be a need for someone with the determination to step up, make decisions, and push a project through.

Like the Greek gods Hermes and Morpheus, change agents are both feared and revered. No one typically volunteers to be a change agent, because the job can be frustrating and tedious. But the rewards are often greater than the pain. Being a change agent is not for people seeking instant gratification; most real change can take a long, long time. But be patient, persistent, and unwavering, and someday you may even get your own statue or temple.

Bibliography

A Better Solution, Inc. Trigger information. http://www.abs-consulting.com.

Augustine, Liz. "How Technical Writers Use Rational ClearCase." *The Rational Edge*, IBM Rational Software, January 2001.

Baker, Bryon. "Business Modeling with UML: The Light at the End of the Tunnel." *The Rational Edge*, IBM Rational Software, December 2001.

Covey, Stephen R. *Seven Habits of Highly Effective People*. Simon & Schuster, 1990.

Davis, Adam. "Using Requirements Management to Speed Delivery of Higher-Quality Applications." *Rational Developer Network*, IBM Rational Software.

Deming, W. Edwards. *The New Economics*. The MIT Press, 2000.

Durden, Benji. "The Path to Marathon Success." *Runnersworld.com*, Rodale Inc.

Humphrey, Watts S. *A Discipline for Software Engineering*. Addison-Wesley, 1994.

IBM Rational Software. *ClearCase Reference Manual*.

Kitcho, Catherine. *High-Tech Product Launch*. Pele Publications, 1999.

Lynch, Jerry. "Mind Over Marathon." *Runnersworld.com*, Rodale Inc., 1998.

McLaughlin, Mark. "Saying Hello to CAL (the ClearCase Automation Library): The ClearCase COM Interface Isn't So Scary After All." *Rational Developer Network*, IBM Rational Software.

Merriam-Webster. *Merriam-Webster's Collegiate Dictionary, 11th Edition*. Merriam-Webster, 2003.

NASA Glenn Research Center. Drag coefficient definition. http://www.grc.nasa.gov.

Object Management Group. CORBA IDL specification. http://www.omg.org.

Pender, Lee. "Hard Times Are the Best Times." *CIO Magazine*, CXO Media Inc., August 2001.

Requadt, Walter E. Definition of entropy. http://www.rationality.net.

Rosenberg, Doug, and Kendall Scott. *Use Case Driven Object Modeling with UML*. Addison-Wesley, 1999.

Scott, Kendall. *UML Explained*. Addison-Wesley, 2001.

Snyder, John. "Honoring the Forces of Transformation." http://www.thinksmart.com.

Steele, Lowell W. *Managing Technology: The Strategic View*. McGraw-Hill, 1989.

Stroustrup, Bjarne. "International Standard for the C++ Programming Language Approved!" http://www.research.att.com/~bs/iso_release.html.

"Windows NT Domains and ClearCase." *Rational Developer Network*, IBM Rational Software.

Index